The Caregiver's HANDBOOK

A Self-Help Love Story

The CAREGIVER'S HANDBOOK
– A Self-Help Love Story
Copyright © 2009, 2019 by Paul Lane. All rights reserved.

No part of this publication may be reproduced, stored in a retrieval system or transmitted in any way by any means, electronic, mechanical, photocopy, recording, or otherwise without the prior permission of the author except as provided by USA copyright law.

Unless otherwise stated, all scripture quotations are taken from The King James & The New King James versions of the Bible.

Published by:
Lane Enterprises
www.PaulLane.net

ISBN: 978-0-9841473-1-1

Category: Self Help | Christian Living | Love Story | Caregiver

Written by Paul Lane | info@paullane.net

Edited by Ruthie Urman, Mitchell McConnell, and Debi Owens

Cover Design & Layout by Eli Blyden | CrunchTimeGraphics.com

Printed & Published in the United States of America | Tampa FL

Disclaimer

This book details the author's personal experiences and opinions with and about emotional intelligence. The author is not a licensed psychologist. Except as specifically stated in this book, neither the author or publisher, nor authors, contributors or other representatives will be liable for damages arising out of or in connection with the use of this book. You understand that this book is not intended as a substitute for consultation with a licensed legal or accounting professional. Before you begin any change in your lifestyle in any way, you will consult a licensed professional to ensure you are doing what is best for your situation. This book provides content related to emotional intelligence topics. As such, use of this book implies your acceptance of this disclaimer.

The CAREGIVER'S HANDBOOK

To:

From:

The CAREGIVER'S HANDBOOK

This book is dedicated to those who sit tirelessly at the bedside of dying loved ones and literally sacrifice their own lives in doing so.

Who selflessly serve the needs of the sick and dying and never give up.

Also, I dedicate it to the children of the terminally ill.

Losing a loved one is painful for anyone, but for a child (or adult), losing a parent is perhaps one of the most difficult, and perplexing happenstances life can present.

The CAREGIVER'S HANDBOOK

Table of Contents

Dedication vii

Introduction 1

CHAPTER 1
Amanda's Unforgettable Birthday Wednesday,
June 21, 2006 5

CHAPTER 2
Surgery and Prognosis Thursday, June 22, 2006 17

CHAPTER 3
The ICU Waiting Room Friday, June 23, 2006 35

CHAPTER 4
Recovery Saturday, June 24, 2006 43

CHAPTER 5
Treatment July, 2 2006 51

CHAPTER 6
Chemotherapy 63

CHAPTER 7
It Could Have Been Worse Wednesday,
September 19, 1979 71

CHAPTER 8
The Decline 79

CHAPTER 9
Support Group 99

CHAPTER 10
The First Trip to California 113

CHAPTER 11
How to Alienate Everyone You Know 119

CHAPTER 12
The Second California Trip 145

CHAPTER 13
A Feeling Like No Other 159

CHAPTER 14
Been Knocked Down? What Do You Do Now? 165

CHAPTER 15
The Stepchild of all Cancers 171

CHAPTER 16
The Second Surgery 177

CHAPTER 17
Depression 187

CHAPTER 18
Pain and Grief 199

CHAPTER 19
Etiquette 207

CHAPTER 20
Never ask a Dying Man how he's Doing 233

CHAPTER 21
I've Learned that Most Men Are Asses! 245

CHAPTER 22
Stranger Than Fiction 257

CHAPTER 23
Forgiveness and Closure 295

CHAPTER 24
She Should Have Been Dead by Friday 313

CHAPTER 25
The Magnitude of Solitude 325

CHAPTER 26
The Dance 335

CHAPTER 27
Family Dynamics 343

CHAPTER 28
Serve Others, Serve Yourself..355

CHAPTER 29
Poor, Poor Pitiful Me 359

CHAPTER 30
I'm Nobody's Hero 365

CHAPTER 31
Is There Life After Death?..373

CHAPTER: 32
A Most Beautiful Death 377

In Gratitude: Loving Hands of Grace 387

References and Further Reading:...............................389

I'd Have Gotten More Kisses 391

Contact Paul Lane 397

The CAREGIVER'S HANDBOOK

The Caregiver's HANDBOOK

A Self-Help Love Story

BY PAUL LANE

The CAREGIVER'S HANDBOOK

Introduction

If you told me five years ago, that terminal cancer would one day affect my family, I would have never believed you. The closest thing to a medical emergency in our house was the occasional cold. A bottle of Tylenol would last five years or more and any prescribed medications were usually outdated and ended up in the trash.

My name is Paul Lane and I was married for twenty-eight years. My wife and I met in 1978 at a local disco in downtown Denver, Colorado. Rita and I were married in 1980, two months after my enlistment in the Army ended. Our first house was a quaint three-bedroom bungalow located in central Denver.

I was working as a gas pipe fitter for the local utility company and Rita worked as a commercial account representative for a large insurance firm. Our first daughter was born on June 21, 1984 and we named her Amanda. Stacey, our youngest, was born four years later in 1988. We were considered a model family by many of our friends and relatives. We raised our daughters in a strict yet loving manner. Unlike most families we still believed that dinner should be eaten together with the television off. We shared our daily experiences and always gave God praise and thanks before every meal.

In 2003, I owned two small businesses: a construction company and a urethane spray-foam insulation business. I specialized in kitchen and bathroom remodeling, but because it was difficult to find quality employees, I ended up doing much of the work myself. I faced many challenges, both financially and physically, because of the many costs associated with the construction industry and the time it took to get established. Furthermore, finding time to do anything was difficult because I was working sixty to seventy hours each week. Owning my own business was a great experience but in the end the burdens outweighed the benefits. Consequently, after three and-a-half years, I decided to close both companies in the spring of 2006.

Rita was a very petite woman, standing a mere five feet tall, and at a height perfect for kissing her on her forehead. Her fingers were so tiny I could hardly fit her wedding ring onto the tip of my pinky. She had a contagious laugh that will forever remain in my heart and I can still hear when I close my eyes. She had a subtle smile reminiscent of the Mona Lisa and her green eyes always brightened up my day. Because of her diminutive size and mild manner, my daughters and I called her, "Precious." I considered her a classy woman who possessed much wisdom and insight. There was never an uncomfortable silence between us and we always cherished this fact. Though most people thought of her as a quiet and reserved person, those that knew her intimately knew she was a wonderful, intelligent conversationalist.

During the time I decided to close both companies she had just taken a position with a large international insurance company. Her new job included a substantial pay increase. She had only been there four months when our earth-shattering journey began.

Previously, our emergency room experience had been limited to stitches for Amanda's hand and when Stacey had slipped off of a retaining wall. Amanda's incident occurred on our thirteenth anniversary; she sliced her hand on a broken glass milk-bottle, and Stacey was treated for the removal of several long, creosote splinters from the inside of her thigh. We had never experienced any kind of traumatic occurrence aside from these two events. The daily routine of our family life was as pleasant and worry-free as any family could hope. What we had come to accept as normal would be completely redefined on the afternoon of June 21, 2006.

Originally, this book started out as a journal and eventually developed a life of its own. I've written an account of my experiences as a caretaker with the hope that you, the reader, may benefit from its pages. I trust that the information I present will help you better cope with, and understand, the dynamics of a debilitating illness. If a catastrophic illness were to occur in your family, I trust that this book will help you to be emotionally and maybe even spiritually, prepared. Also, this book may aid you in deciding to invest in insurance, whether it's health, life, or another sort. Statistically, one out of every two people in America will eventually require long term care. Based on the current rate of declining health in America it is possible that you too will one day be forced to see life through a caretaker's eyes.

CHAPTER 1

Amanda's Unforgettable Birthday
Wednesday, June 21, 2006

The morning of June 21, 2006 will remain permanently etched in my mind forever. Rita's face was brimming with excitement that morning when we woke up.

"Paul," she said, with a smile, "You know what today is, don't you?"

"Of course," I chuckled. "It's the first day of summer." Of course, I knew–it was Amanda's birthday. How could I forget? Amanda reminded us the full week before.

Rita looked at me from her side of the bed, tilting her head as she grinned. "You know honey, you're sure getting old." The sun was already pouring in through our bedroom window. I loved the way it made her green eyes look almost golden. They seemed to turn colors in different light.

"Old man," I retorted. "Look who's talking?" She giggled when I jumped out of bed and ran to her side.

She pulled the blankets around her so I couldn't get my hands in. "Give me a kiss right now or I'll tear those blankets off of you!" I said.

"No way, morning -breath!" she laughed.

I was excited and ready to start my third day at the new job. It may not have offered the same freedom I had while running my own companies, but I wasn't burdened with the stress of paying all the bills, either. Making cold calls by telephone wasn't my forte but I had experience doing it before; besides, when I was hired they told me most of the leads would be provided by them. I was just starting to get the hang of the office and I liked that they would soon be providing me with a company truck. Everyone there was friendly and there was a team atmosphere. Though I had never worked in an office before, this felt like it would be a great place to work. My boss's name was Dave. He looked like a body builder. His face was so square, he reminded me of a Rockem-Sockem Robot. I liked him right away. He was soft-spoken and seemed to really like me, too. Best of all he knew the roofing business inside and out. I knew right away I could learn a lot from him.

Right after lunch, I tried to call Rita on her cell phone but she didn't answer. I wanted to see how her lunch date went with Amanda. That morning she told me she was going to Wendy's to pick up a birthday lunch for Amanda. I guessed it must have been going well because she didn't answer her work phone, either. Oh well, I thought, I'm sure she'll call me when she gets back. I sat at my desk and started my afternoon phone calling session.

I don't know exactly what time it was, but shortly after I started making calls, my cell phone rang. It was an unknown number. It looked like Rita's work number but it wasn't her direct line. Expecting to hear Rita's voice on the other end, I was surprised when it wasn't Rita, but her supervisor. I sensed nervousness in her voice. She told me that Rita had had a *mishap* at work; she suffered a seizure at her desk. She was being rushed to Presbyterian/St. Luke's Hospital in an ambulance. My heart jumped as her words reverberated in my ears. Seizure? Ambulance? What the heck was this woman trying to say to me? I asked her to repeat herself at least two times before I totally got it. A hundred scenarios played out in my mind. Had she gotten sick from her Wendy's meal? Could it have been a heart attack? Was it Epilepsy? Her boss assured me that Rita was talking to the EMTs while they put her on the gurney. She said it seemed like Rita was confused but at least she was talking.

I frantically called both of my daughters as I drove to the hospital. I could hardly hold back my tears as I told them the news. I knew I had to sound calm so they wouldn't panic and have an accident. My heart seemed to be beating at twice its normal rate. Everyone seemed to be driving so slow, I could hardly stand it. Every red light was like an eternity. I didn't care about running them and I kind of hoped a cop would see and escort me. I kept in constant contact with Stacey because I knew she would never find the hospital alone. I looked in my rear view mirror and saw her behind me. I felt relieved because she didn't know her way driving around Denver, yet. When we got to the admissions desk, I was stunned when the clerk said there was no record of a Rita Lane being admitted. A nurse told us she *might* be at St. Joseph's Hospital, about a block away, so we went there immediately, but she wasn't there, either. We met Amanda outside of the emergency room of St. Joseph's Hospital. My daughter's faces were filled with an unmistakable fear. I could tell by her make-up, that Stacey had been crying.

"Girls, come here," I said, "we need to pray right now." My voice trembled. My face grew warmer as my stress level rose. "Oh Heavenly Father, please protect Rita at this moment," I said. "Lord, give us comfort and peace." Almost instantly, a peace filled my heart. I could tell that my daughters were on the verge of panic and so I added, "Oh, and happy birthday Amanda." How silly it must have appeared for us to be walking down the street laughing as we cried.

I pinched myself to make sure I wasn't having a horrible dream. *Oh God, oh God, oh God!* I repeated to myself. My wife was helpless and I couldn't be there to protect her. My mind wandered from memory to memory: *Our wedding day; the look on her face during the birth of our daughters; the day we got the keys to our first home; the way we spooned each other at night; cooking dinner as a family; holding hands while we watched movies.* It was as though our entire life together was replayed in a single instant.

This time, an emergency room nurse searched all records of ambulance activity in the Denver area within the last two hours. It was as though Rita never existed. After calling five hospitals, and thirty agonizing minutes, the nurse told us that Rita had in fact been taken to Presbyterian/St. Luke's. We returned to the Presbyterian/St. Luke's information desk. They told us that Rita was there but had not been officially admitted. We rushed to where she was located and she looked at us as if nothing was wrong. We were greeted with her familiar warm smile and the, "Hi guys!" she so often used. She sounded completely normal, and a tremendous sense of relief swept over me. *Everything is going to be alright,* I thought to myself. I told my daughters it looked like their mom was going to be just fine. Right then, a triage nurse joined us. She had overheard our conversation and told us that Rita was having some memory problems most likely due to the seizure.

"Ask her some questions." the nurse told me. I looked at the seemingly blank, but peaceful expression on Rita's face. There was no sign of distress or pain.

"Do you know me?" I asked. She looked at me with a puzzled look and shook her head.

Amanda then said, "Hi Mommy, do you know who I am?" And again Rita's face showed no sign of recollection. I looked out into the waiting room where Stacey was, thankful she couldn't hear the conversation.

Rita looked like a little girl as she sat up on the gurney, her legs dangling as she looked at the curtain that separated her from the other patients. The pale green paint and the contraptions on the walls seemed to catch her eye. I remember a man was having some kind of heart trouble in the adjacent exam room. His moans and groans were loud and distracting. I sat down and buried my face in my sweaty hands. I wanted to run away from it all. I didn't want to be there. I wished that this whole situation would end.

About fifteen minutes later, an orderly came in and told me that Rita needed a CAT scan. I told him I wanted to go with her. He said that that would be fine; I was allowed to stay in the scan room throughout the entire process. I remember watching her being scanned: Suddenly there it was, on the left side of her brain, a spot, about the size of a walnut. I remember thinking *there must be a spot just like it on the other side of her brain.* It never really occurred to me that the spot could be a tumor. The orderly rolled her bed back into the ER exam room, and the whole time I remained by her side. I couldn't let go of her hand. Looking back, I think it may have been more for my comfort than for hers. A doctor pulled me aside and said he had to talk to me about the results of the CAT scan. The news wasn't good. He said there appeared to be a mass in the left frontal lobe of her brain. In the background, I could hear a nurse asking Rita questions, "What's your address? What's your name? Do you know why you're here?"

Rita's face appeared confused and disoriented as the nurse inundated her with questions; she couldn't answer a single one. Suddenly she let out a horrific and high-pitched whine. Her mouth twisted uncontrollably as though she was trying to say something; her voice became a siren. Her eyes rolled back into her head and her hands curled into her abdomen as though she had an uncontrollable tightening of her limbs. Her legs contorted through the bars of the hospital bed. Her involuntary movements were so strong that we couldn't remove her leg from between the bars. The emergency room attendant quickly injected her with a sedative. She was out in seconds. I was relieved that my daughters weren't there to see their mom in such a terrifying state. They rushed Rita to the MRI room to better determine the size and shape of the mass.

I found myself standing outside the MRI room beside Rita's gurney; I could not remember how we got there. As I peered into the room I saw the massive machine and felt completely overwhelmed by its size. Seeing the sliding platform on which they laid my wife was simply unreal.

Tears welled-up in my eyes. I didn't want Rita to go in there alone so I asked the technician if I could stay in the room while she underwent the procedure. He pointed to a locker and directed me to place all metal and electronic objects in it before I would be allowed to enter the room. I was given a set of yellow foam ear plugs and hesitantly placed them in my ears. Rita was motionless as the platform slid into the tube. The machine started slowly at first, and developed into a deafening crescendo of clicks, ticks, and humming sounds. The noise was rhythmic and consistent. My palms were sweating profusely as I watched. Even with the ear plugs in place, the pandemonium of the machine penetrated my entire being.

I looked into the tube where Rita was and I could see her trying to turn her head; just a little at first, but then she began to squirm. Suddenly, she began fighting the blankets that covered her. The technician came into the room and said, "We're going to have to sedate her again, otherwise we'll never get the proper images. Can I have your permission?" The ER physician was called in and gave Rita another injection of the drug she had been given before. She was out in seconds. The technician continued the scanning process but in a matter of minutes Rita stirred again. Once more, the attendant called the doctor who injected four more milligrams of sedative into Rita's I.V. This time I had to interject—I feared that Rita couldn't handle any more of the sedative. The doctor looked at me in amazement.

He asked, "What are you afraid of?"

"I'm afraid you're going to *kill* my wife." My anxiety level skyrocketed. After much coaxing from the doctor, I was assured that she couldn't be in better hands or in a better place. All in all, Rita was given nineteen milligrams of sedative.

After her MRI, Rita was wheeled to the ICU ward. A neurosurgeon came in and explained that there was a three centimeter mass in Rita's left frontal lobe. He explained to me the possible nature of the mass and said that he would perform an emergency surgery the next morning. It was either an infection, or, a tumor. But, in either case it would need to be removed. An ICU nurse came in after the doctor left. She was about 55 years old and seemed to have had a bad day. She wasn't very friendly at first, and told me I would have to leave the ward at seven o'clock pm and I wouldn't be allowed back until eight.

"There's nothing you can do here, you might as well go home," she snapped. I glared at her.

"This is my wife. I'll stay with her as long as she's here," I snapped back. She took Rita's wedding ring off and started to hand it to me but pulled her hand back.

Half smiling, she said, "I've learned not to simply hand a wedding ring to a husband, let me put this on a safety pin so you don't lose it." She handed me the ring and asked if she needed to pin it to my shirt. We both chuckled as I took the ring.

> If you ever find yourself in an ICU or emergency room ward, remember that even though you have little control over the situation at hand, it is important to remain calm. You must realize that you are working with professionals that have dealt with situations similar to yours, countless times. Therefore, it's a good idea to think before you speak or react. At times, I was gripped with so much fear and uncertainty that I couldn't think straight, much less function in a logical manner. Calling upon the peace and wisdom that God has to offer gave me the comfort and peace that I desperately needed. Though your religious or spiritual views may differ from my own, the burdens of your situation should not be faced without support. Call upon the hospital chaplain/clergy or social worker to help you cope better and understand the chaos you will have to endure. I know that there is no way I could have overcome the horrors of any of my ER/ICU experiences without God's divine guidance.

The ICU waiting room was an unbearable place. The seats were beyond old and extremely hard. The room was cramped and the bland décor was mesmerizing. The lights were the dull, florescent type that further dampened our moods. The air-conditioner blasted, and in a short time, my joints had grown stiff because of how cold it was. There were old toys, magazines, and books strewn about, and the constant flickering of a single light was annoying me to no end. Yet, there was not a single Bible to be found. *Was this really a place that dealt with healing and treating people?* I thought. My daughters, Amanda's boyfriend Josh, and I spent the entire night in the waiting room, keeping shifts of bedside vigil with Rita.

CHAPTER 2

Surgery and Prognosis
Thursday, June 22, 2006

The drugs that Rita had been given took their toll. She hadn't stirred the entire night. When she finally woke up the next morning she was able to recognize us, and for that we gave thanks to God. We soon realized that even though she knew our names, she had no short-term memory recall and couldn't remember any of the events from the night before. She queried, again and again, as to where she was, and why she was there. I was unnerved by her persistent inquiries but patiently answered her each time.

By ten a.m. more than thirty people, most of them family members, had gathered on Rita's behalf. An orderly had come to prepare Rita for surgery and shaved several small areas on her head. Next, she began placing Cheerio-sized sensors on the spots that she had just shaven. She told us that Rita needed another MRI prior to surgery and that the *Cheerios* would assist the surgeon in mapping her brain. She had also shaved one large area where *the* incision would be made. After she finished the preparations I noticed Rita's hair and thought about how grey it had gotten over the years; her youthful face a striking contrast.

I told the orderly that Rita would not want to have her entire head shaved and she assured me that the doctor didn't need to shave her head. When the orderly finished, she placed a lock of Rita's hair in a plastic bag and taped it to the wall. As I stared at the bag the infinite reality of death gripped my thoughts. I almost hyperventilated. Is that all there would be left of my wife? Would it be used for forensic testing? What on earth was it for? Surely it wasn't a morbid souvenir of some sort.

My mind wandered from the ICU room to a foreboding image of me, standing alone at the foot of our bed. I was looking at the place where my wife and I slept together each night. I noticed the family photos that decorated our bedroom. But something was missing. The room seemed dark and unwelcoming. Rita's image was in almost every picture but her presence was completely absent. Now, the words *till death do us part* resounded through the hollows of my mind. I couldn't stop thinking about life without her.

A short while later Rita was taken for her second MRI. On the way to the scan room she started to repeatedly ask where she was and why she was there.

When we reached the MRI room Rita was placed onto the sliding platform and into the tube. She began to squirm and struggle as she was moved into the small circular opening in the face of the machine. The emergency room doctor was called to sedate Rita. It was the same doctor from the night before. At first meeting, he had struck me as a humble man and had a calming bedside manner; I was relieved to see the face of someone who knew Rita's situation. This time, she was out long enough to complete the MRI without further sedation and became semi-conscious as soon as the process was over. When Rita was slowly rolled out of the tube she was wide-eyed and mumbling. I wondered if she was somehow mirroring how I felt.

Amanda and Stacey were at the door as Rita was wheeled out of the MRI room. She looked at the girls and managed a half smile.

"Where am I?" she asked. "What happened?"

Sensing their distress, I gently took Rita's hand in mine and smiled at her. Then I glanced at my daughters, took a deep breath, and said, "You were in an accident, Honey. You were skating and you hit a skier with your surfboard." Our nervous laughter broke the tension.

The process of the pre-operation briefing can be overwhelming and especially confusing. Remember to ask as many pertinent questions as possible. Ask questions not only for your own peace of mind, but to have a better understanding of what can or will happen to your loved one. Based on my experience, good communication is essential. First, you will likely meet with a nurse that will talk to you about their role during the procedure and what to expect, i.e. the duration of the procedure, keeping you updated during the procedure, and where your loved one will be after everything is completed. The surgeon will also want to have a word with you about the surgery and everything they want to accomplish. They will go into detail with regard to the size of the incision, the possible outcomes of the surgery, and the risks involved. Finally, you will meet with the anesthesiologist.

If your loved one is incapacitated, as in Rita's situation, they will ask you to sign a waiver form in order to proceed with anesthetization. There were times when the medical jargon combined with the gravity of the situation simply left me dumbfounded. So, I encourage you to get clarification on any terms they use until you clearly understand.

Surgery and Prognosis
Thursday, June 22, 2006

Rita looked bewildered and asked, "I was skating?" Her response sent us into a fit of tear-filled relief. Our half-attempt to hug her was overshadowed by the fact that the time for her surgery was drawing nearer. When the anesthesiologist finally came to take Rita for her surgery, our previous moment together was completely dashed away by thoughts of the incalculable outcome. He introduced himself and told me he would administer the anesthesia during surgery. He was an enthusiastic gentleman with a contagious laugh. The nurses and orderlies that accompanied him seemed to like him. He must have seen the concern in my eyes as he repeatedly assured me that Rita would be in good hands during the procedure. He then handed me a document and explained that it was a waiver form for using anesthesia. The risks involved included the possibility of death and I reluctantly signed it.

In jest, I said, "Will you promise me you'll take as good of care of her as you would your own wife?"

He smiled and said, "I couldn't legally anesthetize my own wife, but I promise you, I'll take as good of care of her as I would my own mother." He smiled at me again and said, "I'll be coming out to talk to you once the surgery is complete—to tell you how it went." He and his entourage then wheeled Rita to the awaiting elevator.

My girls and I stood there crying while the doors of the elevator slowly closed. A part of me felt as though it would be the last time we would ever see her again. Down-trodden and worried, we wandered through the endless maze of hospital corridors to the surgery waiting room. When we walked in, we were met by some forty family members and friends.

The procedure was scheduled to last one-and-a-half hours and the surgical nurse had stated that we would be receiving an update after the first hour. My nervousness had me pacing all the while. Even though it was comforting that our family and friends were present, the tension in the room was palpable. Each time the door to the surgical ward opened, prayers were halted and the room grew silent and motionless. Three-and-a-half hours later, there was still no word of Rita's condition. At last, the neurosurgeon appeared. He removed his surgical cap as he walked through the doors and motioned for me to follow him into a small, private family room. Amanda and Stacey followed as I closed the door.

Without a shred of emotion, he said, "We were able to remove the entire mass." He explained that a sample would be sent to the forensics lab for an evaluation. It would take at least forty-eight hours for the results. He turned and walked out of the room, leaving me and my girls in a state of contemplation as the three of us hugged tightly and cried uncontrollably.

Surgery and Prognosis
Thursday, June 22, 2006

We walked out into the waiting room, our tear-tracked faces met by over seventy others that had waited, anticipating the results. The room was silent as I worked my way into the middle of the group. I took a seat next to my father-in-law and calmly stated, "They got it all." Irrepressible tears of joy and relief gushed from my eyes. I was trembling so badly that when I tried to, I couldn't stand on my own. I don't remember who it was, but two people came to my sides and supported me by my arms. Passionate tears of gratitude spread from person to person like a gust of wind. The overwhelming emotion in the room was beyond anything that I had ever experienced in my life. The wait for the forensic results would be like a lifetime.

We were told that Rita was in the recovery ward but no visitors were allowed. Even though we were told that she would be moved in an hour or so, an eternity passed as we waited for her release to the ICU. Of the seventy people that had gathered, some had left to get food, while others had followed me to the ICU waiting room. The sheer volume of followers surprised even the hospital staff and one clerk even questioned multiple times whether we were all in the party. Finally, after more than an hour, we were notified that Rita was out of recovery. Only two visitors were allowed at a time but my daughters and I went in straight away.

The first thing I noticed was the ventilator protruding from her mouth, her chest rising each time the machine pumped air into her lungs. It was agonizing to see her lying there; unconscious, with a large cotton bandage wrapped around her head, an IV tube in her arm, and eight bags and bottles feeding the IV. A bag hung on the side of her bed, fed by a tube that rose up her leg and disappeared into her gown. Her wrists were restrained by her sides. Her visitors each agreed on ten-minute shifts and could only watch as her machines beeped, hummed and pumped. She was never alone except for the one hour we were required to leave the ICU ward each morning and each night.

The next day, Rita had slept until one p.m. and by that time everyone but Amanda, Stacey, Josh, and I were gone. When the neurosurgeon and a respiratory nurse came into her room, Amanda and I watched as he ordered the nurse to remove the ventilator. We watched, horrified and helpless, as the nurse frustratingly tried to disengage the ventilator. She was turning it off so that Rita would begin to breathe on her own. But for some unknown reason she would not, or could not, inhale. After forty-five motionless seconds, the machine would automatically pump another breath into her. Watching Rita struggle on the gurney as the machine stopped and started over and over again, was tortuous. Each time, her attempts to breathe caused her to writhe and pull at her restraints. It was crucial that Rita start breathing without help from the machine before it could be completely shut down and removed from her airway.

The neurosurgeon became visibly annoyed after he repeatedly ordered that the machine be shut down. The nurse insisted that Rita needed to breathe on her own before she could remove the machine. The underlying dynamics of their professional relationship became clear and I sensed an unmistakable animosity between them. After perhaps twenty minutes, their words became hostile. The nurse would not concede and their discussion became so heated that they went out into the common area and began yelling at one another. Finally they returned to the room and the ventilator was completely removed...then nothing. The seconds were like hours as we waited and watched. Twenty-one, twenty-two, twenty-three, twenty-four... Finally, after thirty seconds, Rita inhaled deeply as though she had been held underwater the whole time.

For some reason the nurse had also removed the restraints on Rita's wrists. That's when the battle to protect her from herself began. She was constantly flailing and struggling to remove one thing or another. Her hospital gown, oxygen tube, IV, and sensors became the focus of her involuntary thrashing. Rita's hands had to be held down every second. Somehow, she even managed to pull her IV partially from her wrist. It was as though she had four hands and she was astoundingly strong for her size and condition. Over and over, she kicked her legs and tried to sit up. She yanked at her IV tubes, and tried to climb over the bed rails. Her personal assault was so relentless that after a short time I was completely exhausted. I cried out for my daughters to help me. It took every ounce of my strength just to fend off her self-destructive onslaught.

About twenty minutes into the ordeal, the neurosurgeon walked back into Rita's room and gave my shirt a tug. He asked me to go out into the common area *to talk*.

Without a shred of compassion or concern for the situation at hand, he revealed the news, "Your wife has a Grade IV Glioblastoma Multiforme."

"She has a what?" I asked perplexed.

"She has a very aggressive type of malignant brain tumor." Everything he said after that sounded like a foreign language. His piercing words were deliberate, blunt, and crude; I nearly fainted. A nurse brought a chair for me to sit in. Tears filled my eyes and I felt a lump rising in my throat.

"I-i-is it terminal?" I stammered.

Through the confusion I heard him say, "Yes."

"What am I going to tell my daughters?" I asked robotically. Without hesitation he turned and headed toward the room.

Looking back on it, I never should have let him enter the room alone, but in my daze, I didn't think to stop him. He gave the girls the bad news. I entered as he left. Both of my daughters were standing there, staring and pale as though they had seen a ghost. First, Stacey began to cry, then Amanda. I could hold back no longer. Our already worn souls had been pushed to the limit. We didn't see the doctor again until the next day and I was glad. His bedside manner was unacceptable. Maybe it was because he was the one who had given us the news, maybe it was because of the way he did it, but from that day forward, I disdained him.

Both of my daughters left me alone with Rita shortly after the doctor had walked out. I didn't realize either of them had left. The news was probably too much for them to grasp and I could hardly perceive the events at hand. All I could focus on was to do my best to hold her down. After what must have been fifteen minutes, I could hardly stop her flailing hands and feet.

Then, I sensed someone behind me. I turned, and there in the doorway stood Rita's good friend, Mercy. I don't know why, but at first, I felt angered by her presence. She was focused on Rita and me. My hands held down Rita's hands and my right leg was thrown over her legs. In my mind I knew Rita was in no condition to receive visitors. In a stern and unfriendly voice, I said, "Please leave us alone!" I could see the mixture of fear and hurt on Mercy's face. She turned and began to walk away and it felt as though I was alone in the world. I realized I was out of gas.

"Mercy!" I shouted, "Can you please, come back, I could use your help." She must have heard the desperation in my plea. She reluctantly entered the room and placed her hands upon Rita's wrists and I held her legs down. Neither of us spoke and the tension of our situation seemed to fuel the awkwardness. Mercy left a half-hour later; her face pale and her hands trembling. Luckily, Amanda returned just as Mercy had to leave, and though she and Mercy were good friends, neither of them said a word.

Soon after Mercy left, Stacey returned. We found ourselves trying to keep Rita from removing her robe. This time she was speaking incoherently.

Stacey tired to loosen Rita's grasp from her gown and said, "Mom, you don't want anyone to see you naked do you?"

Rita belligerently retorted, "*Yes,* damn it!" It was surprising to hear that come from her mouth; Rita was never one to swear. She was so combative she wouldn't listen to reason. By seven o'clock, the IV tube had been partially pulled from her wrist and the dressing that covered her incision was lying on the bed. The exposed area on her head throbbed with every beat of Rita's heart. The wound was half-moon in shape and blood was seeping slightly from the countless staples. No one had suggested that she be re-restrained, but thinking back on the experience it would have been easier to have restrained Rita than to have put ourselves through the whole ordeal.

When Amanda and Stacey returned at eight, they discovered that Rita had removed her gown and was lying naked in bed. Stacey called the ICU nurse and said, "You wouldn't want my dad to see her like that. If I were you, I'd get her some scrubs before he gets here." The nurse quickly found a set of cotton scrubs and before I got there they had carefully dressed Rita. The nurse even made special cuts so that the catheter, IV tubes, and electrodes would not be hampered.

The IV tube which first protruded from her wrist was now inserted and stitched in place below the left side of her collar bone, and the bandage she had removed from her head during the ordeal was never replaced. There was a surreal feeling of duress and exhaustion. I felt as though I had just been baptized in black, sludgy engine oil without hope of ever being clean, again. My daughters, Josh and I took turns watching Rita that night. We took one-hour shifts, two at a time, while the other two tired to sleep.

Around three a.m., Amanda came into the waiting room as I half slept. In an excited voice, she whispered, "Dad, are you awake?" I thought I was dreaming at first.

"Dad, are you awake? Mom finally settled down; she's resting." My eyes shot open. It was my turn to go in and stay with her. This time when I walked in, I noticed a child-sized blood pressure cuff on her petite arm. It was programmed to take a reading every five minutes and the nurse explained that it was because her blood pressure had become dangerously low. I looked at the readings on the machine; 62 over 45. I gently grasped Rita's hand and began to pray. I was awestruck when I noticed that within two cycles of prayer, her blood pressure had increased. Within five cycles, twenty-five minutes later, her blood pressure went up to 107 over 70. I knew in my heart, that even in her unconscious state, Rita was comforted by my presence and prayer. God's mercy and healing was so apparent that I was overcome by His promise of peace that surpasses all understanding.

Around five fifteen a.m., Rita began stirring. Though she was very groggy, I looked straight into her eyes and asked, "Who loves you?" It was a question I had always asked in the years we spent together. She would always answer, "You do," and I was terribly worried that she might not remember.

Not all medical professionals will exhibit the same level of sensitivity. Know that at some point during your experience you may be disappointed, or possibly appalled, by the way you are treated. I have heard from many families, stories of how other doctors delivered their prognosis in a heartless and brutal manner. There will, of course, be other healthcare providers that will be constantly mindful of your family's situation. Remember, if you're treated disrespectfully or unprofessionally during your stay, there are other good doctors and hospitals. Though you may be limited by your healthcare provider if the need to transfer arises, you still have a voice with the hospital social workers and administrators. Keep in mind that good communication is essential for good service. Don't be afraid to ask questions or do research on the illness you are facing. When it comes to you or your loved one, you are the one in control.

Lastly, I happen to be an emotional man. Perhaps you don't have the ability or need to let your emotions flow like me. That's alright too; just remember we each need to do what makes us feel comfortable. There are no wrong answers. For me the tears were a therapeutic relief.

She gazed at me and in a strained and raspy whisper, said, "You do." I was so thankful to God for giving me another day with her. I laughed and smiled while Rita laid there, oblivious to my elation. After I calmed down, I raced out to the waiting room. I found the girls and told them the words I had just heard from the lips of their mother. I had a renewed hope that everything was going to be fine.

A few days after the diagnosis, Amanda did a Google search on Glioblastoma Multiforme (GBM). She came to see me that afternoon at the hospital and was obviously very distraught. She asked me to walk with her to her car and as we walked, Amanda's voice started to crack. Her eyes filled with tears and she began to cry. She told me that she found out that on average, the life expectancy of a GBM patient, after their first diagnosis, was twelve to eighteen months. The doctors same words came to mind, but when Amanda said it, for some reason it seemed even more devastating. I remember I could hardly stand after hearing those words the first time, and now it was as if being hit in the face with a board. I was dizzy and nauseated. I knew that I would have to go back into Rita's room in a few minutes and I was afraid to have to face her, tell her, and possibly lose her.

I remember I went home that same afternoon to shower and mow our lawn. It had been some time since I last mowed and as I pushed the mower, all of a sudden, the words of the song, "Honey," came to my mind. It's a song about a man whose wife died unexpectedly and in the refrain, the song says "…and honey I miss you, and I'm being good. I'd like to be with you, if only I could..." I couldn't help but picture Rita lying in a coffin. The scene of me, our daughters, and our families crying became vividly etched into my mind. There was sweat beading up on my face coupled with overflowing tears. I suddenly went through a dry area in the yard and a dust cloud rose up as the mower stirred the ground. The mixture of sweat and tears on my face were a magnet for the dust. My face was caked with a thin coat of mud and when I finished, I went into the bathroom and looked in the mirror. The dirt was thickest where tears had flowed from my eyes and the surrounding area was a smooth layer of mud. It looked like I had intentionally made a mask of mud. After taking a shower and putting on a clean set of clothes, I headed back to the hospital.

CHAPTER 3

The ICU Waiting Room
Friday, June 23, 2006

I couldn't bring myself to leave the ICU ward except to eat, change clothes, and bathe. Over the next five days every time I left Rita's side, even to be relieved by one of my daughters, there seemed to be a magnetic force compelling me to return. I think my real fear revolved around the thought of being alone; alone without Rita, and alone with my turbulent necessity to have to leave her when the situation called for it. The time between leaving the ICU and the time I was able to rejoin my ailing wife was endless. Whenever I was in the waiting room I would notice other families. They would filter in, a few at a time. Their faces too, were laden with worry. Some seemed irritated to be there, while others were as dazed as I. Simply put, I was scared out of my mind. There was a constant feeling of uncertainty and aloneness. It was like winning the lottery, but in my case it had the worst possible outcome: my daughters and I living without our Precious Rita.

We found ourselves constantly praying and I reminded the girls that the Bible promises that God will give us, "A peace that passes understanding."

I also trusted that God would bless me with an *unshakable faith*. The thought would cross my mind during our prayers countless times, *unshakable*. What is unshakable faith? What is peace that passes understanding? *Could I count on God to give me peace that passes understanding? Would He give me an unshakable faith?* Could faith heal Rita's cancer? From the onset, people were telling me of how their church was keeping Rita in their prayers. The parishioners from one church would call one another and give word of Rita's need for prayer, then that person would pass along the information until a chain of prayers was formed. In the first three days there must have been at least ten prayer chains spanning almost the entire U.S., Canada, Mexico, and even Australia to name a few. *Please God, make our faith strong and give us peace.*

After three or four families came and went, I wondered if maybe they too needed support and prayer. Perhaps they longed for a fellow soul to help comfort their pain. I eased my way over to a young couple sitting opposite me. I asked them if they had a family member in the ICU. They told me that their daughter had stopped breathing. We got acquainted and spent the next fifteen minutes sharing our hospital experiences. We wept together and felt stronger despite our grief. I asked their daughter's name and if I could pray for her. They agreed and we prayed for their daughter and Rita. This went on for the next four days with many different families. When I went to the cafeteria, people I had met in the ICU would often wave and smile at me. I would be greeted by warm, empathetic hugs and questions about Rita's condition.

One time a woman whom I had visited with came to see me in the ICU ward. I had met her in the ICU waiting room while she waited for her husband. He was having pacemaker surgery and we prayed for a successful outcome. It was two days after her husband had been released to his non-emergency room, when she visited. Her visit and encouraging words were very uplifting. After our brief visit I decided that I was doing right by making friends in the waiting room.

The emergency/ICU waiting room is a very daunting place. Everyone there is suffering a personal tragedy, including you. The most important thing to remember is that *you are not alone*. Most people rely on their family for support, but what they don't realize is that life can't always stop for your issues; nor can you expect people to just drop everything and cater to you. I found the most relief by talking with others. I started talking on a whim and didn't expect anything in return. It was a blessing to be able to share my support, and honestly, I felt as though I received more support than I gave. Though you may not be capable of approaching a total stranger, especially in a dire situation, I encourage you to try. Perhaps you don't know where to start or what to say. I understand because I felt the same way. I decided to carry a cooler of bottled water and soda pop. Whenever I approached someone I offered them a cold drink. By using this approach I had great success getting acquainted with people. Even those that would not accept a drink were more receptive to what I had to say. Of course, some people refused to even look at me much less speak to me. But I was okay with that, too.

> I have come to the conclusion that if I see someone in pain or any situation where they might need prayer, I pray for them at that very moment. I'll stop whatever I'm doing or drop whatever I'm holding and ask if I can pray for them. Not only is it an awesome testimony to God's mercy and grace, but it's a great way to witness your faith. Most of all, God will be *glorified.* You may not realize it, but by comforting others, a simple conversation or prayer may start a chain reaction of kindness and caring.

One thing that always struck me as interesting about the waiting room was how everyone created a perimeter of chairs to mark their territory each night. It was like being on a camping trip; only no one really wanted to be there. We did our best to make the other *campers* feel welcome. We would set up camp each night using a 3x3 chair formation with one chair missing, to go in and out. In our makeshift camp ground we would spread out mats for sleeping, eating, playing games, doing puzzles, and of course, waiting. Each night there was never more than two or three other families, but they too would adopt the chair-perimeter campsite. One night while I was praying with the girls, I was overcome with an urge to find a Bible. We searched the entire ICU waiting room and could not find a single copy. We went to the surgery waiting room, several common areas, and the ER waiting room to no avail. Finally, we looked in Rita's room and that too yielded no results. There was not a single Bible to be found.

The next morning when the hospital social worker came in, she asked how we were doing and whether there was anything she could do. I told her about our search for a Bible and how we couldn't find a single copy and how the temperature in the ICU waiting room was just too cold to bear. She left the room and came back accompanied by a chaplain who was carrying three Bibles. Two would be left in the waiting room and one in Rita's room. I felt it was a blessing to see such quick action in such a trying time of need. Shortly after that an engineer came into the waiting room and adjusted the temperature to a more comfortable setting. Their quick response was a surprise given how much we had experienced in the last two days. Everything had seemed to take forever, even the simplest of tasks like waiting an hour until we were able to return to Rita's bedside. That social worker was a blessing in an otherwise dark and distressful time.

Another thing I remember is how our family and friends brought all kinds of food and drink to the waiting room. There was more food than anyone could ever, or should ever, eat. Because of the stress involved, I found that I was never hungry. So instead, I would offer food to anyone that entered the room. They had their pick of sandwiches, vegetable trays, cookie trays, nuts, seven or eight types of potato chips, pizza, and even candy. Sharing our food was very rewarding because we were able to help people that didn't have the same sort of support we did. Some people were from out of town and had little or no resources to draw upon, especially for food. Some were living in the Ronald McDonald House and didn't know of any restaurants in the Denver area. For those that were too afraid to navigate the city, the food must have been a blessing. We also gave directions and helped many people find their way back to their hotels and temporary housing locations. It's funny how the more you help others the better you feel, and the better you feel, the more you are willing to help others. The Bible talks about how giving will be met with a reciprocation that is pressed down, shaken together, and overflowing (Luke 6:38). I can honestly say I received more blessings than I gave in my ICU waiting room experience. Some of the most significant things we learn about life are not from books at all, but from our own experiences and God's hand in them.

In the end, some of the friends I made while I was waiting in the hospital changed my life forever. People from different walks of life came to my side in a time of need, and I will always be grateful. I only hope they were as blessed as I. I sometimes think about the word unshakable and I wonder *how did I fare?* I hope that I was able to show God the proper devotion and set an example that other people could follow. But in all truthfulness, in that chaotic period, I'm sure I made many mistakes. Thank God for his mercy and forgiveness. I once heard that unshakable faith is faith that *has* been shaken. If that holds true, I can honestly say that I have truly experienced *unshakable faith*.

CHAPTER 4

Recovery
Saturday, June 24, 2006

On Saturday morning, when Rita started to regain some sense of consciousness, I asked her if she'd like me to brush her teeth. With a slow drawl and a raspy voice she accepted. My daughters and I chuckled each time she spoke. Her voice sounded almost like the character from the movie E.T. because of the ventilator tube. There was a cart containing various medical supplies in the room, and I found a toothbrush designed for patients that could be attached to a suction hose in the wall. When the patient brushed it would suck up excess fluids.

I hooked up the toothbrush, Rita opened her mouth, and I brushed her teeth. When I tried to brush her molars her tongue would interfere. It was kind of funny at the time, but I couldn't help but wonder about the prospects of her recovery. She was obviously frustrated that she had to depend on me to brush her teeth. She repeatedly grabbed for the toothbrush but her coordination was completely discombobulated. She was completely unable to get the toothbrush to her mouth.

When I finished, I asked her to tell me about the details of her life. She responded slowly and most of her answers were incorrect. It was evident that she had lost, or forgotten, many of the details of her life. Even small details like everyday objects were difficult to identify. She had trouble with people too, like the time my nephew Mitchell and my sister Rosa visited. I asked her who Rosa was and she grinned and said with complete confidence, "That's my daughter, Stacey." Upon hearing her response I didn't know what to think, and even though most of her answers were wrong, I was still pleased to hear her try.

A while later, a woman walked into the room. She introduced herself as a speech pathologist. She explained that Rita would progress slowly at first and that healing after the surgery was not an exact science. There was no way of knowing how fast she would recover. It was likely she would improve rapidly once the swelling in her brain went down. Later, a physical therapist came. She said she would be bringing some liquids to see if Rita could keep them down. She also said she would test Rita to see if she could sit up by herself. If she were able to sit up unassisted, the therapist would then have Rita try to stand and walk.

Soon after the short meetings, Rita's liquid breakfast arrived. I spoon-fed her some broth and she gulped it down. Then, without hesitation she reached out for her tea. Carefully, her hands trembling awkwardly, she lifted the cup to her lips and drank its entire contents. She then devoured her gelatin and looked up at me. I told her how proud of her I was. There was a childlike innocence in her gleaming eyes and the way she smiled that I can still picture in my mind.

Within an hour, the physical therapist was back. They helped Rita into a sitting position and she was able to stay upright without assistance. The therapist told Rita to try standing while holding onto the bed. She could hardly stand without losing her balance but managed with a little help. Then, she was instructed to walk toward the head of the bed. Rita was able to move, ever so slowly, from one end of the bed to the other. Then she was told to move back to the center. Afterward, she was carefully eased back onto the bed. It amazed me that she could do all this less, than twenty-four hours after brain surgery. It was clear that she had a spirit of strength and a strong desire to live.

Shortly thereafter, more family members and friends began to arrive. When my mother came to see her, Rita squinted as she tried to focus on her face. I asked if she knew who the visitor was. She thought for a moment and said, "Yes, that's my mom." I could see loving tears in my mother's eyes. Then, Rita laid back and fell fast asleep. My mother was delighted. She and Rita had always been very close. Throughout the rest of the day she continued to mistakenly identify family members, but in the later hours her responses became more accurate and she laughed as often as she would have before the surgery.

The following evening, our good friends Lindsay and Julie Heyer came to visit. As soon as they walked in, Rita recognized Lindsay and called him by name. It seemed that her recall was progressing just fine considering we hadn't seen the Heyers in several years. I mentioned to them how well her recovery was going and I asked if she could tell me who the president was. After a short pause, she said "Lance, President Lance." At first, I was confused by her answer, but after I thought about it for a minute I realized that she was actually remembering the name of the Heyers' eldest son, Lance. During their visit Rita could identify almost every item shown to her. For a moment, I completely forgot about the devastating news we had received just one day prior. It felt as though we were getting our Precious back. A young intern assigned to her told us that her recovery was nothing short of miraculous. On Tuesday, when she was finally discharged, her personality had returned and she was almost able to walk without her walker. When I asked her about the hospital she had no recollection of her stay.

About two days after Rita had been home, two therapists came to interview the two of us. The occupational therapist visited in order to conduct a house survey and determine the best way to accommodate Rita. She compiled a list of things that needed to be addressed and adjusted. She recommended that I install grab bars and rubber bath-mats in the shower. She also told Rita to stay away from the stairs, and since our laundry room was in the basement, that meant that I would have to do the laundry. During the therapist's second visit, Rita asked if she could stop using her walker. A trip around the house was enough to prove that her balance was sufficient. As long as she didn't look up or down, while walking, she was fine. The physical therapist followed up on the recommendations of the occupational therapist by assessing Rita's limitations. This included everyday tasks that Rita should be able to perform and those that would pose the most difficulty. The therapists showed her how to get in and out of the bathtub and how to access the kitchen cupboards. She advised against sweeping and trying to get into any of the upper cabinets.

Family began to visit as soon as Rita returned home. Initially, most of the visitors were her parents, siblings, and their spouses from southern Colorado, where Rita had been raised. Every weekend someone from her family visited. I would videotape portions of each conversation as often as I could. At first I thought the flood of visitors would overwhelm Rita, but she graciously welcomed each guest. Her friendly smile and contagious laugh made everyone feel welcome. She and her guests would sit on our couch and have small talks about days passed. After three or four weeks, however, the number of visitors began to dwindle. After five weeks, visitors were rare. Rita became more and more withdrawn and quiet. At first, I thought that she might be depressed but I couldn't tell whether her behavior was a result of the illness, or, because of what she had been through. The possibility of her dying never crossed our minds. Family and friends would come and see her in high spirits, and assume that her recovery was inevitable. In the months following the surgery, everyone thought she would completely recover, including me.

But in private, it became apparent that Rita's memory was in decline. Her ability to focus and stay on task, diminished. Even from the time she came home from the hospital, I discovered she could no longer remember the voice mail code; so I changed it to make it easier.

The recovery period can be very taxing. Having support is crucial and helpful. From what I learned at our brain tumor support group, recovery can be a long and tumultuous period. Remember, no two illnesses are alike, The recovery period can be very taxing. Having support is crucial and helpful. From what I learned at our brain tumor support group, recovery can be a long and tumultuous period. Remember, no two illnesses are alike, nor are surgeries. It's best to remain calm and pray for wisdom and comfort. You may have to limit the number of guests depending on whether your loved one can handle it. Some patients may not want to socialize at all. Your visitors may even stop coming, so be sure to appreciate those that have made the effort to help. Ultimately, sincere encouragement is good for both patient and caregiver. It's most important to realize that caregiving is tremendously stressful, especially if the prognosis is bleak. Therefore, try to "read" each situation and keep an open mind; *you do not know how the caregiver feels*, nor what they are going through.

Come October of 2006, Rita's behavior began to noticeably change. At night, when we got ready for bed, she would aimlessly wander into the kitchen or sunroom as though she were searching for something. I asked her what she was looking for, but she would never reply. She no longer felt comfortable taking her clothes off in front of me and would insist I left the room while she dressed or undressed. Sometimes she would pull out a piece of cookware, place it on the stove, turn on the burner, and walk away. I would often have to stop her from going out into the cold sunroom and into the garage or the backyard. I continually worried that she would make it outside while I was in the shower, or using the bathroom. Leaving her alone for even a minute was a risk. Thankfully, I am a light sleeper.

CHAPTER 5

Treatment
July, 2 2006

Rita's first appointment with a radiologist was two days before the fourth of July. She had been referred by her neurosurgeon and that whole week I had a knot in my stomach. Each night I would toss and turn, all the while worrying about Rita, my daughters, and the mounting costs. Feelings of solitude and desperation overwhelmed me daily and I wondered what would become of our family. I feared we would lose our home and wondered how Rita could be so calm with all that was happening. How could she not be frightened? Even when I questioned how she felt, Rita would show no signs of emotion. The *unknown* had taken hold of our lives entirely. And I wondered if Rita had succumbed to the psychological terrorist we knew as GBM.

In the days leading up to her appointment, Amanda and I spent countless hours, *googling* and researching

GBMs, the abbreviated term for the Glioblastoma Multiforme. We looked up "left frontal lobe" to better understand the part of the brain where the GBM had been removed. We desperately searched for hope that there was an experimental treatment or cure, but to no avail. We went to the bookstore and library and found every book we could find, relevant to cancer. Surprisingly, there were few books related to brain cancer and we discovered that brain tumors are relatively uncommon. In fact, they represent only ten percent of all tumors. Soon, we had a good grasp of the situation Rita faced and though we never told Rita, we knew her odds were not good.

 I didn't sleep a wink the night before the appointment. I was already awake, staring at the ceiling when the alarm sounded. There was stillness as though I was dreaming. The prayer chains that we had heard so much about crossed my mind and I was certain that Rita would be healed. Yet, there was a lingering feeling of doubt and utter peril beneath my hopes. We got ready without saying a word and though there was never nervousness in our silence, this was different. We both knew this was serious. I silently asked for divine healing and as I finished, Rita spoke up. She finally admitted that she was kind of scared. I was somewhat relieved to see that she was mindful of her situation and I started praying, again. This time I prayed exclusively for Rita's peace.

Treatment
July, 2 2006

The drive to the hospital was a blur and I barely remember parallel parking a block from the doctor's office. We sat in the car for a short while and then slowly headed to the entrance of the building. When we walked in, I noticed that the decor was dull and the receptionist was frowning. Rita was handed a clipboard and told to answer the questions to the best of her ability. In the past few days I had filled out so many documents it made my head spin, and now they were asking Rita to deal with the same. There were approximately four to five pages of questions and Rita was fatigued trying to come up with the answers. About half-way through, I took over as Rita sat quietly. Next, we were led into a pillbox of an examination room. It was so cold that it seemed as though the air-conditioner had been turned on high and left on all night. I wrapped my arms around Rita's tiny shivering frame to warm her as we waited, goose bumps covering her arms.

After the obligatory half-hour wait, the oncologist entered. His slumped shoulders and constant frown told me that he was not a happy person. His answers were blunt one-word responses and when he spoke, he seemed to take great care not to make eye contact. His pale skin accentuated the red marks on his face and I wondered if he too might be battling some type of cancer. He had placed Rita's x-rays on the lighted wall-viewer, and while he went on about the three centimeter mass that had been removed from Rita's head, they were a constant distraction. He would prescribe forty-two rounds of radiation in conjunction with chemotherapy and told us that the radiation treatments would likely exhaust Rita's immune system. Each treatment would further compromise her health. He told us she might have to take some other medications in order to keep her blood count up.

I listened carefully to his recommendations. "Tell me doctor, what's your prognosis?" I questioned. He hesitated for a moment, and fidgeted with his hands as if he wished I hadn't asked.

With an abrupt jerk of his head, he looked away and said, "I've never seen anyone survive more than three years with a GBM." His tone was monotonous and without compassion.

"Then I guess we won't be seeing you again; we want someone who can give us hope." I snapped, his words echoing in my ears. Saying that I wanted to run from that place was an understatement. He told us there would be no co-pay for his services since it was a consultation. My thoughts were clouded and my heart was heavy. On the way out, the receptionist asked if we needed to schedule a follow-up visit. I didn't answer or even look her way. Somehow, I guess I wanted to treat her with the same rudeness as she had shown us with her frown, earlier. Although I thought I'd feel better about it, I soon realized I was just angry at the whole world. We walked out of the office and never gave it a second thought.

It was drizzling lightly when we walked out and I felt an emptiness I'd never known. The cloudy skies seemed especially grey as we slowly walked to the car. The rain droplets were just enough to hide the tears that fell from my eyes. During the drive home neither of us spoke a single word. My hands were trembling and I couldn't tell if it was the rain or my tears that blurred traffic. I knew I had to keep my cool despite the repeated bad news.

We had a family meeting that night and decided it would be best if we could find a neuro-oncologist specialized in treating Rita's illness. We hoped to find someone with a more positive outlook. The next day we started our search and Amanda found a neuro-oncologist at Colorado University Hospital. The hospital was located on the other side of town and was touted as one of the most state of the art facilities in the nation. When we went in for Rita's first appointment, we were impressed at how nice it looked, inside and out. The hallways were beautifully decorated and there was even a grand piano in one of the large open entryways. The waiting area felt warm and inviting and the receptionists were enthusiastic and understood how frightening it was for us to be there. After Rita had filled out the required paperwork a nurse called her name. She smiled and put her hand on Rita's shoulder as she escorted her to the lab where she took a small blood sample and other vital information. We were then taken to a small examination room to meet Rita's prospective doctor.

The doctor was a younger woman and greeted us with a smile. She seemed positive and made us feel comfortable. Rita liked her right away and we could tell she was sincerely happy to meet us. She also recommended forty-two radiation treatments followed up with an aggressive course of chemotherapy. In the days prior, Rita had expressed her concern about the toxic treatments because we had witnessed the debilitating effects of chemotherapy on others; after all, it seems like everyone has known someone that has had cancer these days.

As we talked, I thought about cancer, radiation, and chemotherapy. Even with all the advancements in technology, doctors continue to treat cancer the same way as they did fifty years ago. Surely, I thought, there had to be some new treatment. I hoped that the doctor would just give us a "magic pill" that would take all of Rita's cancer away.

The doctor listened to our concerns. Humbly, and in a soft voice, she said, "Whether you take the chemotherapy or not is up to you. However, it is my opinion that the chemotherapy drug she would be taking is cutting-edge. I would strongly recommend you consider it." I asked how much time it would give Rita.

She hesitated for a moment and said, "The survivability of this type of cancer is very low. I could not estimate exactly how much time it would buy, but any time it could add to her life would be worth it." The doctor then explained that Rita would be treated at the Anchutz Medical Campus located on the Colorado University Hospital campus. It was in the final stages of completion and we would have to start Rita's radiation treatments at the older facility. Rita left the decision to undergo chemo up to me. Three weeks later her treatments began.

Rita's first radiation treatment was literally terrifying. The facility was located in the basement of the old hospital. The aged elevators took forever and the drably painted hallways reminded me of something from a science fiction movie. The low pile carpeted floor looked like it was well worn and ready to be replaced. There were hard plastic chairs facing one another and the look of fear on people's faces gave hint to the terror that is radiation. When the receptionist announced each name, loved ones held their breath.

Before Rita's regime, she was fitted for a mask which would keep her head from moving during the radiation process. It was a hard mesh fabric that became pliable when saturated with water. It then conformed to her face and head before it hardened. There was a flat plate at the bottom that had several small holes in the perimeter. The flat portion would be screwed to the table to hold her head down while focused beams of radiation would bombard her brain. I asked if I could go into the room with her, but I wasn't allowed. Even though it only lasted about fifteen minutes, it was like an eternity waiting for them to finish.

Each time she went in for radiation she would always come out with a smile. I think she was trying to make me feel better. After the first few treatments her hair hadn't fallen out and we were optimistic. Then one day a patch of hair fell out on the left side of her head. Over the next seven days, large bunches of hair would be left in the bathtub each time she finished showering, and after combing her hair, there would be large clumps on the ground. As soon as I noticed any hair I would bury it in the trash can so she wouldn't have time to ponder the loss. I figured her not seeing the hair might keep her from becoming too distressed. There was also a bald spot on the back of her head where the radiation exited her skull. Obviously, the radiation beam wasn't stopping at the tumor. It passed through every inch of her brain. More than once, I was tempted to stop the treatments, but the doctor assured me they were necessary. It was weird to think about how much hair had fallen out, and yet the two spots were almost unnoticeable if combed over properly.

We contacted the American Cancer Society after the two spots had gone completely bald. Luckily for Rita, they donated two wigs. But because of how the large bald spot was situated, it made the wig look too low in the front so she decided to have it all buzzed. We went to our local Great Clips and they shaved it off for free. Josh and I shaved our heads in support, the following day. My good friend Franco and his brother shaved their heads. Then we got a call from Rita's brother and nephew. They too had shaved their heads. It was comforting to know that others were trying to understand our pain and they wanted to do whatever they could to lend support.

You may be asking yourself whether or not radiation and/or chemotherapy are right for you or your loved one. I cannot give advice since everyone's situation is different. But, I can say that it is best to find out as much as possible about the drug(s) that will be given as treatment. Find out about survival rates and the patient's quality of life while taking the drugs/radiation. Learn about the side-effects and make sure you ask if there are medications that may ease the discomfort caused by chemotherapy. It is also important to have a positive oncology team. They must believe the treatment they recommend will best serve your needs. A second opinion, and even a third, may give you peace of mind, but I wouldn't go past a third. Time is of the essence at this juncture.

Make a decision and stick to your plan. Finally, if you're the caretaker, you may be frightened by the effects of the treatment or certain aspects of it all; especially if the patient is someone very near and dear. Do your best to conceal your fear, and remember—if you show any doubt concerning the outcome, your loved one will certainly recognize it. Don't get me wrong, there is a time and a place to express your

> fears, but you must choose them carefully. Talk to someone who is empathetic and supportive. For me, a brain tumor support group was my best outlet. A chaplain or other clergy is another option, or even a close family member or friend. Don't hold back your fears or doubts, and don't bear the entire brunt alone. Last, and most important, *pray*. The Bible says we should "Pray without ceasing" (1 Thessalonians 5:17) and also "...The effectual fervent prayer of a righteous man availeth much." (James 5:16b)

Rita's attitude during her treatment was very inspirational and I was proud of her. She never complained about being nauseated, losing her hair, or even her illness. When we met with the doctor after she started the chemotherapy (which I will discuss more in-depth later), the doctor asked, "How did your first couple of nights go?"

Rita half-smiled and said, "Oh, I got a little nauseated."

I was stunned by her answer and said, "If *that* was a little nauseated, I'd hate to see *very* nauseated."

Whenever anyone asked her how she was, her standard reply was, "I'm doing *fine*." Then she would always follow up with, "How are *you* doing?" She would take the focus away from herself. If she was talking to someone and they started getting negative, she would almost always say something like, "Life is good." If someone said they were praying for her she would always say, "I'm praying for you, too." And she really meant it. I've never met anyone who was so unassuming or selfless. Though the treatment was very hard on Rita, she held her head high and faced every day with a positive attitude. I only hope that if I ever have to face a circumstance as daunting as hers, I'll have half the courage and stamina she did.

CHAPTER 6

Chemotherapy

Shortly after her radiation treatments began, Rita also started chemotherapy. Her treatments were in pill-form and supposed to be taken in twenty-eight day cycles; five consecutive days on, and twenty-three days off. She was instructed to take her anti-nausea medication forty-five minutes before going to bed, at bed-time she was to take the Temodar. The neuro-oncologist seemed very confident that it would be beneficial and insisted we try it. She said that Temodar (Temazolomide) had been showing promise and that it was a cutting-edge chemo treatment. When I asked her what kind of success we could expect from the Temodar, she said it would add an average of three months to the patient's life. I was stunned. I was expecting her to say it would kill some of the cancer. How could this be happening—only three months? I looked at Rita and thoughts of her dying overwhelmed me. All I wanted to do was tell the doctor she was wrong. I was filled with an indescribable anger. Three months? Three months for a dying person must seem like an eternity, but compared to the twenty-six years Rita and I had been married, it was a brief moment! All we could do was accept it. I wanted every minute I could get—no matter what. On the way home, I thought about the scripture where God says our time here is but a vapor. I reflected upon that idea—our lives are nothing more than a brief instance of vapor, like a passing cloud. I was so dazed that I drove right past the pharmacy and had to turn back around. We filled the prescription and the pharmacist told us about the precautions for handling the chemo. He said that the chemotherapy was so toxic that we needed to wash our hands thoroughly if we handled it. I held the bag containing the three small bottles of drugs and looked at the actual cost listed on the receipt: $4,000. How could twenty pills cost $4,000? We were relieved to have to only pay $200. Thank goodness for good insurance.

The first night I had placed a small trash can near Rita's side of the bed and lined it with two bags in case she got sick. At around one a.m., Rita began thrashing around as though she was struggling to remove her blankets. At first I thought she might be having a bad dream or perhaps she had to go to the bathroom. But she didn't get out of bed. Then suddenly she sat up and pulled the trash can to her face. She began to tremble as though she were having convulsions and vomited so violently that it shook the entire bed. Her vomiting went on continuously for two hours and by then there was nothing left to purge. Each time she tried to vomit, she would gag so hard there was not a single breath coming out of her. Yellow fluid was all I could see and it had a bitter chemical odor to it that permeated the room. Her eyes were filled with tears and she looked so weak I was afraid she might not be able to withstand any more. All I could do was watch and pray. Between her attacks of nausea I asked if she wanted me to rub her back.

Exhausted, she whispered, "Please don't touch me, I'm afraid if you do, I'll get sick again." The nausea went on throughout the night and continued each of the first two nights. Even after her nighttime nausea subsided, and she was between chemotherapy cycles, she often suffered sudden bouts of vomiting. Her appetite decreased daily, and her weight dropped from 139 pounds before becoming ill, down to 111 pounds in just four weeks. I was most concerned because in addition to losing body fat, Rita was obviously losing muscle tone. She had lost all motivation for exercise and convincing her to eat was nearly impossible. By October of 2006, her weight loss caused her to become very sensitive to the cold and consequently, she was always bundled up in extra clothing or blankets; she didn't even want to go outside. Within the first month of starting chemo, Rita's whole face broke out with severe acne. She also began to show signs of depression and became withdrawn and unmotivated to do anything. I felt like all I could do was encourage her. I suggested that we start exercising and after much coaxing I convinced her to go on short walks with me through the local mall. She walked very slowly at first and would get tired after a few minutes. But, by the end of her second chemo cycle, there were noticeable improvements in her state of mind, her endurance, and even her complexion.

Given the way she improved, it made my daughters and me optimistic. For a while we started believing it was possible that Rita could beat the cancer. But then, after her third chemo-cycle, her energy waned once more. The daily walks too, were taking their toll, and soon she was too fatigued to walk. Still she enjoyed her mall visits very much and so we began using one of the mall wheelchairs. I would wheel her around while talking to her, but Rita never spoke a word. Even two weeks after her monthly chemo cycles ended, she was in decline. She would sometimes have bouts of nausea where she would just vomit without warning. She wouldn't have time to turn her head or even cover her mouth. The doctor called it "trajectory vomiting."

My daughters had never seen their mother during one of her vomiting bouts or while she was having a very bad day, 'till late October when we all went for a ride. When I was a few blocks from home, I saw Rita lurch forward as if I had suddenly slammed on the brakes. Without warning, vomit exploded from her mouth. She couldn't roll her window down or even turn her head. The vomit was spread across the windshield and all over her car door. Her face, chest, and legs were covered. I pulled to the side of the road as fast as I could. Stacey opened her door and ran to the curb and vomited as well. There was a frustrating feeling of helplessness as I cleaned the mess and wiped Rita's face. Up 'till then, both girls had denied their mom's decline. But now, they seemed to realize just how severe their mother's illness had become.

Shortly after she started chemotherapy, Rita developed a slight rash on the backsides of her hands. Not scratching the rash was unbearable for her and soon it spread to her arms and neck. Next, it appeared on her legs. Rita scratched the rash so frequently that it began to bleed. The more she scratched the more it spread. Before we knew it the rash covered everything but her face and scalp. We made an urgent appointment with a dermatologist. They prescribed a series of products starting with Aveno brand oatmeal baths and Cetafil cream. The products worked for a short while but neither was able to get her through a whole night without scratching 'till it bled. No matter how much I discouraged her from scratching, she persisted and no matter what product she applied to the rash, the itching continued.

As demonstrated in my experience with Rita, chemotherapy can be a devastating experience. There's no telling what will occur and some people may even have a more positive response to the drugs. If you or your loved ones become concerned about the changes in daily life because of the chemo, it is important to understand that the changes are even more difficult for the person experiencing them. Have a group discussion with your family. Find out what everyone is thinking. If you are alone with your affected loved one, don't wait to seek help—talk with your doctor. They may be able to recommend support that you may not be aware of, such as a hospital social worker(s) or psychological counseling and support groups. In my experience, support groups are one of the best resources you can draw upon. Your feelings are valid and need to be addressed. Support groups are perfect for sharing, advice, and support, of course. Don't hesitate to take care of yourself, or feel like you're alone in the world... remember: *You are not alone.*

In our many visits to the cancer center, we learned that some chemotherapy drugs may cause the patient to lose every hair on their body. I met one young man who had lost all of his hair but wasn't concerned. Conversely, a woman I knew was thrown into a deep depression from the same result. She couldn't stand the thought of having lost her beautiful long braids. Losing one's hair can be very devastating and in some cases even create feelings of hopelessness. If this is the case I would recommend a good supply of scarves and hats, or better yet, wigs that can provide a sense of normalcy. Of course, some people are fine with no hair at all. Furthermore, if your loved one is taking food supplements be sure to let your doctor know what specific products they are taking. Some vitamins and herbs are known to react negatively with chemotherapy drugs. The last thing you would want to do is negate the function of your chemotherapy.

By that time, we were seeing the neuro-oncologist on a semi-weekly basis. We were desperate to rid Rita of the itching that had plagued her for a week and-a-half. The doctor suggested that Rita might be allergic to Dilantin, the anti-seizure drug she had been taking so she prescribed another drug named Keppra. Rita hadn't had a decent night of sleep for two weeks and I could see her becoming weaker by the day. Even after being off of the Dilantin for thirty days, the rash still persisted. Then one night, it occurred to me to try using some therapeutic grade essential oils on her rash. We had been using oils for several years prior to Rita becoming ill and had successful results for everything from burns to scrapes, skin infections, and even headaches and diarrhea. I alternated oils of lavender and frankincense. The lavender was easy on the nose and gentle on her skin. It also helped her sleep better and longer. The aroma of the frankincense filled the room with a sense of peace and calm. Rita would moan, in pain as well as relief, when I applied the oils. Starting with her shoulders and working downward from there, by the time I reached the soles of her feet, she was usually in a relaxed state of semi-consciousness. Most times, she slept through the entire night without moving or making a noise. From then on, and for as long as she was receiving any treatments, I would break out the oils and apply them liberally to her back, shoulders, legs, and feet. Rita's rash began to disappear within three days of using the oils and was completely gone in two weeks. The scars on her legs, neck, and back were visible for months after.

CHAPTER 7

It Could Have Been Worse
Wednesday, September 19, 1979

In September of 1979 I was stationed at Fort Carson in Colorado Springs. I was in the Army and had been dating Rita for almost a year-and-a-half. A few months earlier, my brother Joey had gotten married and Rita stood up with me at his wedding. We walked down the aisle together and I remember coming to the realization that I was in love with Rita. I decided to ask Rita for her hand in marriage and bought an engagement ring from a nearby jewelry store in Colorado Springs. Then I hitchhiked my way to Denver to visit Rita at her apartment.

When I finally got into Denver I still had quite a distance to walk to get to her place. There was a lake near where I was dropped off and I happened to see my friend's mom jogging. I decided to say hi and showed her the ring. I placed it in my shirt pocket and jogged a short way by her side. I was a few blocks from where Rita lived and when I checked to make sure the ring was okay, I realized it was no longer in my pocket. In a panic, I retraced my steps. I looked under trees and bushes and asked people if they had found the ring.

Eventually I realized I wouldn't find the ring. I knocked on Rita's apartment door, distressed and heartbroken. I told her my story and asked for her hand without the ring. Despite the fact that I had lost one of the most important symbols of marriage, she still said yes. She was very understanding and even reacted as though I still had the ring. Sadly though, within a couple of hours I had to get to the bus station to go back to Fort Carson. The rest of the week I had a hard time thinking straight, all I wanted to do was return to Denver and find the ring.

The following Friday, during my free weekend, I hitchhiked back to Denver because at that time, I didn't have a car. A young man pulled to the side of the road and as soon as I entered his car I noticed that he had fresh bandages on his left hand. The bandage covered his middle and ring finger and the first and second joints on both were missing. He told me the story of how he had lost his fingers in a freak accident while working on his car. Coincidentally, it happened the same day I had lost Rita's engagement ring. All of a sudden I had a profound realization, *it could have been worse.* I had lost a ring; he had lost two of his fingers.

It Could Have Been Worse
Wednesday, September 19, 1979

At times when Rita would reflect upon her experience with the treatments and the illness she would say, "It could have been worse." She always had a way of seeing the bright side of things and did her best to keep a positive outlook. I think her optimism helped me get through some of the toughest of days. I would sometimes think that if I had even half of Rita's attitude I would make it through this, too.

In some of the most troubling times in my life I would often read a poem that I had kept handy since my younger days. I would read it to remind myself that though things may seem bad at the moment, I've got so much to be thankful for and to thank God for everything he has done for me. The story of the young man I met the week after losing Rita's ring is very similar to the experiences in the poem which is why it seemed so pertinent throughout my life. That is why I would like to share it with you, and hopefully, you will draw upon the same wisdom I have come to know through reading the poem:

The World Is Mine Oh God, Forgive Me When I Whine

Today, upon a bus, I saw a girl with golden hair.
I envied her, she seemed so gay,
and wished I was as fair.
When suddenly she rose to leave,
I saw her hobble down the aisle.
She had one leg and wore a crutch.
And as she passed...a smile.
Oh God, forgive me when I whine.
I have two legs, the world is mine.
I stopped to buy some candy.
The lad who sold it had such charm.
I talked with him, he seemed so glad.
If I were late, it'd do no harm.
And as I left, he said to me,
"I thank you, you've been so kind.
It's nice to talk with folks like you.
You see," he said, "I'm blind."
Oh God, forgive me when I whine.
I have two eyes, the world is mine.
Later while walking down the street,
I saw a child with eyes of blue.
He stood and watched the others play.
He did not know what to do.
I stopped a moment and then I said,
"Why don't you join the others, dear?"
He looked ahead without a word.

It Could Have Been Worse
Wednesday, September 19, 1979

And then I knew, he couldn't hear.
Oh God, forgive me when I whine.
I have two ears, the world is mine.
With feet to take me where I'd go.
With eyes to see the sunset's glow.
With ears to hear what I'd know.
Oh God, forgive me when I whine.
I've been blessed indeed, the world is mine...
~ Red Foley

Considering Rita's situation from another perspective, I am reminded of the following story. Perhaps you have already read it since it was a popular forwarded email. It was sent to me at a time during Rita's illness when I needed an uplifting of sorts. Though I chuckled when I read it, it was more enlightening than anything else. It helped me face the day and the fact that Rita too must have had a similar outlook as the woman in the story to stay as strong as she did. Even as Rita started becoming more and more incoherent she would be optimistic. She would never say the words seizure, tumor, or cancer and would definitely never personalize the illness as so many doctors these days would have you do. I hope that this story inspires you as much as it has me, because really, it can be applied to anyone's life and not just those that are suffering a terminal illness:

There once was an old woman who woke up one morning, looked in the mirror and noticed that she had only three hairs on her head. Well, she said, I think I'll braid my hair today. So she did and she had a wonderful day. The next day she woke up, looked in the mirror, and saw that she had only two hairs on her head. Hmm, she said, I think I'll part my hair down the middle today. So she did, and she had a grand day. The next day she woke up, looked in the mirror and noticed that she had only one hair on her head. Well, she said, today I'm going to wear my hair in a pony tail. So she did and she had a fun day. The next day she woke up, looked in the mirror, and noticed that there was not a single hair on her head. Yea! She exclaimed, I don't have to fix my hair today!

After the ring incident, Rita and I ended up purchasing an inexpensive wedding band for the ceremony. It may not have had the same monetary value, but the sentimental value was the same. We were married on February 2, 1980. About five years later we bought another ring, this time with a nicer diamond and higher price tag. Oddly enough, the new ring ended up having a faulty claw mounting and Rita lost the diamond! That ring too, was replaced. All in all Rita had four sets of wedding rings. Though some had cost more than others, the value of each remained the same. After all, it's not about the price tag of a ring that makes it special, it's the meaning. One thing I will always remember about Rita was how she too cherished the rings that I bought her—for their meaning. So much in life is judged by value and cost these days that it seems like the true meaning of everything has been toned down. The lost ring story simply reminds me that I had many reasons to be thankful. Rita was alive and she had a great attitude. We had a successful marriage and two healthy and beautiful daughters. Most of all, we had hope. Hope that Rita would be healed and made whole, again. My decision to do my best to keep a more positive outlook no matter what happened made it much easier to keep my eyes firmly fixed on the Lord. Now, whenever I'm in a bad situation or mood I try to remind myself of those most memorable words Rita used to say: *It could have been worse.*

CHAPTER 8

The Decline

One day I found several unopened envelopes addressed to *The Lane Family*. I opened them and discovered cards containing checks, cash, and gift cards that had been donated by the people from our church. The pile of letters on the desk had turned into a small mountain and I had been so wrapped up in the illness that I didn't pay any attention to the obvious happenings around the house. It seemed that Rita had been piling all the mail on the desk in our bedroom for the past five months. In addition to the actual mail there was a pile of junk mail nearly a foot high. Soon after my discovery, I received a letter from our insurance company after coming home from work one day. It stated that they hadn't received payment for our health insurance and that our family's coverage would be dropped if payment wasn't received immediately. I looked for the late notice in question and came across several. It never occurred to me that Rita would be so nonchalant about important things like the bills, and trying to keep up with work and the illness had left me completely unaware. If I had not received the letter from the insurance company we may have found our entire family without insurance. Thank goodness I was able to pay the bill by phone. Losing our coverage could have been yet another catastrophic event.

One morning in February of 2007, I got a call from our second mortgage company. The woman making the call sounded stern as she explained that our second mortgage was in foreclosure. A payment had not been received in five months and a late notice had been sent two months prior. The letter was to inform us that we had thirty days to correct the situation. I was mad at myself for not having been more responsible with the finances throughout the years. I explained my wife's situation and the financial hardships we were facing, and after I politely pled my case, I asked if there was anything they could do for us. At first, the woman seemed surprised—then she paused and said, "I'm going to put you on hold for a minute." The next thing I knew, her supervisor was on the line. She told me she would place us in a special hardship program where all of the late payments would be rolled into the back end of the loan. Then she said she would get our interest rate dropped to zero percent. All of this was possible because I asked if there was anything they could do for us.

When someone has had brain surgery, or another mentally debilitating illness, they may say and do things that make little or no sense. You must understand that even they can't explain their actions. For the patient, letting go of their independence is like admitting that the illness has gotten the best of them. Your decisions in the next few months, or years, may be the toughest you will ever have to make. Remember, the patient is probably as frustrated as you are so it's best to be patient, loving, and kind. When I discovered what Rita had done with the mail, my first reaction was anger. But then I realized that my only option was to step up and take care of things, not get angry at something of which we had no control. So, I took care of the most important delinquent bills and got things straightened out as soon as possible.

If you find that your expenses are too overwhelming, don't avoid your debtors. Face them head-on and tell them about your hardships. The people you will deal with will most likely be understanding and compassionate. Chances are they know someone in a similar situation. In our case we were able to have our second mortgage payment lowered to just fifty dollars a month at

> zero percent interest. This was a crucial factor when Rita was ill, since illness is the number one cause of bankruptcy in the U.S.

After the close-call we had with our mortgage and insurance I asked Rita if I should be the one to manage the bills. She insisted that she was still capable, plus, I had never gotten involved with the finances. After a while, Rita became incapacitated to the point that even simple tasks were too much for her. Looking back, I wish I would have participated more with the household finances but I just never did. Even the junk mail seemed too much to deal with at that time and I didn't touch it for almost six months. By the time I did get to it, it was almost three feet high.

Before Rita had the seizure that started everything, she weighed 139 pounds. She had always been in good health and had no history of disease or illness. Unfortunately it seemed as though the GBM was the culmination of everything she never had to worry about, health-wise, throughout her life. When she was in the hospital, I didn't tell her the prognosis because I didn't want to burden her with it. We talked about how she couldn't remember a single minute of her stay in the hospital when she finally came home. I always made sure that she wasn't in pain and told my daughters how important it was for them to be with her.

We were living the best we could from day to day, and I still continued to work. Rita, on the other hand, never returned to work. The doctors told her that she would never be able to work again because of the severity of her illness. I don't think Rita ever considered why she wasn't allowed to return to work, but she never asked why, either. She would spend her days just sitting around, watching TV, and talking to people on the phone. When the visitors started coming she would converse as though nothing were wrong and there was no indication of her ever having surgery. I would spend my nights after work on the internet and researching every option available. I would compile lists of books, literature, and information about food, treatments, herbs, and alternatives having to do with cancer. Sadly, I found almost nothing about brain tumors. I was sitting in the middle of nowhere with little hope to spare, and almost no options.

After Rita started chemotherapy she began to eat less and less, for obvious reasons. Her weight dropped steadily to 120 pounds, then to 115, and soon, 111. When I took her for an MRI on April 3, 2007, ten months after the first surgery, she weighed just 106 pounds. I looked at her that morning and noticed how frail and weak she seemed. Her shoulders slumped and her legs were very thin. Her neck looked old and layered, as though she had aged into a senior citizen. My once lively, vibrant wife had lost more than just her personality and health. She would spend her days in silence sitting in front of the television, staring blankly as though she had no comprehension of the world around her. Her conversations were limited to one-and two-word sentences and she only spoke when spoken to; I was alone like no one else could understand.

When I would talk to our daughters on the phone, they would chastise me for even hinting that their mother was in full decline. They were in complete denial and I would wonder if they didn't visit for weeks at a time because they didn't want to face what was happening to their precious mother. I can only imagine the pain and heartache that they were going through. The painful reality was that Rita was literally wasting away right before our eyes.

Sometimes I would sit up at night and I would think about cancer. It was like a brilliant invader that could fool even the most renowned doctors of the world, and take lives as though it were created to kill. It seemed like an intelligent being, yet so foolish. How could it eat away at its host to the point of its own demise?

I wondered how long it would take to find a cure, or if one even existed. Would the cure be found before Rita's life was ended? Each visit, I would ask the doctor if there was a new experimental treatment or drug. I would inquire about things I had researched like scorpion venom and red clover, zeolite, burdock root, and blood root to name a few. Yet, each time they would tell me that anything I did would most likely counteract the chemo, and leave me once again at an impasse. My frustration left me in an abysmal state for months at a time. I didn't know where to direct my anger and so anyone and everyone, including my own family, became a target. It wasn't something I could control or have them understand; I was lost in a solitude that went beyond family ties or love. Unfortunately, my disposition was a key factor to my own isolation and I didn't have the mind to consider repercussions or others' lack of understanding.

As for Rita, she seemed to be lost in a world of her own. She was neither the woman I knew, nor someone I could get to know once again. I've heard it said many times before by other caregivers in my support groups, that patients will go into their own worlds. There is no telling what is going on with them. If they don't want to eat, that's that, forget about convincing them, their mind is made up. Losing weight is almost a given and becoming withdrawn is a sign of depression. Participating with the world in any way is not something these patients do. What I heard seemed reminiscent of what I had learned about Alzheimer's and dementia patients. Often, brain tumor patients, like some Alzheimer's patients become hostile and violent. With each story I became more and more heartbroken for the people dealing with situations far different from my own. I would read online forums about brain tumor sufferers and their caretakers, and immediately there was an unspoken, yet shared pain. I grew to hate cancer and everything associated with it; the support groups, hospitals, treatments, doctors, visitors, and even life. Everything became another target for my hatred. I had to force myself to go to church, and as I sat in the pew it seemed as if I could feel pity-filled eyes staring through me. All I wanted to do was avoid that place, but it was my only solace; my only peace came from God and yet I didn't want to be there. Luckily my pastor was never judgmental and had wisdom that I so desperately needed. I would call him often and he would always take my call. He would patiently listen to my gripes and settle my spirit with his prayers and advice.

Sometimes my anger was so misdirected that I would even find myself angry at Rita for being sick. My overwhelming sense of abandonment and helplessness was probably the root of the situation, but at the time it just wasn't apparent. I had many sleepless nights and I would fall to my knees and cry to God. The weirdest thing was that neither Rita, nor I, asked God "why?" or question "why me?" If she did, she never voiced it out loud. I just always knew He was there and I had to continue to remind myself of this fact. I would think about people who didn't know the Lord and wonder how difficult it must be for them. Thank God for his mercy. But on top of it all was the fact that everything I tried to do to help Rita proved futile, and she continued to disappear.

> A nutritionist was available to patients at no cost at the cancer center, so we scheduled an appointment in early May. I was hoping that they would be able to convince Rita to eat more steadily. The nutritionist showed Rita, mathematically, why she was losing so much weight. Rita's caloric intake was at a minimum and her body needed to supplement the loss of calories by consuming the fat and muscles of her own body. Yet, Rita still insisted that she wasn't hungry or only required very small portions. Sometimes, she would pick up a single grain of rice on the tine of a fork, eat no more than fifteen, and that was her meal. She would eat a single green bean and say she was full. It seemed like she was starving herself intentionally. Then I would go to my support group and learn that

others were doing the same thing. The stresses I had to endure were incomprehensible and to this day I know that only God got me through it all.

Rita's weight leveled off at 106 over the next three months and the doctor told us that as long as her weight stayed above 100 pounds she would be fine. When we were first married she had weighed about 100 pounds, so I quit pestering Rita and she stayed at that weight until July of 2007, when she had her second surgery.

One day, while shopping, Amanda discovered a book entitled *A Cancer Battle Plan* by Anne E. and David J. Frähm. It's about Anne and how she battled an advanced terminal cancer by drastically changing her diet and lifestyle. Frankly, it was the number one inspiration for writing this book and the information it contained was extremely helpful and easy to understand. Frähm recounts that she had been experiencing severe back pain for many, many months. Of all the doctors she visited, none could properly diagnose her condition. Finally, after getting an x-ray, she found out that she had advanced breast cancer. By the time she was correctly diagnosed it was realistically too late to save her by medical standards. The cancer had metastasized, meaning it had spread to many other parts of her body, including her skull, shoulder, pelvic bone, ribs, and all along her spine. She said the doctor gave her two years to live. She underwent surgery, chemotherapy, and radiation; commonly known in the medical world as the "big three." Eventually, when her cancer became resistant to the chemotherapy, and it looked like she was going to lose the battle, she opted for a bone marrow transplant. Anne's immune system was so compromised that she was confined to a small, sterile room for several months after the transplant. The chemotherapy she was given during the treatment almost killed her. When the doctor finally sent her home it was basically so she could die peacefully. But, miraculously she fooled them all and survived. She was able to overcome the cancer through diet, exercise, and detoxification practices. She had explored and studied the link between cancer and diet as well as possible environmental factors. Anne went on several juice fasts where she would have juice as her sole source of nutrition for days at a time. After reading about Anne's juice fasting I decided to implement a regimen of juices for Rita. Unfortunately, Rita was stubbornly against foregoing solid food, even though she was barely eating anything at the time.

    I discovered another book entitled *Fit for Life* by Harvey and Marilyn Diamond. After reading this book I learned that when we improperly mix our nutrition we can create a toxic buildup of undigested food in our bodies. It was then that I decided to take Rita off of all meats (especially processed meat), dairy products, and sugars. I placed her on a diet of organic fruits and vegetables. In the mornings she would eat the organic fruit and in the evening the organic vegetables for lunch and dinner. I carefully planned her diet based on what the book suggested to detoxify her body. What I didn't take into account was the fact that she was continually on chemotherapy, so the toxins were always building up in her liver. I didn't ask her to go on this diet alone, though. I ate everything she did, only in larger quantities. Our weight went down considerably as our body fat levels decreased. I dropped from 189 pounds down to 176 two months after starting the diet and I was feeling great, physically. Rita was very opposed to the dietary restrictions. We would have long discussion about how she should be taking her health into account and that the dieting would be beneficial. But no matter what I did or said I could not get her to change her mind. In time, Rita told me that she didn't want to be on any more restrictive diets. She wanted to eat whatever she desired. Since I didn't know how much time I had left with her I decided I didn't want her to feel unpleasant in the short time that she had left. So, I took her out to dinner that night. She ordered a rib-eye steak but only ate a bite or two. Still, it made her happy and I was glad to see her smile again. Even though I wanted to do anything and everything to save her life I didn't argue with her decision. Still, I believe that proper diet is critical for surviving any cancer. The diet you or your loved one decides upon should be of your own choosing. I am *not* a nutritionist so I do not recommend choosing a dietary battle plan before consulting your physician or nutritionist. I do, however, recommend reading both of the books, mentioned earlier, if you or your loved one has cancer.

> No matter what situation you and your loved one are facing, it would be in your best interest to learn as much as you can about all aspects of the illness. Rita's doctors had warned me not to do too much research about the illness because they said it might be too scary. We quickly understood why they said that. The outlook was not good. The average survival rate for a grade IV GBM was only twelve to eighteen months. The doctor had obviously known how bad things actually were and in fact, the week following her first surgery, we went to our family doctor to tell her about the diagnosis. Her expression suddenly became sullen.
>
> She paused momentarily then said, "Oh…I'm so sorry." I had already learned a bit about the

survival statistics, but I hadn't considered that the illness could ever take my wife's life.

I looked at the doctor with a puzzled look and asked, "Why do you say that?" But she didn't respond.

As a result of my research and determination to know as much as I could about GBMs, I think I am extremely knowledgeable, compared to most of the American public. From what I learned I feel that I had done everything in my power to prolong Rita's life. Though I did all that I could, unfortunately, Rita was rarely willing to cooperate in saving her own life. I had never really given it much thought as to why she was so uncooperative, but there were underlying reasons that no one could ever have predicted. It is something that haunts me 'till this day and left a permanent scar on my heart and soul.

The Fundraiser

Soon after Rita started her radiation treatments we realized that the medical bills were going to become pretty significant. Even though Rita's insurance was decent, we were overwhelmed with co-pays for the radiologist, our family doctor, the neurosurgeons, and dermatologist visits. Co-pays for the chemotherapy drugs, anti-nausea and seizure drugs had also affected our financial stability. If we hadn't had insurance, the actual cost of the drugs would have been so totally devastating that even if we had sold our house, two cars, and stopped living as normal as possible we still couldn't have afforded them. For example, the Temodar for chemotherapy would have cost $4,800 for a five-day dose! The anti-nausea drug called Compazine would have been another $600, and that's not even figuring in other medications or treatments. By June 1, 2007, just eleven months after her original diagnosis, Rita had already taken over $100,000 worth of chemotherapy prescriptions. I also had her taking a large variety of vitamins and food supplements, all of which we paid for out of pocket. We soon realized we were about to experience some long term financial difficulties unless we did something drastic to increase our cash flow.

Then one day, one of Rita's cousins suggested that they would be willing to host a fundraiser dinner; it just so happened that their family owned a Mexican restaurant in Denver called Serrano's. Though I hate to admit it, at first I felt too proud to consider their proposal. In the past it was I who helped other people with fundraisers and I preferred being the helpful organizer. For example, years before, I had helped some of the guys in the company I worked for adopt a family for Christmas. We raised enough money to buy them a new television, new clothes for their kids and countless toys. We made their Christmas a time of joy. It seems ironic now that the wife of the family we adopted was suffering from brain cancer, but that just goes to show how much we're connected in life. And now, my family was the one in need, and I realized that without help we would eventually go bankrupt. So, I called Rita's cousin Carol, and asked her if her parents were still willing to host the fundraiser. She said she would talk to her family and after several meetings we came up with a plan. We decided on the date, the price per ticket, and a basic ticket design. It was agreed that we would pay for the cost of food and the remainder would be donated to our family, but we had not considered the wages for servers, dishwashers, and cooks.

The dinner was scheduled for September 17, 2006 at ten pm. That morning when I woke up, I felt humbled to think that we were going to be helped by so many of our friends and family members. On the way over to the restaurant, I still struggled with my pride, but I kept reminding myself that we were truly in need of this assistance. Besides, in the week leading up to the fundraiser I received calls from people that I hadn't spoken to in years. They called to express their anticipation for the dinner and being able to see me and Rita and how glad they were to help. So it wasn't as difficult to accept this generous gift of kindness in our time of need.

Shortly after we had arrived, a small crowd started to form in front of the restaurant. When we opened the doors tons of people flooded in, each with a smile and warm greeting. There was a spirit of joy in the room and old friends and family greeted Rita and me with hugs and well wishes. The place was completely packed by six-thirty and everyone was excited and hungry for the buffet-style Mexican banquet. The room was alive with chatter and good feelings all around. Though I was hardly able to visit with everyone, I went from table to table doing my best to spend a few minutes with each family. The food was delicious and everyone seemed satisfied. After all was said and done, we were able to raise $2,475. Ninety people had come to support Rita and our family. When we went to settle our cost for the food and service with the owners, Ben and Joanne, they refused to accept any money. The servers and waitresses also declined payment. I am so thankful for Carol's parents Ben and Joanne Madrid and their entire family for their love and support.

After the fundraiser, we had an unbelievable amount of financial support. One family member sent us two checks for $1,000 and another sent seven checks for $100 each. Though it was humbling, we let the gifts of caring friends and family be a blessing to us. And Lord willing, some day we will be able to repay those favors; if not to the original gift givers, to someone who may need the same. We also received a huge outpour of help from our church and I don't know what we would have done without their help, too. I became a true believer in the *pay it forward* philosophy. It is my ultimate dream to one day, be able to do what Rick Warren, author of, *The Purpose Driven Life*, does; he donates ninety percent of his income to charity and lives on ten percent.

Changes in Personality

Several months after her surgery, it became apparent that Rita would never be the same person, again. At first, we noticed she had some short-term memory loss. We would ask her to remember three items: book, dog, and chair. After three minutes, she couldn't remember even one of them. We believed her inability to remember would only be temporary, a cause of the surgery and procedures. But even after three weeks she would struggle just to remember our dog's name. One of the most disheartening and terrifying sights is to see someone that you know and love slip into an oblivion of the mind. I also began to notice she was more impatient than before. Sometimes she'd snap at us for little or no reason at all. There was one time when Stacey and Rita were driving to the hospital for a radiation treatment and Stacey wasn't driving to Rita's liking, so she began to strike Stacey repeatedly; it was something our Precious Rita would never do. When I got to the hospital I could tell by the distressed looks on their faces that something had happened. I questioned them and learned of the episode. Another time, while ordering breakfast at a restaurant, the waitress told Rita that they ran out of a certain item on the menu. Rita literally snarled at the waitress and we ended up leaving without even ordering. My heart knew that the angry stranger we now saw was not Rita, but instead a monstrous invader—the GBM.

As the illness progressed, however, Rita became very subdued and almost never showed any sign of impatience or anger. She would even say, "Excuse me," to our dog when she crossed paths with it. I'm told patients who go for brain tumor treatments are, for the most part, the most pleasant to deal with from a hospital-worker perspective. They rarely complain and tend to be very passive and, consequently, are easy to please. Rita was no exception.

CHAPTER 9

Support Group

In August of 2006 we began attending a brain tumor support group. At first we had mixed feelings about going because we didn't want others' thoughts and opinions forced upon us. We didn't want to be told what to do or how to feel and we didn't know how the others in the group would react to us. But, since our doctor was adamant about us attending we decided to give it a try. The meetings were held at Swedish Hospital in Denver, on the first Wednesday of each month, and were sponsored by the hospital for brain tumor patients and their families. Most of the patients that attended had GBMs, but there were other people that had different brain tumors, also.

At our initial meeting we were the first ones in the room. The facilitator introduced herself as Stacey and told us to help ourselves to some pizza and drinks that had been set up on a table in the room. We talked briefly about some of our fears and she told us not to worry because everyone was very understanding and welcoming. More and more people started to arrive and soon, the entire group had filled the room. Once everyone was settled, we went over the ground rules for each session:

- Everything said in the room would be kept confidential.
- Everyone would be able to have a chance to talk.
- Sessions had to be attended in a sober state of mind, so no drugs or alcohol.
- And, never, in any circumstance should someone attend if they are sick.

   Since each patient-attendee had a weakened immune system, rule four was the most important, because catching a cold could be like a death sentence. Once the ground rules were explained, the patients stayed in the main room and the caregivers went into a separate room. It was set up this way so that the patients and caregivers would be able to speak freely about common fears, concerns, and problems. Also, it allowed each person to share how they dealt with their issues at hand without having to worry about their loved ones' feelings.

   At one meeting there was a woman, who was taking care of her husband, who also happened to have been diagnosed with a GBM. She told us about a condition called *anticipatory grief*. She explained that there is an emotional mechanism that causes us to prematurely grieve the loss of a loved one. It is a grief reaction that occurs in response to an impending death, usually of someone close, like a spouse. So, according to this theory, the day we had received the initial prognosis, we subconsciously started marking our calendars eighteen months in advance. Even though we all understood what she was saying, it was very hard to grasp. When I got out of the support group, I told Rita what the woman had said. Rita looked at me and said "Honey, I'm not dead. Don't mourn my death until I'm dead." That statement brought everything together for me. Although I still had many bouts of *anticipatory grief*, I was usually able to refocus relatively quickly.

Throughout Rita's whole ordeal our lives seemed like we were continually readying ourselves for a funeral. As a result, my daughters and I found ourselves in a static state of sadness and desperation. No matter how hard we tried, we could not shake the reality of the situation for more than a brief period of time. I couldn't help but feel a constant empathetic pain for her. Even on her *good days*, there seemed to be a looming feeling of despair in our home. I've always been a pretty emotional guy and I even cry at sad movies and get emotional at weddings. But, the grief I felt was so overwhelming that it seemed like I couldn't go forty-five minutes without breaking down.

At first, I apologized when I cried in front of other people, especially men. After a while though, I began telling people that I had "earned" the right to cry. After all, I had spent more than half my life with Rita and we always shared an undeniably special kind of loving relationship. In fact, over the years, people had told us they wished they could develop the kind of love we shared. It was always very humbling and an honor to hear.

One day while talking with a friend, he reminded me of a very comforting Bible verse. In II Timothy 1:7 it says, "For God hath not given us the spirit of fear; but of power, and of love, and of a sound mind." Unfortunately, my flesh seemed to be overpowering my spirit. My faith was too weak to truly hear those comforting words, and as I look back, I understand. God **does not** give us a spirit of fear—we only need to be reminded of it. I believe having God in the picture is important for one's sanity.

By our third month we were pretty much regulars, and before each meeting people would come and make small talk with us. Most of the time, the same group of families would attend regularly, even though there were always new attendees, but for some strange reason none of us ever exchanged phone numbers. Perhaps it was because no one knew for sure if they or the others would be alive the following month; it was a fear that was on everyone's mind but never brought up in general. Or maybe they were tired of the barrage of concerned callers, each asking the same questions over and over. Maybe we all felt like being with another family outside of that room would cause us to re-live the pain we had been experiencing. Regardless, we got to know each other's situations very quickly and it wasn't long before we were pouring our hearts out to one another. Tears were often the norm in each meeting and emotions always ran high. Overall, each meeting gave us new courage and useful information. It truly was a support system that we could appreciate on many different levels.

As time passed, caretakers and family members would describe the symptoms their loved ones exhibited and it became clear that there were definite similarities. Some people would tell of how their cancer-stricken husband or wife would wander aimlessly through the house. Some patients would place empty pots or pans on the stove and turn the burner to high. Others would exhibit hostility toward their family and friends, or like Rita, become as docile as a baby. The feeling of hopelessness and frustration for doctors/medical professionals was certainly a common aspect. Some talked about being angry at the illness, while others were angry at their families because they felt abandoned in their time of need. It was also common to hear of anger directed toward loved ones for having gotten sick. Most of us were concerned with the exorbitant costs for medical care, and it wasn't unusual to hear of families losing their homes. Some were desperate because they couldn't afford the cost of surgery and could do nothing but watch helplessly as their loved one's life was slowly extinguished.

> We learned that, if you survive three-and-a-half years with a GBM, they classify you as a *long term survivor*. There were several long term survivors in our group. One woman had survived over eight years and was still symptom free. She would bring homemade cookies to the meetings, as if to say that she was still capable and alive. The long term survivors were the ones that gave us hope and inspiration. Sometimes, when a regular didn't show I would wonder if they were ill or if they had passed away. Regardless, it would remain a mystery because legally, the facilitators weren't allowed to tell us about the other members.
>
> When Rita was first admitted to the hospital we were asked if she had an "Advanced Directive." I wasn't sure what it was. The

attending nurse explained that an Advanced Directive is a document that explains what your wishes are should you ever become incapacitated and cannot make medical decisions for yourself. So, during our first night at the support group, when the facilitator handed out a document called "The Five Wishes," I was very interested to learn more.

Paraphrased, The Five Wishes on the sheet included:
- The person you want to make care decisions for you when you can't.
- The kind of medical treatment you want or don't want.
- How comfortable you want to be.
- How you want people to treat you.
- What you want your loved ones to know.

When I first began filling in *The Five Wishes* booklet it was very difficult. I didn't know why, but I guess the reality of my own eventual death had never been so real to me before. Rita also had a hard time filling hers out, to the point that it took her over two months to fill out.

No matter how hard it may be, an Advanced Directive, A Living Will, or a *Five Wishes* booklet will benefit you should anything ever occur. Fortunately, the *Five Wishes* booklet serves as all three. You can obtain a *Five Wishes* booklet by calling 1-888-5WISHES (888 594-7437) or by visiting their website www.agingwithdignity.org.

Right now you may be saying to yourself, "I don't need that," or "That sounds too morbid." If you feel any reluctance to have such a document prepared, consider the following story.

It was the second week of December 1997, and one day we received a phone call. Someone we loved very dearly was in the hospital and was probably not going to make it. My family and I rushed to the hospital to see him. While we were there a doctor came in and asked if he had an *Advanced Directive*. No one knew what it was. Then the doctor suggested that they keep him on life support for no more than seventy-two hours. If he hadn't gotten better, the family needed to consider removing him from life support—since he would have little or no chance of survival. Seventy-two hours came and went. No one wanted to be the one to say "Ok, let's do what's right for him." Everyone thought he would get better the next day.

Eventually three days turned to seven, and seven turned to ten. Suddenly, there we were on Christmas day. Still, **no one** wanted to make the decision to remove him from life support. By this time he had suffered kidney failure, liver failure, respiratory failure, and was about to suffer coronary failure.

More than thirteen days had gone by since he had been admitted and he had zero chance of recovery. The doctor told us that even if he did recover, he would certainly require a kidney transplant. Even then, they were sure they couldn't keep him alive long enough to get a new kidney. His liver was so badly damaged it too would have to be replaced. And, the level of oxygen he had received over the last week had damaged his lungs beyond repair.

His brother and sisters were emotionally distressed. Even though I wasn't his son or brother or even blood family, I finally went into the room where they were meeting and told them he had suffered long enough. There was no way he could survive and have any kind of normal life. In essence, I told his family they had to let go. The family decided to have a private meeting and they asked me to leave the

> room. I was heartbroken. They came out thirty minutes later and made the announcement. The decision had finally been made to disconnect his life support. So much could have been avoided if only he had made an Advanced Directive.

Incidentally, when one of our favorite families, Mike and Judy Bahm, were absent for the meeting of February 2007, I felt a strong need to keep them in prayer. During the January meeting Judy had told us that Mike's tumor had spread to his brain stem. He had been in the ICU ward for a whole week. But then, on Tuesday, the 13th of February, I checked my email and learned that Mike was in the Porter Hospice Center in Littleton. The email was from Stacey, the group facilitator, and it said that he was about to finish his battle. Judy had contacted her and asked if she would contact Rita and me to tell us the news. She also asked if we would be able to visit.

When we had first met a few months prior, Mike was a tall, strong-looking man. He and his wife had been married for over thirty-five years. You could see that they loved each other very deeply. But their lives changed one day when Mike had been operated on and diagnosed with a Grade IV, GBM. They removed a large tumor from his right frontal lobe and his scar started from behind his right ear and extended to the top of his head. He was a senior engineer at the time, and was still working, even after his surgery. We had actually met at a prayer group before the support group and learned that we were Christian families and that we trusted in the Lord for peace and wisdom. We had even planned to get together some time, but for some reason, it never worked out.

Rita and I went to the hospice center the next day, which happened to be Valentine's Day. When we walked in, Judy was sitting at a table in a large family room near the entrance. When she looked up at me, her teary eyes told the story of her inconceivable grief. She looked tired and downtrodden but through her tears, managed a smile as she hugged us. We slowly walked down the noiseless halls and she told us how much Mike had declined since we last saw them. When we walked into his room I was astonished to see how much weight he had lost. He wasn't even a shadow of his former self, and he seemed so empty that I wondered if this was really Mike. Judy told me that his condition was rapidly worsening each day. His eyes were rolled back into his head and he was unconscious, but the nurse told us he could hear us. We spoke softly to him and visited with Judy and their daughter. We stayed with Judy and Mike for about half-an-hour and I knew it was time to leave.

I had wanted to give them words of comfort, but somehow, as we left, I realized I had failed. The possibility that Rita could be in Mike's position within a month, a year, or at any time in the future, was suddenly painfully real. I couldn't bear the thought of seeing my lovely wife in that state and blanked on any sort of comforting words for my friends. As we drove home, not a word was spoken. I didn't think Rita understood the harsh reality of our situation. I was afraid to ask how she felt. I was so overwhelmed that I couldn't focus on anything the rest of the day. We never spoke of what we saw.

Two days later, Rita and I went to visit, again. This time, I was determined that I would be more supportive, but when we went into Mike's room his bed had been cleared off. The Bible that was beside his bed, the picture signed by all of his friends that hung on the wall, the flowers he had ordered for his wife prior to his being incapacitated (as it was Valentine's Day)— everything was gone. My heart pounded so loudly that the rushing blood nearly deafened me as we walked to the administrative office. The nurse on staff looked up from her work as we stood in the doorway. I stammered, "Mike Bahm?" I almost couldn't mouth the words without breaking up. Then she told us the news, *Mike was not with us anymore*. This time, the ride home was longer and quieter than the last. My eyes were misty and

I was afraid if I said one word, I would have a nervous breakdown. I don't think either of us wanted to say or hear anything from the other. When we got home I couldn't bring myself to call Judy. My heart ached so badly for her and her family that all I could do was hold Rita close and cry uncontrollably. Yet, Rita showed no sign of emotion.

The next morning I woke up with an awesome feeling of joy and excitement. The promise of God's salvation reverberated through my head again and again. Halleluiah!! *Mike was not with us, anymore!!* I saw him laughing, praising God, and dancing in a dream that night. I clearly envisioned him with a healthy body, like from the first time we met, and I knew in my heart that the message was from God. His eyes were filled with the most joyous look one could ever imagine. Halleluiah!! **Mike was not with us, anymore!** The peace of knowing God's promises made the whole experience much less painful. I got on the phone right away and called Judy to share with her the comforting message from God, which I had just received. Though she was understandably sad and sorrowful for her loss, she was comforted by my call.

When we went to the funeral service there was standing room only, even though the church was very large. Several men, including pastors and friends, eulogized Mike as a model Christian, father, and husband. Judy greeted us as though we were family and though it was incredibly sad, there was a spirit of joy. Knowing that Mike was in paradise in the bosom of the Lord was very comforting for everyone. We ended up meeting many other families through the support group, but sadly, none were ever as special to us as Mike and Judy had been.

CHAPTER 10

The First Trip to California

In November of 2006, Rita told me she wished she could go to California to see the ocean; in case it was her last chance to see it. We had a family meeting the next day and we told our daughters their mother's wish. We decided we would find a way to take the trip and make sure that everyone went, including Josh. Within a couple of weeks we almost had enough money, from donations, for the five of us to go. Since our funds were so limited we found ways to minimize our costs as much as we could, and luckily, using the internet was very helpful to us. I booked everything online including our airline tickets, rental car, and hotel. We ended up having to skip the house payment for that month, too. I figured that there are times in life when fulfilling a last wish is more important than a house payment, and this was one of them. Besides, in the back of my mind I knew there was a good chance Rita would not be with us much longer, so it was a now or never situation.

When we finally touched down in Los Angeles the green landscape sharply contrasted the dull brown plains of Colorado. The warm temperature and blue skies felt welcoming compared to the brown haze that hung over Denver. It reminded me of Dorothy stepping into the brilliant world of Oz from the black and white of her home in Kansas. We felt energized and giddy as we walked from the terminal to the rental car place. Even Rita was in good spirits, especially when we got to our gun-barrel grey Dodge Charger. Hilariously enough, the trunk was almost too small to accommodate everyone's luggage, but in the end we managed. All of us were hungry too, so after we drove around for a short while, we settled on a restaurant called Dinah's in Culver City. I thought it funny that though it was supposedly famous for its ribs, yet no one ordered them. After eating we checked into our hotel, tired, yet excited about going to the beach the next day.

We had two adjoining rooms, one was your average room and the other was for people with disabilities. The two rooms were pretty similar except that our bathroom had a shower seat and hand-held shower head. The only thing that really stood out was the fact that we could look out and see palm trees, but other than that our view was nothing more than a parking lot. Once we had settled into our rooms we took a short ride down the Pacific Coast highway headed south. Everyone was disappointed because we couldn't see the ocean from the highway. It was nice to see the palm trees though, and there were so many fancy cars that Amanda and Stacey were practically hanging out the windows as we drove down the street. After awhile everyone was getting tired, so we returned to the hotel around nine o'clock. It felt nice to be able to fulfill Rita's wish to visit California, but even better because we were there as a family.

All through the first night I tossed and turned. I kept thinking about Rita and hoped she would be able to enjoy her time in California. Before we went to bed, I asked her if she was glad we had come. She looked at me and said, "Thank you for bringing us honey, it means a lot to me." At times, Rita would remind me of a child when she looked at me. She'd have a big smile on her tiny face as her wig hung crookedly. She always had trouble keeping her wig on straight, and no matter how many times she adjusted it, it always managed to slide to one side or the other. When I think of her—her innocent looking smile and "where did you go" look as she tilted her head back to peer with one eye through the artificial bangs—I can't help but smile. Yet, the reality of her condition was never far from my mind. Thankfully we timed our trip so that she wouldn't have to take chemotherapy.

The next morning I thought for sure that the girls and Josh would wake up first. But as usual, Rita and I were already bathed and dressed and had to wait for them. Finally, after everyone was ready, we headed out to the Santa Monica pier with bathing suits under our clothes. The first thing we saw was the Ferris wheel. If the girls weren't so excited to swim in the ocean we probably would have spent the whole day in the small amusement park. After watching people swim for a short while we decided to rent a body board from a small shop on the pier. Josh and Rita watched as Stacey, Amanda, and I swam in the cold November waters of the Pacific Ocean. People on the shore seemed shocked to see us swimming since it was so cold and everyone else was wearing wet-suits. Since Rita had never learned to swim, she decided her one time knee-deep tromp through the water was enough. Plus, her immune system had been compromised by the chemotherapy and the water was much too cold for her to tolerate. None the less, it was like a dream vacation being there, together. Knowing it could be our last trip, we treasured not just every day, but every minute as if it were our last.

After four hours of exhaustive fun, we were so famished that we went to a seafood restaurant near the pier. From there we drove from one beach to another until finally stopping in Laguna Beach. By that time it was already sunset and we had visited five or six other beaches. We decided that Laguna was the best and swam all afternoon. Eventually we found another seafood restaurant that was so delicious that the parking ticket we received made it all worth it. Throughout the vacation we went everywhere from Hollywood to Rodeo Drive and ate at many nice restaurants. All in all, the trip was extraordinary and relaxing. When the pilot announced our final approach upon our return, and we saw the barren landscape and brown cloud hover over the city, it put a damper on things. We were somewhat saddened by the fact that we had to return home, to the lives we had so briefly left behind.

CHAPTER 11

How to Alienate Everyone You Know

During our battle for Rita's life I experienced many personal trials, in particular, keeping my mouth in check. Looking back, there were many times when I said things I would rather not have said, but as the proverbial saying goes, you can't un-ring a bell. A friend of mine once told me I was "letting my bulldog mouth over-run my poodle ass." When Rita's mental condition declined, and her physical health followed, I found myself becoming less and less concerned with what other people thought. I would often just tell it like it was. I felt justified in being blunt and abrupt and I didn't care who knew it. After all, when the day was done and everyone else was safe in their own perfect little lives, I was left alone to take care of Rita. I would think to myself, a day for me was like a week for someone else. Though I am not trying to justify my fickle and resentful behavior, I believe that if anyone was in the position I was in, they too would exhibit similar behavior.

Anyone who knows me knows that I am a "what you see is what you get" kind of guy. I learned a long time ago I would never try to be someone I'm not.

> Once, when I was in the eighth grade, I had a huge crush on a girl named Loretta. She was the prettiest girl in the whole school. I wanted her to like me so much, yet I was very shy. She did like me as a friend, and I was sure I never had a chance with her. Then, we ended up in the same science class and she was assigned to the seat next to me. One day I overheard her talking about how she liked boys with hairy arms. I decided then and there that I would be that kind of guy, but how? By doing the logical thing and shaving my arms so they would become hairy. So, I went home that very day and I shaved my arms. I just knew I'd have hair growing on them by Friday. The next day I went to school and when it came time for science class, I walked in and took my assigned seat. Of all the outcomes, she happened to look at my arms and noticed that I shaved them. So what does she do? She yells to her friend across the room, "Hey Inez,

> look! Paul shaved his arms!" Before I knew it, the whole class was laughing about my clean-shaven arms. Long story short, she never became my girlfriend. Worse yet—*the hair never grew back*. I think it would have been better if I had just been myself. I'm just glad she didn't say she liked guys with hairy chests.

There was once a six-month period when not one of my wife's sisters or brothers even visited. Though they would call weekly, I felt it was their familial duty to honor Rita's wishes of having them as regular visitors, regardless of her condition. Finally, I became so upset that I took it upon myself to call one of my sisters-in-law to give her a piece of my mind. I was utterly frustrated with the whole lot of them for not caring enough to visit their own ailing sister.

Maybe I never took into account that they didn't know what to say, and I never considered whether they were afraid to be a burden. Deep down, maybe it wasn't Rita I wanted them to visit, but me. I was even more indignant to the fact that my own family had also neglected to visit. There was even a time I felt the need to call my mother and tell her that if the family didn't visit that night, I would never speak to any of them again. This, of course, was during one of many times when I thought Rita was on her deathbed and I was desperate for anyone to talk to and be with. And even though my family showed within the hour, after that it was literally the last time I saw most of them for the rest of Rita's life. Throughout the rest of the ordeal I never received a visit, a card, or even a call from all but one of my siblings. Even though I was volatile with the way I reacted to people not visiting, I feel that I reacted the way I did because I wasn't going to change who I am. Be aware that being yourself can come with a price, especially in turbulent and stressful times. In any case, I was guilty of alienating my entire family and many of my friends.

As kids our mother would make us raise our hands to talk at the dinner table because we were so loud. And though our family isn't huge we have always joked about how boisterous we are when we're together. So in February of 2007, when I decided to host one of our monthly family gatherings, I didn't take into consideration just how loud we usually get. At this particular family gathering everyone was well aware of Rita's condition, so we had many more visitors than usual. Unfortunately, most weren't aware of Rita's need for quiet because they hadn't really been around her. So after everyone had eaten their fill, and started to relax, the noise level became a little too elevated. Everyone seemed to be speaking at the same time and I kept hinting for them to keep the noise down. And though everyone was having a wonderful time, it seemed that the more I asked everyone to quiet down, the louder they became. It was evident by the tone of my voice that my frustration level was peaking. I wanted silence so my wife could relax and yet, they wanted to have a good time. I refrained from making a fool of myself that day, but there was no mistaking that I felt like no one respected my request for silence. Finally, when the last guests left I was bordering on livid. I admitted to them my frustration, and thinking they understood, I later found out that the news of my frustration had spread to the entire family. They probably felt uncomfortable after that, because there was never any suggestion of my hosting another family gathering. My family acted as though I said, "I don't want you here, anymore." But what I meant was that I wanted my wife to be able to have some peace and quiet. I felt it was in her best interest, and honestly, I didn't think anyone would act so callously to such a request. However, I seriously don't feel like they considered their actions to be of any consequence. Therefore, it has become apparent that both of us were in the wrong. We didn't have enough communication to understand the needs of one another.

After the noisy family gathering, I didn't want too many people from my family in one place at the same time. I told my mom to let the family know I didn't want groups over to see Rita, for awhile. I didn't know it then, but that gesture was instrumental in isolating me from my family. In my own anger, I figured that since they never called or came over anyway—I'd just make it official.

Then, for Thanksgiving of 2007, I received only three phone calls; one from my two daughters each and one from my mom. Considering that we had spent almost every Thanksgiving with Rita's family for over two decades, and given the fact that I didn't even get an invitation, was completely devastating. So of the twenty-five brothers and sisters-in-laws I had in Rita's family, and seven from mine, I only got one phone call from one of my three sisters. Not even a call from her parents. It now seemed that both families were somehow writing me off. I was so depressed I just wanted to crawl into a hole and die. Eventually, I called my niece, Lisa. She and her parents graciously invited me over for an early Thanksgiving snack, and then I was off to Amanda's for our official dinner. Overall, I had a lot more control over things than I would admit then, but of course, hindsight is 20/20.

I now know that this feeling of alienation is a common experience for caregivers and their families. I believe that caregivers experience the worst feelings of rejection and despair during the holidays; especially if they're used to attending large gatherings each year. If you're a caregiver, I suggest you guard heavily against self pity, which was my personal biggest enemy. All the time I was focused on those who had not called me, I should have been thanking those who had.

Attitude

Sometimes I teach a motivational exercise on attitude to young and old audiences. I've been told that even though it's a simple exercise, it has impact on the participants. For example, I ask the participants to name all of the things it takes to be successful in their particular situation. If I'm doing the exercise with students, I ask what they could do that would make them a better or more successful student. If I'm in a workplace, I ask them to name all of the things it would take for them to be a better employee. Participants would always give me a typical list: being on-time, not calling in sick, learning to do their job well, and getting along with the boss. Once the list is made, I ask the participants to tell me whether the items listed are skills or attitudes. Starting from the top of the list, I work my way down to the bottom. Each and every time the results are the same. Ninety-eight percent of the items on their list are directly related to attitude. Only two to three percent of their success is based on the skills they possess. Attitude is everything when it comes to being successful.

The need for a positive attitude during any time of crisis is crucial. Once a good friend of mine named, Aaron, called me. He said that his brother-in-law had been diagnosed with pancreatic cancer. He then asked me how I made Rita laugh. I thought it was an odd question, but I humored him. As he spoke, it became clearer that he was asking for the sake of his brother-in-law. If the treatments didn't work, the doctors had given him nine months to live. He went on to explain that his brother-in-law was very angry at the world after his diagnosis. He said he had been doing extensive research and it was his conclusion that laughter could heal his brother-in-law. But the brother-in-law had no desire to be around anyone else but his wife. He asked me over and over how to make him laugh. I explained over and over that if someone didn't wish to laugh, nothing Aaron could do, would accomplish his task. I tried to explain that an angry or bitter person must decide to change their attitude before they could improve their state of mind. Soon we were both frustrated due to the lack of clear understanding so I finally stopped him and said that I couldn't explain it in any simpler terms.

I told him that pancreatic cancer is very similar to a GBM and there was nothing that could really be done other than buy time. In his book *See you at the Top*, Zig Ziglar says, "…there are three things you can't do; you can't climb a fence that's leaning towards you, you can't kiss a girl who's leaning away from you, and you can't help someone who doesn't want to be helped." I still believe that if his brother-in-law had changed his disposition to that of a more positive one, he would have had a better chance of extending his life and certainly improving his quality of life.

Regardless of whether someone wants to have a more positive attitude when they're in a dire situation it's best to be as supportive as possible. No matter how ridiculous it may seem, the person you're dealing with has their own reasons for their attitude. With your love and support they may see that their life is important to you and decide that survival is a good thing. Aaron didn't realize that the will to die can be every bit as powerful as the will to live.

I thought I could literally save Rita's life from the beginning. But for Rita, God had other plans. And sometimes, even if a person has an iron will to survive, they can still die. Don't blame yourself if things don't work out like you had planned. I once heard a saying, "If you want to make God laugh, just tell Him your plans."

This is Love

After Rita became ill, my conception of time changed entirely. The uncertainty of her survival, coupled with her condition, also changed the way I thought about our love and our life together. Every night before going to sleep I would hold Rita as much as possible. I would smell her hair, her skin and even her breath, every chance I could. I used every opportunity to keep her memory alive in my heart and mind. Every glance, every laugh, and every smile became another chronicle of our life together. Over the last two-and-a-half decades, my love for her had transcended to levels I never dreamed. Rita became such a part of me that it seemed like I too was ill. The thought of losing her was worse than the thought of losing my very own life.

At times I would wish I hated her so that the despair I felt could be lessened. Other times I would think, *I'd rather this happen to her than to me*; that way, she would never have to experience the unending pain and uncertainty that I had to endure. The plethora of emotions I felt became so overwhelming at times that I wondered if I myself might actually die as a result of the experience. For awhile I went through a phase where I was certain that I would die shortly after Rita.

I once heard a story of a man who was invited to a Canadian goose hunt. But, he had told his friends that he would never hunt again. When asked the reason, he told a story of how one day, many years before, he was hunting Canadian geese. He looked up and saw a pair of geese gracefully soaring past his line of fire. He took a shot and hit one of the two. The dying bird hit the ground with a thud. The man watched as the surviving goose flew down to the side of its fatally wounded mate, completely oblivious to the hunter. The man watched in awe and wondered what would happen next. The grieving goose laid its head upon the breast of its fallen mate and died right then and there. After witnessing such an astonishing act, he collected the birds and dug a hole, and buried them together. The experience gave him a lesson in love and commitment which he would never forget. He went home that day and held his wife tightly. He gazed lovingly into her eyes, gently stroked her hair, and tears filled his eyes. He never wanted to let her go and his love for her had reached an entirely new level.

I've heard of people actually dying from a diagnosed "broken heart" after the loss of a loved one. The official medical term for death from a *broken heart* is Takotsubo Cardiomyopathy. I've even heard of people taking their own life because of their grief. In his book entitled, *Tough Times Never Last but Tough People Do*, Dr. Robert Schuller says that when we face trials and difficulties we have two choices: We can become bitter or we can become better. *We must choose to become better.* We cannot let the enemy win this battle, even if that enemy is ourselves. The outcome of all of life's circumstances is God's will. The way you feel about your life situation and how you respond to it, is your choice.

Hug Them Tight

April 20, 1999 is a day I'll never forget. It was the day of the Columbine massacre. Since we happened to live about six miles from the ill-fated high school, my wife called me at work and told me of the news. She told me that both of the girls' schools were on lockdown because they were within the affected area. Having never heard the term "lockdown," I was unsure of its significance. I remember I stopped working and stood, fixated on the radio news reports. All I could think of was making sure my kids were safe. By the time I got home, I knew there were gunmen loose in the school and that several students had been shot. My heart raced as I thought of the horror the students must have been experiencing. I couldn't help but consider the utter fear the parents must have been feeling. I became more and more nervous as I got closer to home. Fortunately, my daughters were there when I arrived. I remember grabbing them both as soon as I walked in the house. I held them tightly. Like the husband in the story of the Canadian goose hunter, I never wanted to let them go.

With regard to Rita's illness, we developed a heightened sense of the meaning of goodbye. Our goodbyes were always accompanied by a hug, a kiss, and, "I love you." And for good measure, we added, "God bless you." Our greetings and partings had become more heartfelt than before the diagnosis. Now, as a result of my experiences I am more grateful for every day of my life.

What About Fear?

Rita's brother came to see her one day and as we were visiting he casually asked her if she was afraid. Although she'd never said anything about it I had assumed she accepted her illness. She knew the disease was aggressive and would inevitably take her life, but there were a few months when I hadn't asked her if she was afraid. She answered that she was indeed afraid. I asked her why and she replied that she feared what was on the other side. After he left, I asked Rita if she was worried that she wouldn't make it to heaven. She said she was. I went to my Bible and read from Romans 8:11, "But if the Spirit of him that raised up Jesus from the dead dwell in you, he that raised up Christ from the dead shall also quicken your mortal bodies by his Spirit that dwelleth in you." I then read her II Timothy 1:7, "For God hath not given us a spirit of fear; but of power and of love and of a sound mind," a verse I had often quoted. I assured her that God loves her and that He had prepared a place for her. She was comforted by those words and told me that her fears were replaced by God's peace. Although for some reason, her fears seemed to persist.

A short time later, I received an email about a sick man that went to see his doctor. As he was preparing to leave the examination room he turned to his doctor and asked, "Doctor, I am afraid to die. Tell me, what lies on the other side?" Very quietly, the doctor said, "I don't know." "You don't know? You, a Christian man, do not know what is on the other side?" the man exclaimed. The doctor was holding the handle of the door and on the other side there was the sound of scratching and whining. When he opened the door, a dog sprang into the room and excitedly leaped on him. Turning to the patient, the doctor said, "Did you notice my dog? He's never been in this room, before. He didn't know what was inside. He knew nothing except that his master was here, and when the door opened, he sprang in without fear." Then he smiled and said, "I know little of what is on the other side of death, but I do know one thing, I know my Master is there and that is enough."

My favorite Bible scripture is Proverbs 3:5-6. "Trust in the Lord with all thine heart; and lean not unto thine own understanding. In all thy ways acknowledge Him and He shall direct thy paths." In times of uncontrollable fear it's best to keep acknowledging Him in all your ways; good, bad and everything in between. Trust His promise... He *will* direct your paths.

Fear is a natural part of dealing with illness and death, for both the patient as well as their loved ones. Acknowledging fear is important, too. It is a good starting point in helping you to find faith. Faith will develop your strength, and strength will sustain you in troubling times. For me, leaning on the wisdom of God's Word was a great decision. I implore you to read and study God's Word. His promises are real and He truly never fails.

Focusing on Your Priorities

Since the time of her first surgery, Rita went in for an MRI about every five to six weeks. Consequently the scan on Friday, June 22, 2007 was routine except that it was exactly one year after I received the phone call that started it all. After each scan, the doctors would assess and compare the most recent results to the last ones. Then we would be informed of the results during our next appointment. Normally, our appointments were the same day of the MRI and the results were usually uneventful. But when we went in to see about the results this time, they told us to come back a week later. Based on what they found, we were given even more bad news: The MRI showed that the tumor may have spread. The doctor said it appeared that the right hemisphere of Rita's brain had been compromised by the new growth. She said she would be presenting Rita's case to the Tumor Board later that week.

Rita was scheduled for a second MRI, ten days later, only this time she would have what is known as spectroscopy with enhanced screening. This meant that she would be injected with a special dye that was designed to indicate if the new area of concern was what the doctors feared: tumor progression. There was also a chance it could be radiation necrosis, when part of the brain dies from the various treatments, which was just as likely. Regardless, the results of this MRI would dictate their course of action. This meant that there was a chance for yet another surgery.

After finding out about the Tumor Board and the need for a second MRI, we did our best to live our lives as normally as possible. Even though a lot had changed in the year since her surgery, we had tried as best as we could to remain a family. The girls and Josh would usually visit three to four times a week and spend the evenings with me. We would talk, cook, and eat together and it really helped me keep my sanity. We would sometimes have crying sessions together accompanied with prayer. Everything we did was geared toward helping each other through this tumultuous time. Conversely, it wasn't only our emotions that had been impacted. I had to quit my job around the same time as the June, 2007 MRI. The girls, both of whom had been enrolled in college, were no longer able to attend. It seemed that even though Rita was the one suffering, the cancer had managed to affect all of our lives.

Personally, I think I was affected most. Not only because I was Rita's caretaker, but also because I was experiencing everything firsthand. My lack of sleep in the past year had left me with awful bags under my eyes. Typically, I only slept about two to three hours, and when I could sleep it was usually in a restless state. When I woke up each morning all I wanted to do was go back to sleep, but my duties as a caretaker and husband forced me to press on. Consequently, I was irritable most of the time and would snap at anyone who crossed me. The friendliness that I used to exhibit had disappeared somewhere between the insanity of our situation and my insomnia.

Our once neat and organized kitchen was now a wreck of dirty dishes and cookware. The counter tops and sink would become piled with dishes and I would spend hours at a time trying to manage the mess. Normally our lawn would be manicured and green, but now it would go weeks without being cut. In the past I had maintained a productive vegetable garden in our backyard, but that year it had become overgrown with weeds. I rarely made our bed because Rita had been sleeping around twenty hours a day. In spite of the obvious downturn around the house, the laundry was always done. I made sure that we always had clean towels and clothes available, especially since Rita was in no condition to be doing laundry. Of course, by then, she wore little more than pajamas and slippers.

Nothing seemed to matter anymore and if I hadn't had to take care of Rita I don't know if I would have taken care of myself. When I looked in the mirror I almost couldn't recognize the tired, overweight man staring back at me. I had somehow managed to let myself go and hadn't even noticed it happening. My life was in a complete tailspin. One morning I woke up and for some strange reason, decided to shave my head. A few days later, a friend told me that I had done it because I had lost control of my life. She said I subconsciously viewed the action as a way to gain some control, despite how limited it seemed. Her words made sense and for a moment, it was like I had a small grasp on what I was going through.

Meanwhile, Rita had become more lethargic by the day. There was one instance when she was showering for an unreasonable amount of time so I went in to check on her. To my surprise, she was sitting in her shower chair and the water was scalding hot, the hand held shower head pointing at the floor of the tub. The room was filled with steam and she was just staring at the ceiling with a blank look on her face. It was then that I realized that I could no longer allow her to shower alone. I adjusted the water temperature and tried to wash her hair but she freaked out when I put the water on her head. I would have to cover her forehead with my hand before wetting her head because it was almost impossible to rinse her hair without her panicking and it took me several tries before she would let me rinse it. I also had to wash every inch of her body because she wouldn't even make an attempt to do so herself. We had been told that the progression of the tumor could affect her ability to initiate tasks but I had never considered how bad it could get. Not only did I have to bathe her, but I also had to brush her teeth, comb her hair, and help her get dressed. Though I was by her side almost every minute of the day she would rarely acknowledge my presence. I had unwittingly become a ghost to my own wife. Even when I was with her I was all alone.

To make matters worse, the drugs she had been taking caused her face to breakout with rosacea and acne. Before, it was limited to small patches on her face, but now, both were so severe that I believe they contributed to her seemingly depressed state. She would speak to me only when I asked her a question, and sometimes the silence was so unyielding that I found it difficult to focus. In addition to the fact that she rarely answered the phone when I called, I found myself in a constant state of panic. I would feel I needed to rush home to check on her. It was almost impossible to get anything done at work because each day was the same. I feared that she would have a seizure or that she might turn on the stove and burn the house down. One time I rushed home from work because Rita wouldn't answer when I called. When I arrived I found her sitting on the couch holding the receiver in her lap. She sat staring into space paying no attention to the obnoxious phone-off-the-hook signal. She didn't even realize that I had entered the room. I was relieved to see she had been on the phone with someone even though she couldn't remember who it was.

Based on her absent demeanor, I honestly feared that she had given up, and to be honest, there were many times when I wished I could run away and never look back. There would be times when I would call and ask someone to spend an hour with Rita so that I could go out and shoot some pool or grab a burger. I would be fine while I was out and about but when it came time to return to the life I had so briefly left behind, I would intentionally pass my exit. I would drive on past Wadsworth, and Kipling, and just keep driving. I wanted to be anywhere but home. I wanted to completely abandon everything and just keep driving. I didn't know if God had given me the strength to turn back or if I was too weak to run. But I do know that the only reason I was able to return, each and every time, was because of God's grace. I continually had to ask Him to sustain, heal, and strengthen us both. The phrases, "In sickness and in health," and "Till death do us part," would always echo in my mind. Those simple words spoken so long ago were as important now as they had always been. I took ownership of them and embraced them. Renewing my vows in my mind each day seemed to renew my strength even though the fear weighed heavily on my heart and mind.

Even though I knew the importance of prayer and its power, I would sometimes be so lost that I couldn't even bring myself to do so. God was there, but my flesh caused me to try to face my hardships and trials alone. The obvious though unrealized fact is that we don't have to face life's trials alone. So, I found myself on my knees, night after night, begging for Him to give me wisdom and strength. As hard as it was, I knew I had to thank God for my grief and fear as much as my happiest moments. The Bible says in 1 Samuel 15:22, "Obedience is better than sacrifice." It seemed to me this lesson was now what the Lord wanted to teach.

I called my daughters one evening while waiting for word from the Tumor Board, and we decided to meet for breakfast the following Saturday. I was already sipping my coffee when the girls arrived. They walked toward the table and I could tell that both of them were more troubled than I ever remembered. They were afraid now because they too had noticed their mother's decline. We knew that losing Rita after the yearlong battle was now more probable than possible. Such a cruel reality check was simply crushing. As we ate I told them I believed that God would definitely heal their precious mother; whether He healed her on earth, or in His presence in Heaven. We embraced each other and cried at the restaurant table. Then, we prayed, asking God for peace and wisdom.

After the prayer one of the girls asked me what we had done to deserve this. I went through my mind and questioned whether there was something I, or we, had done to cause the cancer. In a weird sort of way, somehow, we felt we needed to take some kind of responsibility. Amanda mentioned the fact that there had been only one case of cancer in either of our families. Rita's grandfather had had stomach cancer. But of all the people in the world, why us? I explained that it was no one's fault and that it's just the way things are. Only God knew the reason for it and it was His Will. We decided to part but prayed again, once more as we stood beside Amanda's car. The two of them got into their cars, broken and afraid, and it was almost more than I could bear. As their images got smaller and smaller in my rear view mirror, Amanda's words haunted me once again—of all the people in the world, *why us*?

As I drove, the thought suddenly came to me. This wasn't happening to me or the girls—it was happening to Rita. How self-centered we were being! I needed to drop the self pity and stop focusing on myself. I went home and watched Rita as she slept. When she finally woke up, I held her close. I promised her I would always take care of her no matter what. I tried to explain to her how we felt. We also spoke of her fear of dying. I prayed to God for strength and wisdom and told her about my conversation with the girls and about her being healed. It gave me peace to talk to her about all of it, although I wondered if she was just as comforted.

Then, later in the week, while we were out, the call came. I checked the voice messages on our phone and recognized the neuro-oncologist's voice. She said that she had presented Rita's case before the Tumor Board and that they had agreed: There was definitely new tumor growth. The tumor had spread to the right hemisphere of Rita's brain and she would require a second surgery. I couldn't believe that she left a message for something so personal and especially serious. *Hearing that Rita would require another surgery from a machine was such an insult.* I was beyond livid, but since we had checked the messages so late at night, by the time I woke up the next morning I had calmed down. And by the time we went in for our appointment I had pretty much forgotten about the whole episode.

The doctor walked in and told us about the results. She explained that Rita would require another surgery but that the final decision would be left to us. I wasn't sure Rita even had the presence of mind to approve the surgery and yet, the last thing I wanted to do was be the one responsible for such a complicated decision. I wanted it to be her decision, but I was unsure whether I would be able to explain it to her. We walked out of the doctor's office with no desire to make a decision. I figured that there would be time to decide later.

In accordance with the doctors wishes we made an appointment to meet with the neurosurgeon. He was another reason we had selected the Colorado University Hospital for Rita and even though we had chose him as her surgeon, it was our first time meeting him. In truth, we had hoped to never meet him because if we did, it meant Rita would require another surgery. So, when the time came the first thing that I noticed was that he seemed to be a very humble man. He was very friendly and enthusiastic and seemed to genuinely care. I felt comfortable asking him any question that was on my mind.

After he explained how the surgery would go, I asked about the risks and benefits. He told us Rita would likely become reclusive and could go into a depression. He also said that the surgery would give Rita as much as one more year of life. I never thought to ask about her quality of life within that extra year, and it is my opinion that he never told me all of the facts. Looking back, I believe that if Rita were in her right mind, she would never have agreed to have more of her brain removed.

When we left the neurosurgeon's office, I knew I didn't have much time to explain the situation to Rita before she completely forgot. I began to tell her about the meeting and everything that was mentioned, even though she had been there. I think she was afraid I didn't want her to have the surgery because it might result in her becoming a complete invalid. Yet, her fears were not entirely unfounded, and though I hate to admit it I was thinking exactly that. I was afraid I might not be able to handle taking care of her if she were in a worse state. All I could do was think about myself. What about Rita's fears? What about her wishes? I took a deep breath and told Rita that I would gladly accept whatever decision she made. Then, in voice no louder than a whisper, she said, "Ok, then. I want to have the surgery."

CHAPTER 12

The Second California Trip

When we got home I asked Rita if there was anything she wanted to do, or anyplace she wanted to go. I told her I would find a way to do whatever she asked. She said that she wanted to go back to California to see the sunset one more time. Coincidentally, a month before I had applied for a loan against Rita's life insurance policy since we were facing certain financial ruin and we needed to pay off some bills. I had been able to negotiate the amounts owed with most of the collection agencies, so we had some money left over. In fact, there was plenty enough for us to go to California, so I secretly booked the trip for June 29, 2007.

We would be staying at the Portofino Hotel and Yacht Club located on the Pacific shore in Redondo Beach, California. Mysteriously enough, even though I had booked a room that faced the marina we were upgraded to a room facing the ocean, at no additional charge. God does work in mysterious ways. Each day, million dollar yachts would sail past our room along with everything from kayakers to sailboats. Rita seemed to enjoy the cool ocean breeze and the peaceful hum of the boat engines as they passed. She would lean forward to get a better view of the silent kayakers gracefully maneuvering their way toward the open waters of the Pacific Ocean. From our third floor patio we could hear sea lions barking from a dock about two hundred yards away, and the sunsets were spectacular. We probably never would have stayed in such a nice and expensive hotel if not for this situation, but this was indeed a very special circumstance.

It happened to be the week of the fourth of July when we were there, so naturally, there were lots of people everywhere. We were also within walking distance of a lot of local attractions and restaurants, so we were delighted to get the freshest and finest seafood each day and night. Both Rita and I loved seafood and she would order shrimp and I would have everything from crab to sushi.

While on the trip I connected with Rita in a way we hadn't in many months. Even though the illness, surgery, and subsequent treatments had taken their toll, she seemed to have more awareness than usual, and she was *present*. Rita showed a lot more emotion, too. Although, I never once saw her cry, she did laugh a lot and it was nice to see her smile. But still, a part of me was afraid she might not survive the next surgery. I don't know if Rita truly understood the seriousness of her illness at that point. It seemed like she had a kind of protective mechanism which made her unaware of her condition. She always seemed calm and never afraid of the situation, no matter how bad. She could have just laid down one day and left this world. When you think about it, there are no guarantees that tomorrow will come. You can be gone in a second.

As we were having dinner one night, I became mesmerized by the large waves that relentlessly pounded the beach. As I watched, I recalled the tsunami that had hit Indonesia a couple of years back. The people vacationing there and those that lived there didn't have a care in the world.

Then suddenly the ocean receded and the shoreline opened up for a mile. Everyone must have stopped to see what was happening. It's hard to imagine what it must have looked like. Suddenly a horrible sound approached the beaches and a giant, 100-foot wave came crashing down, destroying everything in its path. People were probably trying to hold onto their children or other loved ones while screaming, "Hold on! I won't let you go!"...their voices hardly audible over the crashing waves. Yet, all their might, will, and desire could not sustain their grasp. In a moment, all that was sacred to them was lost. For the survivors, the despair was probably incomprehensible. The guilt of having survived after losing their grip had to have tortured the survivors relentlessly. They must have felt tormented by their loss, day after day, for simply being alive.

I thought to myself what it would be like if I had to continue living on if Rita had passed. I kept feeling a random guilt and wondered: How could I overcome the guilt of surviving? Suddenly I was back in the restaurant sitting with Rita and my food was cold. I didn't know what tomorrow might bring but I had to keep in mind that I had today, and that was enough for me.

Take Lots of Pictures

I once received an email that talked about taking a lot of pictures. Especially if there is a situation where someone you love is ill or dying. You can always get the pictures out and remember the good times you shared. You can, at a moment, return to a place long forgotten or recapture a distant memory by simply looking at a photograph. Photos, of course, cannot bring back the person you've lost, or their scent or feel of their touch, but you can at least see and return to the moments you shared, in your mind.

When Rita and I got married in February of 1980, our photographer never showed up for our wedding. We didn't get any memorable pictures of the ceremony, reception, or our dance. At the time we didn't really grasp the significance of the event. We didn't realize we would never be able to look through a photo album and relive the memories like we once hoped we could. All we ended up with was a few snapshots, most of which were given to us by friends and family. We had treasured each and every one, none the less.

Soon after we were married, I went out and purchased a 35 mm camera and photography became one of my favorite hobbies. With each new thing I learned, I would use the camera even more than when I first took it out of the box. I have even been accused of being a shutterbug and have a drawer filled with old pictures to prove it. On the rare occasion that I feel melancholy, I like to go to the drawer and sift through the pictures and reminisce. I may have complained about the cost of developing prints back when I took them, but when I look at all of the wonderful memories I had captured, it made me realize just how worthwhile that cost was. Eventually, I invested in a digital SLR camera because it offered much more than film cameras ever could. Most of our journey during Rita's illness was captured in the digital photos I took and I will never regret having taken "too many pictures." In a situation like this, there is no such thing as too many pictures or too much time spent with one another.

When July 4th rolled around I asked Rita if she thought she could ride a bike. She said yes and I told her we could ride nice and slowly along the beach. I was a little fearful about her ability to ride since her balance wasn't too great, but she assured me she would be fine. So we went to the hotel lobby and spoke with the person in charge of the guest bikes. Within a couple of blocks I wanted to see if Rita could stop the bicycle and get off by herself, so I told her to ride over to where I was. As soon as she stopped, she fell into me. Thank goodness I was able to catch her.

We decided that if she wanted to stop she would ride over to where I was and I would ease her feet to the ground. It went well at first, until we got to Hermosa Beach. The walkway was extremely crowded and there were areas where the people took up more than half of the path. I was concerned that she might fall and I wouldn't be close enough to catch her, so I stayed as close to her as I could. Somehow we made it to the pier which was about a mile-and-a-half from where we first got on the bicycle path. We parked the bikes and locked them up and went for a delightful walk to the end of the pier. She was in high spirits and she said she would have no problems riding back to the hotel. Before we headed off she watched children playing in the waves and on the beach. Since it was a holiday, the beach was completely filled with people. I told Rita we should go one block away from the beach where there were fewer people.

She agreed and we headed to the "safe" area. I didn't want to get too far ahead of her, so I rode very slowly, ever mindful of her position all the while, monitoring her ability to control the bike. It didn't take long to see that she was not doing very well. She kept wandering from side to side, and swayed as though she were drunk. I called out to her and told her to make her way to me so I could help her stop and get on her feet. Neither of us knew why, but all of a sudden, she drifted toward the street. She stopped at the curb and tried to step onto the ground but misjudged the distance. Her foot went to the street, ten inches below the curb. She fell from the bike, face first into a parked car and skinned her knees as she fell. Everything seemed to be playing out in slow motion as I ran to her. I could see every detail of the fall, and yet no matter how fast I ran, I could do nothing to prevent it. Her eyes closed as the rear fender of the car came nearer and nearer to her head. I could see the flesh on her face twist and stretch as it hit the red fender. Her forehead took most of the blow, but so did her nose from my angle. By the time I finally got to her, she was between the car and the curb, twisted and moaning in pain. I helped her to her feet and held her close as we walked the rest of the way back to the hotel.

The next morning, we went for breakfast at a restaurant located a few blocks from where she had fallen the day before. My guilt was eating me up. How could I have not been there to prevent her from falling? Should I have allowed her to ride a bike at all? What could I have done to prevent it from happening? All these questions, along with the guilt, kept running through my mind. I had finished my breakfast as I watched Rita slowly and methodically select which morsel she would eat next. I drank several glasses of water while I waited for her to finish. The waiter was a very enthusiastic fellow who was friendly and had a true servant's nature and I mean that in a totally complimentary way. He kept my glass full as I patiently sipped and each time he filled my glass, he did so with a smile. When Rita was finally down to her last few bites

I was about ready to overflow. The waiter happened by and asked if I needed another refill. I said I only needed half a glass. He deliberately filled my glass to the brim and smiled at me again. With a genuine look I shall never forget, he said, "You didn't say whether you wanted the top half or the bottom half, so I filled them both." As I chuckled, I processed his words. They were both enlightening and encouraging to me. I was seeing the glass *half-empty*.

Later on I thought about the day prior, before we started out on our ill-fated bicycle ride. We had prayed for God's protection over us and for a safe return. As I think back to the accident, I realized there were a series of small miracles that took place when she crashed. The first was that we were away from the crowded beach where there had been other bicyclists and skaters that would pass by at break-neck speeds. If she had fallen at the beach, someone could have easily hit her while she was down. Secondly, there was a car parked right where she fell and although she did hit the car face first, the flexible metal of the fender absorbed much of the shock from the blow. If the car hadn't been there, Rita would have fallen another ten to twelve inches. She would have surely landed face first on the street below. God had minimized the injury and protected Rita from what could have been a catastrophic injury. As if these two miracles weren't enough, right after she fell I looked up and there was a Redondo Beach police cruiser right next to where it all happened. He was prepared to call for an ambulance at a moment's notice. Things truly could have ended up much worse than they actually did, but God had filled both halves of our cup and it was running over. Just like the proverbial, "Footprints in the sand." God was there to carry our burden and make things easier no matter what the case.

A few days later, before leaving back to Denver, Rita mentioned that she wanted to go back to Dinah's, the restaurant we had gone to the last time we visited California. I was amused that she remembered the restaurant and was happy to oblige. When we walked in Rita went straight for the menu as though she knew what she wanted. She looked at it for a minute then put it down. I asked her what she wanted and she didn't say a word. The look on her face was almost a look of mystery but also ornery. I asked her again, but she wouldn't answer. Finally the waiter came and asked for Rita's order. Quickly and without hesitation she ordered a *half chicken*. I was stunned not only because she hardly ate, but because of the manner in which she had ordered it. She had slowly placed the menu on the table, looked straight at me, and said she wanted *a half chicken*. It was just so unbelievably hilarious. And though she only ate a few bites of it, we took it to the airport with us and finished it on the concourse. All in all, she ate only a drumstick.

As a youngster I remember reading a fascinating book called, *Flowers for Algernon*. It was a gripping novel about an experiment on a mouse, named Algernon, which was designed to make it brilliant. The same experiment was tested on the main character, a *mentally retarded* man named Charlie Gordon. The book starts out with Charlie's journal where the author deliberately misspells the words as though they were actually those of Charlie. Charlie undergoes an incredible intellectual transformation but eventually becomes so advanced that he is an isolated genius; isolated just as he was when he was before. Ultimately, it is discovered that the experiment's success is only temporary and Charlie reverts back to the imbecile he once was.

Seeing Rita change from an intelligent, wise, and composed woman into a person that required constant care on a twenty-four-hour basis seemed strangely familiar.

Early on in the illness, I told my daughters again and again that I noticed a change in their mom. Amanda felt that I was being pessimistic and they both felt I was just overreacting. I almost began to question my faith as I noticed subtle but definite changes in Rita that only I could see. Regardless, I promised myself I would make her as comfortable as I could and would do whatever she asked no matter what it was. If she was cold I covered her with a blanket. When she was hot in the summer time, I fired up the swamp cooler. If she asked me to take her out for dinner, I took her out.

She had been a wonderful wife from day one, and I believe if the shoe were on the other foot, she too would have done whatever it took to ensure my comfort and peace of mind. Three weeks before her second surgery, she was little more than a wisp of a woman. Her weight had dropped from one-hundred-thirty-nine pounds before the first seizure, down to one-hundred-six. Later she dropped down to ninety-six pounds, and by the time of her death, she was just about seventy-five pounds. After her second surgery her physical therapist wrote a letter stating that Rita could no longer be left alone. She couldn't feed herself or manage her prescriptions and I viewed it as an honor to take over those responsibilities.

By October of 2007, she needed assistance getting in and out of bed and was no longer able to dress herself. Her sleep patterns were so unpredictable, it was literally impossible to plan any activities. Much of what we did was done on a spur of the moment basis. As a result, we hadn't attended church in several weeks. One time when she decided she wanted to go to church, I woke her up in time to bathe and dress her. We went to church and sadly she couldn't name any of the people we had known for quite some time. I could tell that she didn't grasp the sermon's message but seemed to really enjoy it. As soon as we got home, she walked into the house and went straight to bed. An hour later I woke her up to feed her. She ate a small portion and went back to bed. She slept until two-thirty the next afternoon. It soon became clear that she wasn't physically strong enough to attend church anymore.

Another time, when she was having one of her good days, I asked her if she wanted to go to her old workplace to see some of her friends. The company was in downtown Denver on one of the top floors of a skyscraper. When I suggested the visit she became excited. I dressed her in warm clothes and combed her hair neatly. After we arrived we rode the elevator to the floor where she used to work. She used to know most of the people she worked with, and yet when a group of former co-workers came to say hello she was unable to name even one of them. By watching the way they all gathered around her so lovingly, I could see that Rita had had a significant impact on them.

That day I came to a new realization: I had, over the past sixteen months, lived and re-lived my wife's demise too many times to remember. This time though, it hit me in a way that it never had before. I could not, nor did I want to, stop the inevitable outcome and I came to the conclusion that Rita dying was better than her living as she was now. Oh yes, it hurt deeply to see the one I loved suffering, but in truth I was the one in pain. I was the one who would be left on this earth when all was said and done. Rita would experience physical pain, mostly in the form of headaches, but I was an emotional train wreck. My pain was deeper than physical pain. It was in my whole being, my mind, my body, and my spirit. The feeling of seeing someone you love deeply, in a constant and definite state of decline, is one of the most devastating experiences. It makes you question your very existence and the purpose of life. Like Charlie in the story, my wife's time was also dwindling away. But unlike Charlie, Rita would be gone from this earth and our lives.

CHAPTER 13

A Feeling Like No Other

When it comes to life expectancy most good doctors can give a relatively accurate prognosis after reading a patient's chart. For example, my friend's dad was diagnosed with lung cancer on a Thursday and was given just one week to live. After three days he passed. When my stepdad was diagnosed with pancreatic cancer he was given five months to live and died just a few days short of the prediction. Like doctors, medical professionals in the hospice field are amazingly adept at being able to predict when someone will pass, based on the patient's appearance. They can look at a patient and make an accurate assessment of how their illness is progressing. They can analyze each change in skin color, texture, eye appearance, and so on, and make a relatively accurate prediction as to when that person will die. However, in the case of a brain tumor, it's literally impossible to ascertain even a possibility of survival, much less the duration, or if/when the patient will die.

There was one time, when she first went into hospice, when Rita's appearance was so deathlike and waning that on that Monday, the nurse predicted she would die by Friday—and I agreed with her. Then on that Friday afternoon, she rebounded and became almost completely lucid, again. Rita's condition had become so unpredictable and erratic that we thought we would lose her for sure, more than a few times. She would go three or more days without eating, then, she would become unresponsive and catatonic. She always had dangerously low blood pressure and sometimes I'd even have to reintroduce myself to her five times in a single day. Then, the next day she would be coherent and would greet me with a smile and sometimes she would even call me by name. The changes and contrasts she went through from one day to the next were staggering.

The following story illustrates the feelings I went through in a roundabout way. I remembered the experience one day while I was in the midst of one of Rita's many off days

When I was in the fifth grade I got my first job. I stood on a street corner in downtown Denver and sold what was then called the *Final Edition* of a local newspaper called the *Denver Post*. The work was easy all I had to do was stand there and offer the paper to passersby. The papers were ten cents apiece and I earned a whopping three cents per paper sold.

One day, I decided that I needed a radio to entertain me while I worked, so I went into the F.W. Woolworth store downtown and put one on layaway. The radio was a General Electric AM/FM unit and cost $25 plus tax, which is like $150, today. Diligently I would pay a little bit each week until finally I had enough to make the last payment. I was on my way to being a responsible adult. I was about to purchase something big, something I never would have dreamed of. I went to the layaway department of the store after school one day and paid the remaining balance. The radio was finally mine. I proudly showed it to all my coworkers who also sold papers on the street corners downtown.

This was long before the era of boom boxes, so the radio wasn't much more than a large transistor, but it was mine and I was proud to own it. Everyone was impressed and I was the coolest guy in the place that day. I proudly went to my street corner, and set the radio on the newsstand.

About an hour into my shift, I noticed four boys walking down the street. They were much bigger than I was and were headed straight for me and my radio. I pretended I didn't notice them as they sauntered closer and closer to where I stood. All the while, I felt my stomach tighten and my palms start to sweat. Their voices seemed to become more elevated as they approached. In the blink of an eye they were all over me. One was trying to take my apron, which held the money, and another was pushing me from side to side trying to get between me and my radio. I knew I was helpless and felt very intimidated. I knew I didn't stand a chance, not only because I was smaller, but because I was outnumbered four to one. Suddenly, the worst that could happen, happened. One of the boys grabbed my brand new radio. The thought of losing my treasure suddenly became a mixture of fear and rage. I knew I would do whatever it took to retrieve my radio, but I also realized that I might get beaten up if I didn't back off and just let them take it.

I followed the boys, screaming for them to give me my radio back. My voice cracked and I was trembling with fear as I followed. I was hardly able to hold back my tears. They knew they were bigger, stronger, and that I was frightened. I felt so helpless, there was absolutely nothing I could do but watch as they walked away.

No matter how loud I yelled, or how many bystanders I desperately asked for help, it became apparent that no one was going to rescue my radio or me. Soon we were two blocks away from my newsstand. Just then, I saw an opportunity when the boy holding my radio stopped to taunt me. That's when I ran at him like a madman. He seemed startled and surprised by my speed and the fact that I ran toward, instead of away from him. The radio was within my reach and I knew it wouldn't be there for more than a second. So with all the speed I could muster I snatched it from his hands. They were stunned as I ran away holding my radio. My determination to protect what was rightfully mine had somehow given me the strength and courage to reclaim it.

While running I knew I was in more trouble now than I was before. The boys were chasing after me, only this time *they* were the ones angry and humiliated. I continued to run as fast as I could, and knowing full well that I could never outrun them, I ran into a business. I began to scream for help at the top of my lungs. But it was as if no one could hear me! The boys stood outside the door and I could tell they were looking for blood. I thought for a second they would follow me into the business, but they ended up leaving. I was trembling very badly and I watched as they walked down the street laughing, as though it were a game. When it was all finally over, I fell to my knees and cried uncontrollably. Even though I had my beloved radio again, they had taken away my sense of security.

This story is a good example of how I felt during Rita's illness and the roller coaster of wellness to sickness and back during her stays in hospice. There was something taking my most treasured thing in this world and causing nothing but chaos in my family's life. And I was completely helpless. The illness stepped on our souls and ground them in the dirt like a discarded cigarette. It had bankrupted us financially, physically, mentally, and especially emotionally. All we could do was pray to God that the illness would go away and leave us alone. The reality of our situation was that our bully never relented and never gave us a shred of mercy or opportunity to fight back. In the back of my mind I knew that the only freedom we would ever have was in the inevitable death of my precious, darling Rita. The monster would not die or relent, without also taking her life with it.

CHAPTER 14

Been Knocked Down? What Do You Do Now?

Years ago I went to see a championship boxing match at a friend's house. It was potentially one of the greatest match-ups of the century. The fight would be between a promising young fighter named Meldrick Taylor and the legendary Julio Caesar Chavez. At the time, Chavez was much older and the obvious underdog. Taylor was younger and heavier but nowhere near as experienced. The stage was set and the hype was rampant. The two fighters faced-off and before the second round was over, Taylor had already knocked Chavez to the ground. Chavez, though surprised, was on his feet in a moment. He wailed at every opening he could find. Throughout the fight, Taylor, the favorite to win, disappointed no one. His agility and skill were clearly superior to that of the veteran fighter. By the twelfth and final round, Chavez had been knocked to the mat three times, but Taylor hadn't been declared the winner. There was not a three-knock-down rule in the fight, so in other words, you could get knocked down three times and still win but only by knocking your opponent out. Taylor would certainly be the winner of the fight barring some miraculous finish by the seemingly defeated Chavez.

With the clock winding down, all Taylor had to do was kill time and he would soon win the title he had longed for his entire life. His confidence soared as the crowd cheered. This truly would go down as one of the most awesome fights anyone had ever seen. With seconds to go in the final round, Julio Caesar Chavez came to life. He began to swing with pinpoint accuracy landing punch after punch on the face of Meldrick Taylor. Suddenly, the swelling in Taylor's face began to show. Yet Chavez seemed as though he had never been hit once.

Chavez's countenance seemed to change within seconds. He went from looking old, haggard, and defeated to that of the world champion he knew he was. As each of his punches landed, you could see fatigue setting in on the face of his young opponent. In the last few seconds, Chavez landed the final punch. Meldrick Taylor winced as he received the punch that sent him to the mat. The world was transfixed as they watched Taylor fall hard. His free fall to the mat was stunning. He went completely unconscious at the second the last blow landed. The crowd went wild as the final seconds of the round ticked off the clock. Luckily for Chavez, the match was a no-saved-by-the-bell event, which meant that even though the bell rang you could still be counted-out during a KO count.

Chavez went to his corner. The referee began the count. One ... Taylor's face showed no sign of life. Two... Chavez gazed at his young opponent, lying motionless on the mat. Three... there was pandemonium in the arena. Four... Meldrick Taylor's hand moved toward the mat. Five... reporters were all along the ringside, desperately trying to see if Taylor could recover in time to be the new champion. Six...Taylor tried again and again to position his hands to get up, but he was too exhausted. Seven... Taylor could not regain his balance even from his laying position. Eight... try as he might Taylor was beyond his limit. Nine... the crowd was almost out of control with anticipation and Taylor could not stand to his feet. TEN...Yes, the old man, who was slated to lose from the very beginning, had won. It was a seemingly impossible fight in a match where everyone thought Taylor would be the winner. The determination of Julio Caesar Chavez and his desire to win had overcome the facts.

If you're facing a seemingly impossible situation, and have been knocked down again and again because of insurmountable odds, never forget that the fight is not over until the last second of the last round. In this case, the victory came after there was *absolutely no hope for survival*. Winston Churchill said it best. "Never give up…never give up… never, give up!" On the other hand, there is also one fact that we all must keep in mind. All human beings without exception have one thing in common: every single one of us will eventually die. If and when someone dies, remember, when the coffin goes into the ground there is only one body in it. Don't let yourself become what I call the living dead. If your heart is still beating you are still alive, it is not just your right, it's your responsibility to live.

Sometimes *What Happened* Wasn't Really What Happened

Though the preceding story was very entertaining and intense, it didn't actually happen that way. That's the way I remembered it! I googled the fight and watched it again and Taylor did in fact get knocked to the mat in the final seconds of the last round. He did get to his feet before he was counted out but when the referee asked him to respond, he said nothing. So because he didn't respond, the referee called it a knock-out. Seconds later when Taylor came to his senses, you could almost read his lips as he questioned the referee. He protested the decision saying he was not knocked-out. Chavez was named the winner of the fight, nonetheless. Taylor was later taken to the hospital where x-rays revealed that he had several badly broken bones in his face. He had received the beating of his life. It is also reported that Taylor suffered brain damage from the shellacking he had taken that night. You could see in interviews recorded after the fight that he was not the same fighter who entered the ring that fateful night. Consequently, he never fought again.

Just as Chavez didn't believe in the hype surrounding Taylor, people need to address challenging situations in the same way. When setbacks occur in life there are two possibilities—either stay down and submit or get up and face the situation. A battle is a battle because you fight for what you want, not because you simply accept defeat.

I once heard a motivational speaker named Doug Weed say that, "Man is not great because he has never failed—he is great because failure does not stop him." Whether it's getting the prognosis, or losing the battle, you must get up and live again. Otherwise, you might as well have been buried with the person who died. Remember death is a part of life.

After everything is said and done there may come a time when family members may have memories or misperceptions of what actually occurred. There were times before Rita's passing when I would be talking with members of her family and they would have completely different recollections from my own. It was almost insulting, yet funny at times, the way they would seem to fabricate memories. I have talked to people that remember few, if any, of the details of their ordeal just one year after the fact. If I hadn't documented the details of my experiences, I doubt I would have been able to remember enough to write this book. My advice is to accept the conflicting perceptions and let it be. Arguing will only serve to further aggravate an already difficult situation.

During my lifetime I have heard stories where families were completely torn apart after a death, particularly after the death of a parent. Siblings often disputed over possessions and promises made with regard to everything from money, to jewels, to just about anything else you can imagine. Remember, unless it is in writing, nothing is guaranteed. This is an important reason I believe it is best to have a last will and testament created, regardless of your health. Like insurance policies, a last will and testament is incontestable and can settle any dispute.

CHAPTER 15

The Stepchild of all Cancers

As I was writing this book, I heard news that Senator Ted Kennedy had been rushed to a hospital after having a seizure. A biopsy revealed a malignant brain tumor known as a glioma. In his book, *Living with a Brain Tumor,* Dr. Peter Black explains that there are three types of gliomas, two of which are malignant.

When the news of his condition was announced, I was heartbroken for Senator Kennedy and his family. Encouraging words from senators, congressmen, and other politicians were broadcasted all evening for Senator Kennedy and his family. Yet, given the way they spoke and the words they used, they clearly had no clue about how severe and serious his illness truly was. Likewise, Senator Kennedy and his family had no idea about the brutal monster they were about to face.

It was announced that he would likely undergo the *traditional* treatments given to brain cancer patients—radiation and chemotherapy. What bothered me most was the fact that this is the same exact treatment used on cancer patients fifty years ago. With the exception of a few experimental medicines, the only real difference today is that they now use different types of chemotherapy and more precise radiation treatments. Of course, they no longer use cobalt to treat cancer of any kind, but that doesn't excuse the fact that they still use outdated methods today. With all of the technological advancements made in electronics, automobiles, computers and the like, isn't it odd that we still have the same treatments used so many years ago? As horrible as Senator Kennedy's disease seems, there is a bright side to his diagnosis because brain cancer has finally received some notoriety.

In fact, brain tumors are so unrecognized when it comes to research funding and awareness drives, that I have come to call them the *stepchildren of all cancers*. Furthermore, the more I learned about brain tumors and cancer, the more I came to realize that they are but a miniscule blip on the radar screen of world diseases.

Coincidentally, during the period of June 2007, while Rita was receiving treatments, the Pink Ribbon Foundation happened to have some leftover charity funds. So, a small grant had been allocated for the "less important" or "less common" cancer patients. Because of the leftover funding, the hospital was able to provide Rita the opportunity to take part in a grant that allowed six complementary acupuncture, chiropractic, and/or massage therapy sessions. Thanks to the generosity of the Pink Ribbon Foundation, Rita received a little extra TLC. I hope that one day there will be an organization as recognized as the Pink Ribbon Foundation for brain cancer and research.

Solving Problems Creatively

Back when I ran my own construction company, I met a man who wanted me to install new doors in his home. His budget was limited and he asked if he could pick up the doors himself. I was fine with his proposal and even offered to help him but he insisted that he could do it. When I arrived the next day, he was standing in the doorway. Then, with a big smile on his face he asked me if I ever had trouble getting help at the local Home Depot. I told him that since I was a contractor, and practically lived in the stores, I never really had any problems. He then shared his experience with me. He said that the day before, when he went to the door section, no one was there to help him. He looked around and found an associate but they rushed by and seemed to be helping someone else. He then proceeded to ask every person who looked like they worked there, for assistance. But to his surprise he seemed to be in a kind of Twilight Zone. He wandered aimlessly through the aisles as though invisible and no one even acknowledged him. Finally, he laid down in the aisle of the door section and closed his eyes for a bit. Within seconds, five associates and the store manager were standing around him in a panic. They were ready to dial 911 when the manager asked, "Sir, are you all right?" He opened his eyes and calmly pointed to the upper shelves and said, "Can you get those two doors down for me?"

Of course there must have been a tremendous sense of relief when he responded. This is a perfect example of coming up with a creative way to solve your problems. It's mostly how you approach them and being aware of what's possible. There may be free services available that you don't even know about. If it weren't for the Pink Ribbon Foundation and the hospital administrators, we never would have found out about the grant she ended up receiving.

Look in the hallways for bulletin boards. They list many types of programs, seminars, and resources like support groups. If you are without insurance or suffering financially, you might want to consider asking for information about experimental treatment. Just be sure to know what you're getting into if you do take the experimental treatment route.

There was once a time when Rita and I were helped by the hospital social worker. His name was Michael and he informed us of all the benefits available. He was a very kind man and very knowledgeable. With his help we were able to apply for Social Security benefits and got accepted on the first try. Usually when it comes to applying for such benefits it can take three tries or more.

If you're trying to obtain Social Security benefits, Medicare or any other assistance, I strongly encourage you to contact your hospital social worker. We were also able to talk with the hospital psychologist when we felt as though we needed counseling, so consider the hospital psychologist, too. When Rita began to look like she was getting ready for hospice care, the doctor referred us to a local program. We were also referred to a physical therapist, speech therapist, and occupational therapist, by the hospital.

We were also able to enroll in a wonderful program known as Project Angel Heart. The project, organized in Colorado, allows for patients of terminal illnesses to receive home-delivered meals each week. The meals are made by local chefs, and individually packaged and frozen. Rita enjoyed them very much and with their assistance, our life was a little easier for a time.

All in all, be sure that no matter what, you look into every available option. Though your life and situation may feel overwhelming, there is no reason to think that you cannot get help…even if you have to lay down in a Home Depot just to get a couple of doors.

CHAPTER 16

The Second Surgery

On July, 19, 2007, Rita was scheduled for a second surgery. The surgery was called a *left frontal resection craniotomy*. The decision for the surgery was a consequence of her recent MRI scans that had indicated new tumor growth and the high possibility of radiation necrosis, where additional brain tissue had died—a result of the *success* of the radiation and chemotherapy. Needless to say, the weeks leading up to the surgery were agonizing. We had just gotten back from California and already fear and uncertainty became the norm for us again. The fact that even more of her brain would be removed was horrifying. Even though Rita rarely spoke of her concerns or fears, her decision for the surgery teetered from regret to acceptance regularly. On one of her more lucid days she told me she was afraid because the surgery might leave her unable to talk. She said that if the surgery would significantly impact her quality of life, or if there was a likelihood of her being left in a vegetative state, she would decline.

As the day of the surgery neared, I reminded Rita of the situation as best I could. She understood and seemed pleased to have made the decision for herself. I asked her to explain her predicament to me in her own words. She said she understood that the surgery had risks and she knew she might experience some depression as a result, but she also knew there could be other side effects. As much as I hate to admit it, I felt incredibly relieved that it was her decision and not mine.

We prayed the night before her surgery and I came to a realization: It seemed that the more I tried to rely on myself for comfort and relief, the more the Lord made me depend upon Him. I knew that He was in control, but I "over-thought" everything and was trying to be the rock in the family. When I finally made Him my Rock, He gave me wisdom to cope. I leaned on Him more than ever that night, and as a result, I got one of the best nights of sleep I had had in a long time.

The second surgery was scheduled for Thursday, July 19, and due to the neurosurgeon's demanding schedule, would have to be at six p.m. It seemed odd that the neurosurgeon would be so busy, but after hearing of Amanda's research, we understood why. Rita's neurosurgeon had performed over 300 surgeries, on average, per year. He was one of the top rated neurosurgeons in the nation, and had been performing brain surgery for over twenty-five years. We knew we couldn't be in better hands with the exception of God's. We could have waited till July 31, but the neurosurgeon highly recommended that the surgery be preformed *A.S.A.P.*

The dreaded day finally came. Prior to the surgery, Amanda, Stacey and I got the chance to meet the operating room staff. We met the nurse, anesthesiologist, and a neurosurgeon who was a resident doctor. This time I was much more knowledgeable than before and I had more questions. I asked if they would be doing pathology reports on the tumor and if they would be determining which markers were present so that we could formulate a battle plan after the surgery. I told the anesthesiologist I didn't want Rita on Adivant due to her bad experience with it during her first hospital stay. I asked if she would be given Decadron, a steroid used to control brain swelling. I told them about Rita's low blood counts and low blood pressure and I asked if it would be a factor again this time. I asked so many questions I could see that they were a bit surprised. Perhaps they weren't used to someone being as informed as Amanda and I were, because the nurse asked if I was an engineer. I laughed and asked her why. She said that I had so many questions and was so well-informed that I must be.

We got to the hospital at three-thirty in the afternoon so that Rita could have another MRI to map her brain and highlight any new growth. It would be used to aid the surgeon in making precise cuts in specific areas of her brain during the procedure. During a meeting with the neurosurgeon he told us that he would be using the same incision from Rita's first operation. He also stated that he would probably have to leave some of the tumor behind because some of it would be inaccessible. Apparently, the tumor had invaded her right frontal lobe as well as her corpus callosum. This meant that her cerebrospinal fluid sac could be ruptured if he tried to remove any of the malignant growth in that area. He also advised that we allow special chemotherapy wafers to be planted into the new tumor growth that wasn't accessible. Theoretically, the wafers would dissolve in about three weeks and slow the growth of the tumor. Unfortunately, there was one adverse side-effect, which was the death of the surrounding brain tissue. We consented to his proposal and during the surgery, he implanted eight chemo-wafers in her brain.

    The operating room nurse took my cell phone number and told me she would be contacting me every two hours to let me know how things were going. Rita was taken in at six o'clock for the surgery and I never heard from the nurse again. By the time three hours had passed, I was a mess. I was pacing and trying to keep myself occupied by visiting with the family members that had gathered to support us.

The Second Surgery

It seemed like forever since Rita was taken to the O.R. so I used a hospital phone directly connected to the recovery room to ask the attendant if she could tell me anything about Rita's progress. She was unable to tell anything but instead had someone from the operating room contact me. The surgery was going just fine. Delays had pushed the start time back and they hadn't begun until sometime after nine p.m. Overall, the surgery only lasted about three hours, but by the time the doctor came out of the O.R., it was after twelve-thirty a.m. Everyone was completely drained, but when the neurosurgeon walked out, his smile was all the news we needed. I sensed a sigh of relief from everyone present. I think he was amazed to see so many people sitting there waiting, hoping and praying, for him to give us the news. He told us the surgery had gone very well. They had removed a seven-centimeter mass and he told us that Rita would be in her room in about an hour. Then he said something that stunned me. He said that while she was being taken to the Neuro Intensive Care Unit *she was talking*. And to think that I was certain she would be on a ventilator, unconscious or at best, highly drugged.

Rita was from a family of fourteen children and it was pleasantly surprising to see just how many of her brothers, sisters, nieces and nephews had showed up at the hospital. In addition, my four siblings, their spouses, their children, and all parents had come too. The emotion in the packed waiting room was so intense that no one said a word. Maybe it was because we were all exhausted from the long wait, or for some the long drive, but everyone kept their silence as we herded into the neuro-ICU waiting room. After what seemed like hours, Amanda, Stacey and I were finally allowed into her room. We braced ourselves as we walked into the ICU ward thinking back to how she looked after her first surgery. She recognized us immediately as we peeked in and she managed a crooked smile. She reached out and it was hard to hold back our tears but we managed to keep our composure. I walked to her bedside and asked, "Who loves you?" She softly whispered, "You do." When she responded, we were relieved. A nurse came in and told us we shouldn't rouse her too much, or make too much noise, so we went back to the waiting room and told everyone to please keep their voices low, and their visits to a maximum of five minutes. Amazingly, Rita was able to recognize everyone who went into her room that night.

The next morning when Rita woke up, she was groggy and disoriented. And though she had named everyone the night before, she still had trouble naming common objects. By the second day after surgery, she was able to use a walker and negotiate the halls. A few days later Rita was discharged. Now, we were visited by speech, occupational, and physical therapists.

The Second Surgery

Meanwhile, the tissue samples removed from Rita's brain were sent to pathology for examination.

On our following visit, the twenty-five staples used to close the incision were removed. Later that same day, we went to meet with the neuro-oncologist to plan our next move. From all the evidence they could see, everything had gone exactly as planned. Then she told us the news that haunted me for weeks to come. Forensic evaluations revealed that only thirty percent of what was removed was "viable tumor." The other seventy percent of the tissue removed was what the doctor called "treatment effect." In other words, seventy percent of the brain tissue removed had been killed by the treatments. Their treatments had caused more damage than the cancer! I wondered how a seventy percent kill ratio could be called "successful treatment." How would they define a failed treatment? How could she believe we would be happy that seventy percent of the damage was done by the treatment and only thirty percent from the cancer? It seemed to me that *the cancer was the good guy in this aspect*. Suddenly, I recalled the many sleepless nights, the never ending vomiting, the weight loss, and Rita's diminishing quality of life. I questioned whether it was even a good idea to allow them to keep her on chemotherapy even though the tumor continued to grow. The doctor argued that without treatment there may have been more cancerous growth.

The full effects of the surgery weren't evident at first, but after three weeks Rita couldn't even recognize a tree. She couldn't tell what a leg, arm and hand had in common. She was no longer able to hold conversations, and if you didn't ask her a question, you would never hear a word out of her mouth. As a result of her new personality I felt completely alone and abandoned, even more so than in the last thirteen months. The thought kept entering my mind—*there has to be something better*.

According to her doctors, Rita's tumor was a kind that was highly resistant to treatments. It was almost like it was able to outsmart the chemotherapy and come back stronger. Though chemo treatments will work for a while, their toxicity is too much for most people to handle for an extended period. Temozolomide was no longer effective for Rita, so the doctor prescribed a different chemotherapy. It would be similar to the chemicals in the gliadel-wafers, implanted during the second surgery, which were known as BCNU. The new chemo was a sister drug called CCNU.

Unfortunately, Rita's blood would also suffer from the new chemotherapy, and now she would require blood work on a weekly basis. This was due to the fact that all chemo will inevitably lower white blood cell counts. The blood work this time would determine whether to continue with the treatment or whether a white blood cell booster was necessary. Within two weeks of the first dose of CCNU, Rita needed an injection of white blood cell booster. It wasn't long before Rita told me she didn't want to take any more chemotherapy, especially when it came to the CCNU. She said that the way it made her feel was not worth the few weeks of life it *might* give her. We made a decision to forego the second dose of CCNU. The doctor told us she could only take it two times in her life anyway, and that CCNU is so overly potent that it will stay in someone's system for the rest of their life.

It was a blessing to have Rita off of the drugs and chemicals, and perhaps she felt some sense of normalcy again. Up until the time she went into hospice she was able to live without nausea, MRIs, doctors, or surgery. Rita was relieved that she would no longer have to take chemo and except for blood work, never have to visit another doctor.

CHAPTER 17

Depression

After sixteen months of taking care of my wife and dealing with the burdens that plagued us, I must have had six or more nervous breakdowns. I don't actually know what a nervous breakdown is, but after researching the subject, it turns out that there is no *official* definition. To me, it's when a person loses all concern for being "strong." Sometimes it may involve a physical collapse, or sometimes mental. I feel that I had lost my strength to cope and ability to function, so even without a definition I still believe I experienced some sort of breakdown. For example, I would reflect on a random memory, like Rita and I working in the garden, or cooking dinner together, and I would completely fall apart. Sometimes I would fall to my knees and cry uncontrollably for what seemed like hours. I would drift in and out of depression on a daily basis. With thanks to God, and the prayers of others, I always found a way to seek Him.

I've heard pastors speculate, during sermons, about how Biblical characters may have suffered from depression. Like when Adam and Eve became aware of their nakedness, they probably experienced depression because of falling from God's grace. Even when reading the Bible it's apparent that Abraham, Jonah, Job, Elijah, Saul, and David, must have experienced depression. As I thought about this possibility, I came to realize that I was not alone. Of course, there is no way of knowing if any of these people actually experienced depression, but given their respective situations, how could they not?

Mankind has battled depression at least since Biblical times. David said in Psalms 6:2-3, "Have mercy upon me, O Lord; for I am weak: O Lord, heal me; for my bones are vexed.³ My soul is also sorely vexed: but thou, O Lord, how long?" In verses 6-7, it says "I am weary with my groaning; all the night make I my bed to swim; I water my couch with my tears.⁷ Mine eye is consumed because of grief; it waxeth old because of all mine enemies."

If you ever read the book of Psalms, pay special attention to the number of times David cries out to God. He was *one depressed guy!* I also encourage you to consider how many times God pulled him through, in spite of his many failures. It would be hard to find anyone that God loved more than David. Perhaps the reason is because David loved and trusted the Lord through all of his life. God promised His faithfulness and *His word is good*. Incidentally, I said His word "IS good." You can still call on Him, today.

Although there has been a lot of research on depression, there is no real way of telling when or how it will occur. No one truly knows how to avoid it either, but if you're experiencing depression as a result of your loved one's illness, understand that it's normal for anyone in your situation. I know from my own experience that no one could possibly know what you're feeling, but there is someone out there that can help you deal with depression. If you are experiencing difficult times and depression is affecting you, please seek help.

Once when I was talking to the hospice chaplain, I told him about my depression. He explained that there are several different kinds. The most common is *clinical depression*, which can become so severe and persistent that you essentially stop participating in life. I, on the other hand, was suffering from what's known as *situational depression*. In other words, my depression was directly related to, and caused, by Rita's illness.

After that, when I began to feel the hopelessness that usually preceded my depression, I would think about my situation and the phrase, "This too shall pass." I didn't know if I would continue to battle depression after all was said and done, but I'm glad I was able to gain insight to the devastating effects of this psychological demon.

Depression does not Discriminate

Though you may not know it, some of the most famous people have experienced, or are experiencing, depression. If you think you're alone, here is a short list of famous individuals who have fought/fight depression; Vincent Van Gogh, Abraham Lincoln, Winston Churchill, Billy Joel, Brooke Shields, Robin Williams, Marie Osmond, Princess Diana, Harrison Ford, Jim Carrey, Drew Carey, Sheryl Crow, and Terry Bradshaw. Obviously the condition afflicts everyone regardless of status, race, religion, or age. I believe everyone at one point in their life experiences depression despite some people claiming to never have experienced it. Looking back at the list, I'd say you're in pretty good company if depression hits you.

We must look beyond the depression and uncertainty and focus on the end in store. You must maintain your focus and not lose sight of what is important in the long run, keeping your sanity and holding your life together for your future self. The Bible says, in Proverbs 29:18, "Where there is no vision, the people perish…" Today is nothing more than a passing moment in time. Though you may feel each day lasts forever, keep in mind that tomorrow will come in spite of your pain today. I remember thinking, at times, that Rita's suffering and sickness would last forever. Then, I thought about how I would feel after she died. I figured I'd be saying, "It seemed to last forever and now that it's over, it went like a flash." I challenge you to live as though this day were your last. Make every waking moment with your loved one count. It will pass, and before you know it you will be reflecting on all that you have experienced. Then one day you too will die.

Depression is not an Excuse to Act Stupid
During some of my deepest depressions I was guilty of saying hurtful things. Even when I would say bad things to my friends and family, I didn't seem to care who my words hurt. Normally, I consider myself to be a very sensitive guy, but when I was depressed I managed to somehow say all the wrong things. I was letting my emotions control nearly every aspect of my life and had thrown caution to the wind. Honestly, there is no excuse for rude behavior, ever. Nevertheless, I found myself apologizing, again and again, for offending loved ones with my harsh words. I would sometimes describe my behavior to my cousin Lou and in her infinite wisdom she would reply, "And how did you feel after that?" I hated that she would ask me that question, because I knew what she was really saying was, "Are you sorry

now?" And my answer was always the same, *I know, I know.*

How many times have you heard of someone going into a school, mall, workplace or home and doing the unthinkable? At the time when I wrote this there were four mass shootings in the United States. I think that most, if not every one of the shootings was directly related to depression. Depression is no excuse for harming yourself or another human being, physically or emotionally. In either case it's completely unacceptable. Remember, if you're considering doing something that may harm another, you can't and won't feel better about it afterward and seeking help is an excellent idea.

The Pathway of Pain~

If my days were untroubled and my heart always light
Would I seek that fair land where there is no night?
If I never grew weary with the weight of my load
Would I search for God's peace at the end of the road?

If I never knew sickness or never felt pain
Would I search for a hand to help and sustain
Would I walk without sorrow and live without loss
Would my soul seek solace at the foot of the cross?

If all I desired was mine day by day
Would I kneel before God and reverently pray?
If God sent no winter to freeze me with fear
Would I yearn for the warmth for spring each year?

I ask myself these questions and the answers are plain
If my life were all pleasure and I never knew pain
I would seek God less often and need Him much less
For God is sought more often in the times of distress
And no one knows God or sees Him as plain
As those who have met him on
The Pathway Of Pain.

~Lori Di Maggio

I don't know about you, but this poem, which was written by my dear friend Lori, gives me a lot to be thankful for. It talks about the joy and happiness we feel would not be possible if it weren't for the pain we know. Somehow, in the grand scheme of things, it seems that pleasure and pain go hand in hand.

Should I Take Antidepressants?

If you're a caretaker, or family member of the patient, the topic of antidepressants may have arisen. Amanda happened to be selling private health insurance at the time of Rita's illness, so I knew that when the time came to purchase health insurance, I would go through her. I happened to mention that I had considered taking antidepressants to deal with the many emotional issues I was facing and she told me that if I were ever treated for depression, in any form, I *could* be penalized for it later on. She even told me it was possible that my application for private insurance coverage could be denied altogether because depression is what is called a "pre-existing condition" in the insurance industry. Personally, I think that doctors should be held at least partially responsibile for patients on antidepressants who commit murder or take their own lives. To me, it's not unlike a bartender who sells liquor to someone who is inebriated and then kills someone on his or her way home. If the bartender is liable, why shouldn't the doctor be?

It seems unbelievable that a condition that affects so much of the population in our country could be considered in such a negative manner. It's ironic that hundreds if not thousands of people take their lives every year, and yet there's no *official* definition of a nervous breakdown. It seems every time we hear of someone going on a shooting rampage, the news tells us they were currently using, or had been on antidepressants in the past. I recently saw a commercial from the makers of an antidepressant that said that two out of three people taking antidepressants are not getting the relief they want and expect. Still, doctors readily over-prescribe these antidepressants like they were going out of business. Not just to the adult population any more, but even to children. With all this in mind, I elected not to take antidepressants—for me, the tradeoffs were just too great. Of course I don't deny I have had to deal with my issues head-on and yes, they have been great, but I have used all of the resources I have detailed in this book. By the way, if it is your choice, and if you are diagnosed with depression, do what it takes to get the help you need.

Pets and Depression

During the time of Rita's illness, I noticed an abrupt change in our dog, Sassy. We had gotten her from a friend a few years prior and she quickly became a part of our family. Unfortunately, she changed when Rita became ill and it was clear that Sassy sensed something was wrong. Since the time when Rita first came home from the hospital, Sassy would walk around the house in what seemed to be a confused state. One thing we had always liked about her is how mellow she is, but the way she acted at that time was worrisome. I had been reluctant about taking her home, since I knew that Jack Russell Terriers were high strung, but we never had problems with her. In fact, she had been trained by her previous owner and had been raised indoors. As Rita's illness progressed, Sassy would sit across from her and just stare. It was obvious that Sassy sensed our sadness, and it drove Rita crazy. Sometimes, she would just lay her head on Rita's feet and not do anything for hours. And when people would come to visit, Sassy would sit between the guest and Rita, as though she were protecting her.

Soon, Sassy was eating less and less. She had gone from a plump and healthy little dog, to a skinny and shedding, nervous wreck. It was clear that she was depressed. Then, one day while Rita was napping, I noticed Sassy sitting at my feet as though she were asking me to show her some love. When I picked her up and held her to my chest, she rested her head on my heart. I hugged her tight and cried as we seemingly understood one another.

Based on that experience I believe that dogs can suffer from depression, or at least they sense what their master is feeling and mirror it. I also learned that dogs get as much benefit from contact as you would, by petting them. If you have a pet, or pets, keep a close eye on them throughout your crisis. They can become sick with grief if they don't receive enough attention or comfort, much like a human. Also, it's common during a time of crisis to forget about pets when there is so much happening. Sometimes they may be better off someplace else, so I would recommend asking friends or family members if they can help by taking them off of your hands for a short time. In fact, after Rita had been placed in twenty-four-hour hospice care, I contacted the woman who had given us Sassy. I asked if she would be willing to take her for two or three weeks, and she gladly obliged. But after Rita's hospice stay stretched from a month to two, and there was no end in sight, I decided to take her back.

Family dogs were welcomed at the hospice center so I began taking her when I visited. The first time I took her, she loved it. She would walk right into Rita's room and "smile" at her mom; Rita seemed to recognize her too. Though she never called Sassy by name, Rita would dangle her foot off the edge of the bed to try and get her attention. It was always a cute sight and I could tell that Rita was comforted by Sassy's presence. The best part was that she never even barked while we visited, as though she knew she was in a hospice. When Rita would go to sleep, I would take Sassy for walks and it helped my stress tremendously. Still, I could tell Sassy was affected by the whole situation and that she worried about Rita. Ultimately, having Sassy around was a good way to calm my spirit and I believe the feeling was mutual.

In the end, I was glad that I had Sassy to comfort me when no one else cared to be around or to listen. And though she is just a dog, I feel that she understood me more than a lot of people, during the whole ordeal.

CHAPTER 18

Pain and Grief

Losing a loved one is one of the most horrible experiences ever. I've mentioned in sections prior, how seeing someone go from a vibrant and healthy person then inch closer to death, causes tremendous stress. Personally, in addition to said stress I felt physical pain; in my chest, head, and body, which ached constantly.

When grief would overwhelm me, the result became unbearably intense. I was more fragile than I had ever been, both physically and emotionally. To add insult to injury, I would hear of rumors and lies being spread about me and how I allegedly treated Rita. I heard things like I was wanted/on the run from the police. I was apparently cheating on my wife. I had been seen at a karaoke bar hugging a younger woman, when in fact, I was there with Amanda and had dedicated the song to my wife. I heard that I had been "buying drugs with all the money donated for Rita," and that I had been leaving

Rita alone for hours and hours and keeping her outside in nothing but a diaper, in the cold.

There were times when people would try to give me advice by telling me how to take care of Rita. It all added up until I couldn't take all the lies and rumors and soon I just told everyone to get lost.

Even though I knew better and should have ignored the unfounded rumors and lies, I still ended up alienating many people from my support system. By allowing my pain to preoccupy my life and thoughts, it caused me to be overly sensitive and defensive. For me, the combination of physical pain and emotion were much too volatile to ignore. I became guarded, and didn't care if my words and actions were offensive. If you find yourself becoming blunt or short with people, take it from me, you will regret it if you allow your emotions to control you.

Grief and Anger

When grief and anger mix, there is potential for irreparable harm and it can tear a family apart. For example, when my brother Johnny died and we were preparing for his burial, my younger brother Joe and I found ourselves at each other's throats. Though neither of us remembers what it was, something had sent us both into a rage. We had lost sight of the issue at hand and felt very devastated. We were both hurting because of the loss of our brother and we didn't understand that our anger was associated with our grief.

I remember losing my grandmother, whose unexpected death left us with much pain and grief. Consequently, there was plenty of animosity in the mix. Her siblings had spread rumors and accusations that my mom had taken advantage of her mother's old age. They subtly hinted that she had received a large insurance settlement. In reality my mom was not financially able to afford the high premiums that seniors must pay. My mom's family has never fully recovered from their mother's death, and some of her siblings never spoke to each other again. Sadly, all but one sister has died. The family was divided because thoughts of grief and anger had become more important than the family itself.

It All Comes Down to Fear

In my opinion, the fight between me and my brother was due to fear. Perhaps it was the fear of our own mortality, or perhaps it was because we didn't want to lose any more of our siblings. During the time I wrote this, I was fearful of the thought that I could one day become dependent on someone else, as Rita had of me, or the thought of having to become a caretaker again. Being fearful of what can or may be, is counterproductive and can affect everything in a negative way. Fear can cause you to destroy your relationships, make bad decisions, and even hinder your ability to move forward. People had told me that they were afraid of visiting Rita for fear of saying or doing the wrong thing. As a caretaker, I would much rather have had to forgive someone for saying or doing the wrong thing than to forgive them for not visiting.

One night I received an email from a family member that seemed very judgmental and condemning of my actions. At first, I was furious but then, after re-reading the message, I realized that there was a lot of fear in their words. I responded by writing things of which they were unaware. I made the response as diplomatic as possible and ended it by stating that I would welcome their correspondence. Soon after I received an apology, and they expressed how they now had a much better understanding of the situation. By thinking things through and not going off of emotion, or fear, I had alleviated their concerns and fears that had caused them to act irrationally. By taking the time to respond politely and thoughtfully I had made things better for both of us.

If I had allowed my fear of judgment and condemnation, to influence what I had written in the response, things could have turned out a lot worse. In this case, I was able to overcome my fear by recognizing theirs.

Just Laugh

After my brother Johnny died, my three sisters, my brother, and I went to a restaurant supply store to buy food for the reception which would follow the funeral.

Pain and Grief

As we were walking around the store, my brother Joey noticed a pallet filled with huge bags of noodles, each bag about as big as a king size pillow. They were on sale, and as we walked, Joey bet me that my eldest sister Angie would not be able to pass by without grabbing one. We waited and our two other sisters passed by, but Angie wasn't with them. We told them about the bet and waited for Angie to round the corner. Sure enough, when Angie came to the end of the aisle and saw the noodles, she quickly picked up a bag and hugged it tightly to her chest. We all broke out in a fit of hysterical laughter. None of us had expected her to be so elated by the sight of noodles and it was the perfect remedy for our dire situation.

Once, when Rita was in the Porter Hospice, on one of her middle-of-the-road days, I was brushing her teeth. She wasn't talking, but could answer questions by nodding and shaking her head. Someone across the hall had just died and family members were beginning to gather outside the room. As I finished brushing, I gave her a small sip of water so she could rinse. She then spit it into the plastic pan which I held. I gave her another sip. But when I put the pan to her mouth for her to spit, she looked me in the eye and just sat there. Her cheeks were puffed with water and I told her to spit it out, but she only shook her head to say no. A nurse named Joyce happened to be going by and heard me asking Rita to spit the water out.

She walked into the room and said, "Rita, now you gotta spit that water out." Rita looked at Joyce and again, did nothing. Joyce and I looked at each other and couldn't help but see the humor of our situation. We both chuckled quietly so that we wouldn't disturb the family across the hall.

Joyce asked Rita, again and again, to spit. But Rita had the same look of defiance on her face. Joyce finally smiled and looked at Rita and said, "You're not going to spit that out are you?"

Rita looked at Joyce, then at me. She shook her head, no.

Joyce then said, "You're just going to be stubborn today, aren't you?"

To our surprise, Rita, cheeks puffed up from the water, half-smiled and nodded, to say "yes." The expression on her face was priceless! Joyce and I both laughed so loudly, the people from the grieving family started to walk to the doorway to see what was happening. We shared a robust laugh and had a wonderful moment, all in the midst of such a tragic setting.

These two experiences reminded me that laughter is very important—even in times when everyone around you is crying. It may be hard to find humor in troubled times, but if you look you will find a reason to laugh.

Me Time

I was constantly reminded by hospital workers, friends, and family, about the grueling demands of being a caretaker. In fact, I learned watching the news that one year of being a caretaker is equivalent to six years of life. I'm told that it's not unusual for caretakers to suddenly fall ill, or die shortly before or after the death of their spouse. Because of these facts, I realized that I needed to take time to recharge myself on a regular basis, but somehow, I could rarely pull myself away. When I looked into her eyes I could see she didn't want me to leave. Or maybe I just wanted to be with her every waking minute since I knew what would happen in the end.

One time, on our way home from California, I was listening to one of the flight attendants as we prepared for take-off. She said that if cabin pressure dropped or was lost, oxygen masks would appear from the ceiling. She explained, "If you are traveling with small children, or those in need of special care and the masks appear, you should place the mask over your own face first." Her words faded away and suddenly that's when it hit me: I could never be an effective caretaker if I too was in poor health. I needed *me* time! I needed to put the proverbial mask on myself before putting it on Rita! I finally realized that I too was still alive. I decided then, that I would try to escape, in the little ways I could, to help offset my stress.

So, every once in a while, when I could get someone to stay with Rita for an hour or two, I would go to a local pool hall and play pool. Sometimes, I would go out for karaoke, which was my biggest outlet. I would have loved to take a weekend to go fishing or camping, but finding a free weekend was pretty much impossible. I felt like I was in a revolving door, able to go around, but never able to leave. My friends and family would sometimes offer to help, but somehow it always seemed like our timing was off. People were just too wrapped up in their own lives to make time for us. The times I did ask for help were difficult since asking for help was never my strong point. So I remained in the revolving door of taking care of my wife. Truthfully though, I have no right to complain. I now know there might have been plenty of help if I had only kept asking. Looking back, I'm thankful for every minute I spent with Rita.

CHAPTER 19

Etiquette

Throughout the illness, and long afterward, people would often say things like, "I don't know what to say," or "I would like to help but I don't know what I could do." Therefore, the following section is filled with ideas regarding ways you can help the caretaker. Each suggestion is based on what I experienced and what I feel will be helpful to know. I'm sure there are many other ideas not listed here, but I have compiled a list of what I felt would have been most beneficial for our particular situation.

Keep Your Word

If you tell a caretaker you'll be able to do something or meet somewhere at a specific time, for Heaven's sake, *be there on time.* If you're not going to show, or can't make it, *please* be sure to call and let them know, especially if you can let them know ahead of time. You have no idea how slow time goes by for a caretaker when they have to wait for someone. Care-taking is like being in a constant state of alertness and worry. There are so many things they must be aware of, that having to wait just adds more to their frustration and stress. It is also crucial for them to have free time to do simple things like make a bank deposit, get a haircut, or allowing them to have some *me* time. If you say you will be able to help, and allow some free time for them, then you really need to honor your word—it will help relieve some stress for them. You need to understand that being a caretaker is like being in a prison—you have all the time in the world, no time for yourself, *and* someone you love is dying. If the patient they're taking care of requires round the clock care and is in an unresponsive state, the caretaker is definitely experiencing something that few others else can comprehend. There is no way to describe how eerie it was for me at times, to just sit around as Rita lay there without talking or doing anything and not having anyone else around. I would talk to her and just assume what she would say in response. When I would sing, tell jokes, or reminisce, at times when Rita was in a catatonic state, 99% of the responses were my own. It was then that hours seemed like days and the days were like eternities.

There was one occasion when Rita's family got a glimpse of what it was like for me. They had not visited for a few months, and I became angry with them. Then one day they called and said they would be visiting Rita at the hospice center. Six of them came to visit, and when they entered the room I could see that they were surprised at Rita's almost totally unresponsive state. I was feeding her when they arrived and asked if anyone would like to help. No one said a word and the mood turned awkward in an instant. I slowly continued to feed her as they took seats in the chairs around Rita's bed. I decided that since they were there I would take the opportunity to go to my house for a shower and change clothes. I asked my brother in-law if he would accompany me and we drove to my house. After taking care of what I needed to do at my house, I visited another family member for a meal. In the back of my mind, I knew that the five I left at the hospice must be feeling a little stress being alone with Rita, but I decided to leave them there for a while longer. After just two hours of being out and about, we returned. When we walked into the room, everyone was sitting in silence. All of them had pushed their chairs tightly against the wall and their faces were pale. As for Rita, she was lying in bed, awake and staring straight into space. The tension in the room was almost laughable. After a brief moment, my father in-law stood up and said, "Let's go get something to eat." They all stood up and walked out. Not one of them said anything as they filed passed me and I was alone again. They returned an hour-and-a-half later, full of dinner and cheery, as though nothing out of the ordinary had happened. I sat there in awe at their total disregard for me. It didn't matter that I was hungry or saddened by the fact that no one invited me, or offered to bring me something back. It didn't matter that I was alone, day after day, taking care of their daughter/sister. It seemed to me like nothing really mattered to them except for themselves.

When people would call and say, "If there's anything you need, give us a call." or, "If there's anything we can do, let us know.", I would usually respond, "Just visit Rita and me." Yet, when it came time for them to actually visit, they were nowhere to be found. After it happened a few times I started to just block out anyone who said anything similar. To me they weren't being sincere, it was just a formality or nicety—something to say so that they seemed like they really cared. In my case I told them exactly what I wanted, for them to visit. It's important to realize that as a caretaker it's very difficult to "know" what your specific needs are, but if they ask you to visit, then you visit. Don't think that saying you will do something will make them feel better, or make them feel like you care. Realize that words are nothing, action is everything.

During the time when Rita was in home hospice, four people told me they would come over and visit on the same day. By five o'clock that afternoon I hadn't received even one phone call from any of them. By eight o'clock that night, after no one had come or called, I was pretty much at the end of my rope. My anger and hurt went beyond seething. It was one of the instances that, overall, contributed to my lashing out in anger when it came to people visiting, or not, and telling them to get lost. Under normal circumstances, being stood up is bad, but when you're stood up under the stress of being a caretaker, it's like multiplying it by a thousand.

I know this sounds cynical, but from my experience, I found that there are some people you shouldn't rely on for anything. For example, I used to ask a certain person for help. One time they arrived one hour late, another time, forty-five minutes late, and the last time they never showed or called. What really bothered me most was not only the fact that they had always shown up late, but that I almost missed the funeral of one of my dear friend's dads because of them. I never asked them for anything else after that and I became reluctant to ask for help from anyone. I was too worried about being let down again. This situation isn't only applicable to friends and family. Rita had one certain home-hospice nurse that would stay with her for one hour, two to three times a week. Because of her help I could go grocery shopping and take care of other random things. She didn't have to do anything but sit and watch the television since I had always bathed, fed, and clothed Rita by the time the she arrived. The only problem was that the nurse was always between fifteen and forty-five minutes late. She never called to let me know she coming late and she would just randomly show up. One time when she came forty-five minutes late, I had made lunch plans with Amanda. I was furious because by the time she arrived, my daughter's lunch break had already ended.

I never understood how people could be the way they were when practically everyone has a cell phone. They would tell me empty lies and promises, as though they were helping me out, when in fact they only made my life harder. Simply put: *Follow through on your promises*.

How can I Help? Offer Specific Help

You may be reading this book and thinking to yourself, the caretaker doesn't seem to want me around, or maybe they even yelled at you for no apparent reason at all. Please, don't give up on them. They probably need you now more than ever before, especially if they just rejected you. They're probably feeling overwhelmed and confused, not to mention fragile. Each time they reject you, or others, their emotions get even more messed-up. They start to regret how mean they were and then they realize they're even more alone, and no one visits because of it.

Understand that it's like a vicious cycle that can only end when everyone has abandoned the caretaker. The trauma your friend or family member is going through as a caretaker is a tremendous load to bear. They may have to adjust to new things every day, and that can be extremely trying. The lack of consistency in their life, and the fact that they've had to sacrifice so much to take on the role of a caretaker is incomprehensible. Until you've walked a mile in a caretaker's shoes, *you'll never know how tight they are.*

It may not seem like a big deal, but there were times when I would have loved for someone to come over and say something like, "Why don't you go out for a haircut or a burger? I'll stay with Rita for an hour," or, "I think you should have a day to yourself, so I'll stay with Rita and you go do whatever." It would have been especially wonderful if someone would have given me five or six hours to go fishing once in awhile. Instead, they would say vague things like, "If there's any way I can help, let me know." Then when I would ask them for a favor they would say they were too busy or use some lame-sounding excuse. In the first year, it was rare for anyone to actually help me out in terms of freeing-up time, however in the second year, people's offers were more sincere and they followed through. They were more available and volunteered to do more specific things to help. I was able to recharge occasionally and it was a total blessing. Without *me* time, a caretaker can get really burnt out, so offer to lend a hand and be specific—even if it's only for a short time.

Just Look Around!

I was having a hard time getting my backyard ready for winter in the fall of 2007, and Rita had just started home hospice. Unfortunately, there was no one to help take care of her so I had to deal with the chores as best as I could. On nice days, I would bundle her up and take her outside with me, or she'd sit in the sunroom and watch as I readied the yard. Still, it was difficult to keep a constant eye on her so I toiled in short spurts. One of my biggest concerns, in terms of yard work, was the branches of my Blue Spruce that I had cut off earlier in the season. It had always taken considerable effort to mow around them and I figured that with them gone, I'd be able to mow the lawn quicker next year. After I had cut them, I had been getting ready to gather and tie them into bunches, but Rita's care became too demanding and I couldn't find time to finish the job.

So, the branches stayed piled up under the tree and I figured I'd pick them up some time in the spring. I knew the pine needles would become dry and brittle, and I hated to put it off, but I had no other option. Then one day I got a surprise visit from my cousin, Ely and his wife, Shelly. The two of them, with my Aunt Rose, had driven all the way to Denver from Pueblo, which is about a hundred miles away. I welcomed them and enjoyed their company.

As we visited, Ely quietly listened and seemed to be having a difficult time with Rita's appearance. Without saying a word, he got up and went out to the backyard. I thought he must have wanted to just enjoy the nice fall day and I didn't think twice about it. But after about forty-five minutes of visiting with his wife and my aunt, I began to wonder what had happened to him. I walked out to the backyard, and to my surprise, Ely had gathered all of the branches and was raking up the last of the debris. He had stacked the branches neatly in a pile so I got some rope, and together, we bundled them and took them to the street. He never asked how he could help but instead took it upon himself to get busy.

If you find that you have no idea what to say to the caretaker or how to help, perhaps it's better to follow Ely's example and tend to something that needs to be done. There are dozens of ways you can help the caretaker, and like Ely, you don't even need to say a word. In fact, you can even contribute if they're not home, like doing some light yard work or by taking their dog for a walk. How nice it would have been to come home from taking care of an errand to find that someone had mowed my lawn while I was gone.

Help Them Clean Their House

With Rita as sick as she was, it became very difficult to care for her and do the housework. So from time to time a few family members would come over and clean our house. They would vacuum the rooms, do dishes, clean and sweep and do anything else they thought might help. The help they gave us was always welcome. After they'd leave it was always a comfort to come home to a clean house.

If you would like to offer your help, try something specific like, "I'd like to come over and help with the housekeeping." This time you're not just asking what it is you can do, you're making them aware of what you're able and willing to do. I encourage you to be persistent when offering help even when they say no or seem disgruntled. They'll never forget your thoughtfulness and will appreciate the offer.

Bring Them a Meal

After Rita's second surgery, several members of our church, family, and friends began bringing us meals. Folks would bring us dinners, desserts and snacks. Though it wasn't a daily thing we were eternally grateful, and the food was always so delicious. I think it tasted so good because I knew the people preparing it had made it with love.

Personally, I loved the homemade breads and casseroles which were easy to freeze if there happened to be leftovers. There were some minor drawbacks however. For example, when people brought food in glass or metal containers—I would have to wash them and keep track of who brought what, then returning them became confusing if I forgot who the owner was. So when people would give us food in disposable containers, we were relieved. My sister in law Julia used to bring stacks of delicious frozen meals in disposable containers so that I could warm them up and toss the containers when finished. I also discovered the time-saving value of paper plates and plastic utensils.

Our dear friends, David and Becky, were so wonderful throughout the whole ordeal. They would bring wonderful, one pot meals, and sometimes Becky would bake loaves of homemade bread. She would also bring us homemade fudge, and her brownies were the absolute best I've ever eaten. One thing I really enjoyed was that she never asked how she could help. Instead she would just call and tell me, "What time are you going to be home? I'm bringing dinner over for you guys this afternoon." I can't begin to count the blessings she, and so many others, bestowed upon me and my family.

Though we appreciated all of the meals people prepared for us, it was always my first choice to cook for ourselves when I could. I think people must have been afraid to prepare things Rita couldn't or wouldn't eat, so they would sometimes give us gift cards. Grocery gift cards were among the most welcome blessings because we could buy things people didn't know we needed like fruits and vegetables or toilet paper. Besides, at one point, our freezer was so filled with prepared meals that we could hardly fit anything in else there. We really appreciated gift cards because we were able to buy anything and weren't limited to just food.

Send a Card

Some people choose to send cards. In fact, Rita received so many cards that we needed a large box in which to store them. Many of the cards she received were so touching that they brought tears to my eyes. The cards were comforting, calming, and reassuring. They reminded us of the awesome glory of God and were a welcomed blessing. I believe that everyone has a gift or strength that they can share. One woman from our church named Bonnie, sent many, many beautiful cards to us. Each week when her cards arrived, I would open and read them to Rita. She didn't always know that Bonnie had sent them, but she always enjoyed looking at them and listening to the prayers and scriptures enclosed. The way Bonnie's cards ministered to us was a true blessing and I know of several people in our church that have also been richly blessed by her cards. Her words of encouragement came at the right time and were always relevant to our situation. I will always be grateful to her and the blessings she sent. If you wish to be a blessing but don't know what to do or say, perhaps you could send a card.

Send a Check or Cash

Around 1998, I took a job at an electronics store selling televisions, stereos, and appliances. I had been out of work for some time, so money was tight and it was right around Thanksgiving. Because of all of our financial troubles I had no idea how we would be able to afford our Thanksgiving that year. After a couple of days of working at the store, my co-worker Kerri, out of the blue, told me she had something for me. We went out to the parking lot and she asked if I could park my car next to hers. She said she needed help getting some things from her trunk. When she opened the trunk there were several paper bags so I thought that she might have some used clothes for my daughters. With the way they were growing at that time, I would have been glad to receive them. I pulled my car next to hers and she asked me to open my trunk. Then she told me to move the bags from her trunk to mine. When I looked in the bags I felt uneasy and was literally dazed and embarrassed. Above all, I was humbled in a way I never imagined.

As I glanced into the bags, I could see that she had given us a Thanksgiving dinner, complete with twenty-pound turkey and all the trimmings! I didn't even know this woman, and there she was, giving us just what I had been worrying about! Kerri had bought a Thanksgiving dinner for my family without even knowing our situation. All of a sudden, I started thinking to myself, "I'm the guy who gives turkey dinners away—not the one who receives them." I don't remember if I said it out loud, or if I just thought it, but I kept hearing, "I can't accept this," over and over. I felt my face turning red as I heard myself saying words I never thought I could say, in a situation like this. My voice was cracking and tears welled-up in my eyes. I heard myself say, thank you, as though someone else was saying it.

I learned the true meaning of the word humility that day. I also accepted the fact that everybody needs a helping hand at some time or another—except this time my family happened to be the ones in need. The strangest thing about this story though, is not that she gave me something. It was that she didn't have an inkling of our situation—how could she have known I had no money for Thanksgiving dinner? The only possible answer is that God *is* the Great Provider. He knows our prayers before we even utter them and whenever we found ourselves in dire need of financial help, I trusted that God would provide for our needs.

When Rita was ill, our friends and family would sometimes send us money. And even though Rita's insurance was very good, her medical expenses were sometimes so costly that they were almost as much of a burden as the illness itself. So, each time we received a cash donation I considered it another blessing from God. We learned to be grateful and appreciative every gift. Just like in the Thanksgiving story, there were times when we were hurting financially.

Interestingly enough, money donations always seemed to come in during our most desperate times of need. There was once a time when I had received a bill for $277, and sure enough someone donated an envelope, anonymously, with exactly $277 cash. Perhaps it sounds too good to be true, but that's how it happened.

Sometimes someone would give us a donation and say, "Take this and go out for a nice dinner—on us." We would go to dinner knowing the food was a blessing and it was clear that people loved us and that God was watching over us. I believe that if I had refused to accept the gifts we received we would have been denying blessings. Saying thank you always felt natural and good. I will always remember the kindness and generosity shown to us.

Since the illness, I have developed the philosophy of paying it forward, and will continue to help others just as I was helped when Rita was ill. If you have no idea how to be of assistance, but want to, remember—*everything goes good with green!*

Keep the Knick-Knacks

A lot of the time Rita would receive many nice and thoughtful decorations or gifts. We really liked the plaques that were inscribed with scriptural or inspirational messages. She also received many angels, teddy bears, candles, and other things. Unfortunately, after a few months we were overwhelmed with knick-knacks. It seemed that Rita felt guilty for liking one gift over another, so she kind of set them all aside. But in truth, the money spent on the mementos would have been of better use to us if it were spent on food or grocery gift cards.

In his book, *The Five Love Languages*, Gary Chapman lists five different personality types that determine how we communicate with one another. He says that each of us is driven by one of five distinct personality characteristics: the five "Love Languages." These are: Quality Time, Words of Affirmation, Gifts, Acts of Service, and Physical Touch. If you were hurt or offended by the fact that I said knick-knacks are unnecessary, it is likely that you are blessed with the personality characteristic of giving. As a result of Rita's personality, it was difficult for her to accept gifts. Though we were eternally grateful for every statuette and teddy bear we received, I think it's best to give people more practical necessities. Sure there are people who just love knick-knacks, but in a crisis, the last thing people need is to have to decide where to put all the trinkets. Of course, this is only my opinion. Perhaps you know of someone that enjoys collecting frog statues or teddy bears. If they are sick, perhaps a new knick knack would really lift their spirits.

Golden Silence

After everything that Rita had been through, she became very sensitive to sustained loud noises. They would clearly drain her energy and confuse her tremendously. In the beginning when we were getting visitors, there would be ten to twelve people talking at once. Rita was so gracious she would never complain. She would simply smile and not show how stressed out she was from the noise. When she found herself surrounded by over-stimulation, she would seek quieter surroundings or crash when we got home. Whether it was from loud gatherings or too much noise from the traffic, high-volume settings had a very negative impact on her.

Toward the end, she could hardly stand to listen to anything more than a whisper. Remember, if you're a bit nervous about not knowing what to say, you do not need to overcompensate with nervous conversation or loud voices. When people are very ill, silence truly is golden.

Some people are very uncomfortable with the powerful effect of silence. They seem to feel a responsibility to fill silence with chatter, regardless of whether what they have to say is important or not. They'll go on and on about the weather, crime rates, or maybe the economy. Then, after half-an-hour they'll say their goodbyes and be off. On their way home I would imagine them looking in the rear-view mirror and thinking, "Well, I sure did enrich their lives." Yet the reality of it was that they had simply increased Rita's stress level. Usually, Rita didn't even remember who had visited, much less what they said. So be open and not afraid to enjoy your time, together. It is fine if there are no words, no voices, simply quiet—except for the presence of the people in the room. It isn't necessary to have complete silence at every moment, but I believe there is an incredible power and blessing in the midst of it. Let the silence fill the room until God's power fulfills the needs of everyone present. Be mindful that quiet moments can be refreshing and comforting for both the patient and the caretaker.

Also, while it's nice to be informed, sometimes visitors that meant well seemed like interrogators. If the patient and their family want you to know about the situation, respect them enough to allow them to voluntarily mention said information. If you are the kind of person who has to ask lots of questions, try and remember that the family is going through a very stressful time. Be tactful, gentle and thoughtful. You can always ask how things are going on the phone, or perhaps consult their blog if they have one. As odd as it may sound, asking about sensitive things like how the patient is doing, in front of the patient, isn't always appropriate.

When Rita was of sound mind she had written in her *Five Wishes* document that she wanted to listen to the music she had always enjoyed. So, throughout her time in hospice, I gladly obliged. Many times the music was the only sound we heard for hours on end. Her facial expressions let me know when to turn it down or off, though sometimes the music at a low volume was even too much for her. So remember, even though a patient may have lost control of their life, you can help them by simply being silent.

Leave the Kids at Home

Although Rita used to enjoy talking to kids when she was well, during her illness she preferred not having to deal with them altogether. Due to the fact that excessive noises were extremely stressful for her, a child-filled environment was the last place I wanted her to be. Not to mention that most kids, especially toddlers, can't fully understand the seriousness of a situation involving a very ill person. They will go about being kids and make loud noises. So it was especially difficult when people would visit with their young kids. If you are unable to find a babysitter, be kind enough to let the patient's family know that you cannot visit because you don't want to disturb them with your children. They'll understand your situation and you'll be doing them a favor. This is very important to remember, especially if the patient is in hospice care, home or otherwise.

For Thanksgiving of 2007, there were kids running up and down the halls of the hospice center all day long. The noise continued throughout the entire holiday weekend, and it was taxing for all the patients. I couldn't believe that people would be so disrespectful of others' dying family members, not to mention how unfair it was to the children. After having to deal with the rowdy little kids that weekend, I couldn't fathom ever taking a small child to a hospice.

Of course, as with any rule there are exceptions. The patient may have children, grandchildren or other small children who are special to them. Perhaps the patient wishes to see them. If that is the case, please just be mindful of the other patients and their families, as well as the amount of time the kids are there.

Offer to Take Their Kids

I can't imagine how difficult it must be to be a caretaker *and* have young children. The burden of having an ill loved one is devastating enough, but with children it must be beyond overwhelming. Therefore, if you happen to know someone who has a terminal illness and kids, offer to take them off their hands for a while. Whether it's for an hour, an afternoon, or a whole night and day, it'll be one of the best things for them. Giving gifts, such as food or clothing is helpful, but helping by taking their kids at the right time may be better than any tangible gift you can give. Just as I mentioned in the previous section, kids can be a terrible stress for a cancer patient. Also, the kids may need a break from the situation, too.

Pray

I first learned about prayer when I was eighteen years old and had just gotten saved. I had been in the army for about four months and was transferred to Fort Carson,

Colorado. I happened to be visiting my sister in Denver when I noticed an open Bible on her table. I picked it up, looked at it, and was shocked to find out that *I could read it!* I had always thought that Bibles were in Latin or some other foreign language. Her boyfriend approached me and asked if I knew the Lord. I asked him what he meant by that and he told me that it was possible to have a personal relationship with Jesus. He then said that I could ask Jesus into my heart as my personal Lord and Savior, if I wanted to. Not really understanding what he meant, I agreed and we said a prayer. Within a few minutes I was filled with a joy I had never known and was crying like crazy. I knew that it was a defining moment in my life.

Ever since I asked Jesus into my life I have done my best to always trust in Him and His word. I learned about the power of prayer and how God can answer those prayers. There are even some people that have a natural gift of praying for others. They are known as "prayer warriors." The term may seem a bit daunting, or strange, but in all actuality they are unsung heroes in the Christian world. Prayer warriors are vigilant and steadfast individuals that pray for others in their times of need. For example, when Rita was first diagnosed, there were so many people praying for our family. Like the prayer chains I mentioned earlier in the book, a prayer warrior is like a single person prayer chain.

Prayer warriors are someone who appeals to God on behalf of an individual in need. They recognize God's mercy and pray for intervention.

It may seem odd, but in truth, I believe those who held my family up in prayer were just as important to our lives as any monetary support we ever received. I am humbled and grateful for every prayer for our behalf.

What Not to Say

One of the worst things people could ever tell me was, "I know how you feel." Of course, there was also, "I know what you must be going through," and, "Everything's going to be alright." Each time someone would tell me that they *knew* what I was going through, or *how I felt*, I would want to yell at them. I would often retort, "How many times has your husband/wife been diagnosed with a malignant brain tumor?" I know it seems kind of harsh putting it like that, but seriously, our culture has been stupefied by the superficiality of hollow sympathy. Everyone thinks that they can just say something like, "I know how you feel," and that will make the sufferer feel better. How does that even make sense? I always felt alienated each time someone tried to tell me that they knew what I was going through. Unless you've actually lived it, no one on earth could possibly know what I went through.

Keep in mind that you really don't know anything about what's going on—in the patient's life or the caretaker's. You may have *an idea* of what's going on, but it's not possible to have all the facts. You might think they should have done something differently, but perhaps they have already investigated those options. Your ideas may not be viable or even applicable. You may not like the conditions of their home or their decisions as far as the treatment, but that is none of your concern. Unless you are A) The patient's spouse/guardian, or B) Going to assume the responsibility of the caretaker, whatever it is you disagree with, there is a point where you need to keep your ideas to yourself. At the very least, it's better to make suggestions as subtly as possible.

Remember, every decision made on behalf of the patient is their choice, and not your own. It is bad enough for the family to have to agonize by seeing their loved one so ill. Trying to tell them what to do is going too far.

Keep in mind that the caretaker probably has a lot of pent-up frustration. So, if you make a remark that doesn't sit well with them, and they go off on you, just know that you brought it upon yourself. There were probably people before you that gave the same suggestion, and how annoying it is to be told, over and over again, the same thing. Know that the caretaker is already second-guessing many, if not every one of, the decisions they've made. Besides, if they're not asking for advice, it's probably because they're not looking for it. You may have experience with a similar or even the exact same illness as the person in question, but that doesn't mean you can suddenly be an authority to them. Even doctors who see many people for the same illness know that what works for one patient may not have any beneficial impact on another. Every illness, every patient is different.

Back when I first started taking care of Rita it seemed as though everyone I talked to had some bit of advice, critique, or input. One time, someone visiting told me I needed to give Rita yogurt in the morning. The next day a different person came over and told me she shouldn't be eating yogurt. I was told that her food was too cold, yet another person told me it was too hot. I should move the bed to the other side of the room. I should move it back to where it was. Rita was too ill to take to California. Why was I taking her off of the medication? Someone even once questioned my authority when I stopped her chemotherapy. Every decision I made was questioned by someone else. Almost every bit of advice, that I was so graciously given, was unsolicited and offensive. Not to mention that most advice was idiotic in general, especially when it would contradict someone else's or had little to no importance in the grand scheme of things. In the end I just got to the point where I would ignore any and all advice.

My Friend I Care

Don't tell me that you understand, don't tell me that you know
Don't tell me that I will survive, how I will surely grow.
Don't tell me this is just a test, that I am truly blessed
That I am chosen for this task, apart from all the rest.
Don't come at me with answers that can only come from me,
Don't tell me how my grief will pass that I will soon be free
Don't stand in pious judgment of the bonds I must untie,
Don't tell me how to suffer, don't tell me how to cry,
My life is filled with selfishness, my pain is all I see,
But I need you, I need your love, unconditionally.
Accept me in my ups and downs, I need someone to share,
Just hold my hand and let me cry, and say,
"My friend, I care."

~Author unknown

CHAPTER 20

Never ask a Dying Man how he's Doing

My wife had an aunt named Senida, whose husband Ishmael had passed away in March of 2007. When he was in his final hours, we went to see him. His small hospital room was literally packed full. Along with his wife, children, and grandchildren, there were numerous nieces and nephews. The room was surprisingly silent as we stood beside his bed. The silence was suddenly broken when one of his grandsons walked in and asked, "How are you, Grandpa?" He looked at his grandson, half smiled and said, "Uh…I'm dying." His tone sounded bewildered yet so matter of fact. The room erupted with laughter. I couldn't help but wonder, was the question appropriate for the occasion? Was there a more appropriate greeting? I thought of what I said when I greeted a sick or dying person. It was the same thing, "How are you doing?"

Until Rita's illness, I never even considered the phrase. Suddenly though, I started to notice that every visitor would ask, "How are you, Rita?" After all she had been through she got to the point where she hated that question, especially when she was taking chemo. Somehow, though, she always managed to say something like, "Good, really good!" or "Awesome." She never wanted to let on to just how ill she really was, and I think she would have preferred that visitors start conversations with something other than a question about her condition. In the end, there was no real way to change the outcome, and perhaps people knew, but it didn't make things any better to remind her that she was dying.

Ask About the Caretaker

When I would go to church it seemed the same people asked every week, how Rita was doing. Eventually, I became so frustrated that I began answering that I didn't want to talk about it. One woman would not accept that answer so she would constantly persist that I tell her. Finally, I said, "She's dying." I felt terrible after that, but I was tired of reliving the thought each time someone asked. Allow the caretaker to share as they see fit. Though you're concerned with the condition of the ill person, don't forget to think about the caretaker. The task of being a caretaker is a thankless and demanding position and it's nice to know someone cares enough to ask. Honestly I knew that people were concerned with Rita's well being, but having to answer questions about her dire condition over and over, was like being stung by a bee, repeatedly. If I had a chance to do it all over, I would have given a report of her condition to everyone at the same time, or announced that they could look at my daily blogs that gave details of her condition.

Thank the Caretaker

When people called, they sometimes came off in a condescending way, as though they were my supervisor. They would say things like, "I'm calling for an update on Rita" or, "We just want to know our sister is being taken care of." And yet they never even said thank you when I'd tell them about her status. If I knew my dedication and efforts were being appreciated, I would have felt less insulted by the way I was treated, and I would have been more communicative.

One of the most devastating days of my life was Thanksgiving, 2007. Only one of my wife's brothers called us to say Happy Thanksgiving, and from my own family, only my mom and one sister called. For the past several years, we had spent our Thanksgivings in southern Colorado with Rita's family, but that year we were all alone. The emptiness and loneliness I felt that day was almost as painful as the past seventeen months combined. All I could think was that I must have done something wrong to deserve being excluded from both our families. Then, for Christmas, the same thing happened. And for our twenty-eighth anniversary, only one of Rita's brothers called. I was so disillusioned and disappointed with our families after that, that my heart became very hardened and I struggled with forgiving them for months to come.

For my birthday the following March, I didn't have very high expectations of anyone. Then the phone rang and it was my father-in-law. He told me he had called to ask about Rita and had no idea it was my birthday.

I thought about his question, and instead of answering his question, said, "The girls are struggling quite a bit and I'm doing my best to hang in there." I don't think he expected me to give an answer related to his granddaughters or me. The phone was silent for a moment then I heard him ask,

"What?"

I repeated the comment, only this time in an enthusiastic voice I added, "Thank you for asking!"

After a long pause he finally said, "I really appreciate the care and love you've always given to Rita."

After another long silence I said, "Dad, you have no idea how much it meant to hear you say that."

After that, I didn't care that he had called just to check on Rita. He had told me how much he appreciated the work I was doing and that was enough. After his remark, I felt as though a lifetime of healing had taken place.

Brace Yourself!

It may seem a bit obvious that once someone is terminally ill they will undergo a slew of physical changes, but in reality it's not something people actually consider. Maybe it's some form of denial, or perhaps it is their way of coping. There were always people who visited that seemed to expect Rita to be in perfect health. Even when she was at death's door, people would noticeably react to how different she looked. By the time patients go into hospice they'll have undergone significant changes in not only physical, but sometimes mental states, too. It is important that you keep your composure while visiting. Any slight disturbance can either confuse or frighten the patient. They know they're sick or dying and your response may be too much for them to handle. My wife never wished to be pitied and confided how she resented anyone that treated her as pathetic or sickly.

When Rita first required home hospice care, I called both families to make them aware of her condition. She had been through a definite and steady decline over the prior weeks, so I wanted them to know what was going on. I had told about how in a one-hour period of time, Rita went from walking to needing to be carried. She was able to answer yes or no questions one hour, then wasn't even able to tell me her own name the next. When she did respond, it was sporadic and incoherent. Since it was the first time that Rita had exhibited this behavior I was distraught and afraid. I never really considered how bad it could get or how others might react.

The worst reaction to how Rita looked was when my sister and brother-in-law came to visit. My sister walked into her room and the shock on her face was ghastly. She maintained her composure while she was in the room but as she walked out, she began to wail and scream. She made her way to the adjacent bathroom and closed the door. But her exaggerated sobbing was so loud and disturbing that everyone in the house could hear her. I was standing next to Rita when the whole thing began and Rita was terrified. Even though she was mostly unaware, Rita was severely frightened. I don't know what I could have done to better prepare my sister, but her reaction was inexcusable. The problem in a situation like that is the fact that you don't think about it until it has already occurred.

If your loved one's appearance has changed drastically and someone comes to visit, it's a good idea to warn them, beforehand. In my case, I asked my sister to leave the house or control herself. Consequently, I didn't see them again until after Rita's death.

Never Give False Hope

Please *do not* tell the family of the patient that everything is going to be fine. You may mean well, but you cannot divine God's will. If the patient doesn't happen to get better, your false sense of hope may anger or upset the family. Or worse yet, your well meaning words may cause them to lose their faith in God if their faith is wavering from their trials.

I used to tell Stacey everything was going to be okay. One day I was talking to Amanda and she told me that Stacey was tired of me telling her that everything would be okay when nothing was getting any better. In fact, everything seemed to be getting progressively worse for her. I called her and said that I would like to talk with her. I told her that I didn't mean that everything would get better when I said that everything was going to be alright. What I meant was that if you have Jesus in your life, He will give you the strength to overcome the trials you face. Also the proverbial saying that this too shall pass, was important to keep in mind.

When Rita was first admitted into the hospital, I remember that each time I would leave the emergency room I would call friends and family to let them know what was going on. One friend in particular would say over and over, "She's going to be fine, she's going to be fine… this is only temporary." For the entire first year and part of the second, one of my family members kept telling my mom, who then told me, "Rita's going to be fine," or, "She's going to be healed." Whenever Rita's condition worsened, or if she had an unusually bad day, I would be reminded of those supposedly comforting and hopeful words. It would make me angry when Rita wouldn't improve.

On the other hand, there may come a time when the family realizes and accepts the possibility that their loved one is tired and ready to let go. The family may no longer wish for prayers of healing. They may have met with their doctors and decided to stop all treatments. They may be praying for the Lord to take their loved one—so respect their wishes. You may not agree to pray for the Lord to take their loved one, but you can honor the family by praying for the Lord's will to be done. Honor the family's requests, no matter if they agree with your own, or not.

Over-Sincerity

When I expressed my fears and doubts to others I usually felt better, but I also felt like I was being patronized at times. There were many phrases that I quickly grew tired of when people would talk to me about Rita, such as, "Keep the faith," and "Be strong," or, "Don't let things get you down." A part of me felt like they were just trying to make themselves feel better. For some reason, when some people told me these things I felt like they really cared, but when other people told me the same, they came off as shallow and uncaring.

I felt like everyone in the world would be going home to their perfect little lives without any problems. Then I would hate myself for being so cynical and self centered. I know that people don't like negative news, or thinking about negative things like death, but when a person is in crisis, overly sincere words can sometimes seem hollow and meaningless. It's strange to think how two people can say the same exact thing and elicit opposite feelings.

For me, a simple hug was the best form of encouragement. And though it may seem odd, sometimes I felt better when I reveled in self-pity. At least self-pity was better than having to listen to superficial comfort. Thanks to God, as time went by and I learned to accept the impending outcome, I stopped with the self-pity and started accepting how life is.

Don't Fight it

When I would call my pastor, Scott Josifec, he would listen patiently to my sob stories and never judge me. He would never tell me I was wrong for feeling self-pity, either. His words were wise and gentle, and he was always sensitive to my situation. When I poured my heart out, Scott understood what I was trying to say. When I'd finish, he would explain to me that it was possible that I was fighting *it* too hard. He said that I should find a way to welcome *it,* instead. For months, I didn't understand what *it* was. But then I came to realize that *it* was the *entire* reality of my situation. The good, the bad, and the ugly of everything that was happening, was *it*. Eventually, I realized that I needed to let go of the pain without letting go of the reality. Once I learned to wholly accept my situation, I learned to be more thankful for the good as well as the bad. Most of all, I learned to be okay with *it*.

If you find that you can't function because the illness you're facing is too much for you, I encourage you to take a step back and look at the big picture. Accept the reality of your situation, even though it may be painful and difficult. If you're like me, it may take a month or two before you see what Pastor Scott meant.

When he said not to fight it, his words were not only wise, they were truly comforting once I understood. Before I had resented people for having what I called a "perfect little life without any problems." But I finally realized that everyone has problems. Others' problems may not be life-threatening like Rita's illness, but everyone has problems just the same. My problem was that I was being self-absorbed. The solution to my problem was that I had to change the way I reacted. My reality was that the illness couldn't be changed, but the way I dealt with it could.

The CAREGIVER'S HANDBOOK

CHAPTER 21

I've Learned that Most Men Are Asses!

As a child, I was very fortunate to have several men mentor me as I grew. My mom's husband wasn't willing to be a part of our lives, so she raised my siblings and me alone. My father figures were neighbors, scout leaders, friend's fathers, teachers, and older relatives. They taught me some of the things I should know about life like fishing, camping, and hunting. I also picked up other useful knowledge about things like mechanics and carpentry.

Unfortunately, I never had a male role model to teach me about household responsibilities or how to contribute. Consequently, I was of little help to my mother when it came to the care and upkeep of her home. My mom had unknowingly taught me that it was women's work to do the cleaning. I was never expected to wash dishes or do laundry and I never cooked or cleaned. Why should I—my mom did everything. My mom had inadvertently conditioned me and my brothers to be sexists.

Take Thanksgiving dinner, for example. After my brothers and I had finished eating, we'd go outside to play while my mom and sisters cleaned up. I'm not trying to excuse my behavior, and I now know that we could have helped out, but that's just how it was.

Later in life, when I met Rita and the time came to meet her parents, I wasn't surprised to learn that the same rules applied in their home. After we had finished Thanksgiving dinner, which had been cooked by my mother-in-law, wife, and sister-in-laws, the men would then go into the living room to watch football. It reminded me of my family when we were young. And yet, I never gave it a second thought.

Years before Rita became ill I was employed as a pipe fitter for the local utility company. While I was there, I had the opportunity to do a lot of public speaking, facilitating, and teaching. I also served as a "Valuing Diversity" trainer. As trainers, we taught company employees about racism and sexism. Though I am ashamed to admit it, valuing gender had never completely sunk in, even after teaching the subject for over five years. At home, I rarely helped with housework and I didn't help out with laundry. But I would cook two to three times a week. Usually though, I cooked only when we had company, or when I wanted a dish I knew I could cook better than my wife. Even then, I rarely helped with the dishes. I honestly didn't do my share of the work around the house, and my upbringing had convinced me that it was alright.

I remember looking in my sock drawer one morning and thinking to myself, "This drawer was almost empty yesterday, but now it's full. How does she do it?" I never thought that maybe Rita could use a hand. After her diagnosis, however, everything changed. As I said in the beginning of the book I was baptized by fire! In one day, I went from filled-up sock drawers, to sock-drawer-filler. I was suddenly the cook, the dishwasher, the house cleaner, and everything in-between. As time went on, Rita's diminished attention span prevented her from being able to even sort laundry. Simple household chores became more than she could handle. So I was the only one responsible for all the things I used to take for granted. Everything Rita did for me over the years usually went unappreciated, and for that I feel truly ashamed. I think it would take a lifetime for me to repay the debt I owe her.

I must say though, that once I mastered the art of running a household I became pretty good at it. I quickly got into the habit of washing the dishes right after dinner, or first thing in the morning. I swept and washed the floors, and cooked dinner every night. I washed her clothes and mine, and then put them away. I can proudly, but humbly, say that after one year of being a caretaker our house was as neat and clean as it had ever been. Of course, I had the advantage of being home full-time, and my daughters were no longer a factor since they had moved out.

If you are in a situation where you know in your heart that you don't do your share, please consider helping out. After I started doing the housework I felt a gratifying sense of accomplishment and satisfaction. It will benefit everyone involved and won't take longer than a few minutes a day. You'll also learn just how much others are doing for you. You'll appreciate them more than you ever imagined, and they'll appreciate you in a way you never thought possible. Doing your share will change your relationship forever, *I guarantee it*. If I had it to do all over again, I would have contributed more. I would have insisted on helping with the laundry, and volunteered to cook three or four times a week. I would have picked up the vacuum once in a while, and allowed Rita to have a little more *me* time. What's most important is that you don't allow something terrible like an illness, or death, to open your eyes to how little you do contribute. Unfortunately in my case, it took a terminal illness for me to realize that most men *are* asses.

For Husbands

In early 2007, a dear friend of mine died of ovarian cancer. She was married and had three young children between the ages of six and eleven. Because of their mother's illness they had become quite adept at helping and taking care of her. Sadly, it was due to the fact that her husband had completely abandoned his wife despite still living in the same house.

Consequently, they too had not been prepared to become caretakers and were forced into the demanding role. Like their mother, they were also prisoners of her disease. It was heartbreaking to know my friend had to face the illness alone with her small children. I can't imagine how difficult it must be now that their mother is gone. I don't even know what happened with her husband, or whether he eventually took responsibility as a father. What upsets me is the fact that if the husband had been supportive in any way, the burden would have been easier to bear for both his wife and children.

Hospice Care

Thursday, October 18, 2007 was pretty much like any other day. After Rita woke up I helped her out of bed, dressed her, and fed her some applesauce and juice. She was no longer able to walk without assistance, so I helped her to the couch so she could watch some television. At around noon, I sensed she might need to use the toilet so

I walked her to the bathroom. When it became clear she wasn't going to go, I told her to stand up. She tried to stand, but midway through, her legs seemed to lock up. I could tell she was losing her balance so I held her by her hands. She looked into my eyes as she stumbled back and I was barely able to keep her from falling backwards into the bathtub. She had an expression of fear and confusion. Her eyes cried out, "Please, help me!" I held her close to me so that she knew she wasn't going to fall. I carried her to the sink so she could wash her hands because she could no longer make it on her own.

Sadly, she couldn't stand, either. Every time she tried to step, her trembling legs wouldn't move. When I saw that her knees buckled with each attempt to walk, I picked her up and carried her to the recliner in the living room. I thought perhaps she needed to regain her composure or maybe her oxygen level had dropped, or maybe her blood pressure was too low.

I gave her a cup of water as she sat in the recliner, but she didn't take a single drink. Within a minute she drifted off to sleep. She almost dumped the water in her lap so I carried her back to bed. As she lay in bed I nervously fumbled through the paperwork I had, pertaining to her medical care. I came across the number of the interim organization which was supposed to help us transition to hospice care. I spoke to a woman and explained our situation. She told me that she would be contacting Rita's doctor immediately and that someone would contact us within an hour or so. I didn't hear another word that day.

The next morning, Rita couldn't even answer yes-no questions. She kept holding her head like she was in pain but she couldn't tell me if she was feeling pain or even where it was. She was almost unable to swallow her pain pills. I left a frantic message with our doctor's office saying I needed someone at my house immediately. I explained how Rita was acting and that I was concerned that she was in pain. The doctor returned my call within an hour. She said she would be contacting a hospice center and that they should be contacting me soon.

Less than an hour later, I received a call from a hospice center, in Denver. (for legal reasons I have decided not to include their name) We arranged an in-home meeting for that afternoon which would be with the vice-president, the head of patient care, and a nurse who would do an assessment of Rita's condition. During our meeting I informed the vice-president of my concern for Rita's needs because of her brain tumor. He assured me that they had plenty of experience with brain tumor patients and that she would receive excellent care. So we filled out all of the necessary paperwork. The home hospice care would start the next day.

From the beginning I was dissatisfied with their communication and organization. It took three days for a hospital bed to arrive and the hospice nurse, though nice and professional, seemed detached and always in a hurry. Apparently, her workload must have been more than she could handle.

Because of several complications which I will go into later in the book, I found it necessary to place Rita in the in-patient hospice care program. That meant she was admitted into their building and hospice care on a full-time basis.

The events and conditions I witnessed at the hospice center were less than satisfactory. When Rita first arrived I noticed that the place seemed old and dilapidated. The hallways were small and there were two people assigned to each, already cramped, room. There was one chair on each side of the bed, meaning one person could sit in her room at a time. Anyone else had to either wait outside or stand. Also, there were always lots of people wandering around unattended. It reminded me of some kind of correctional facility, like the movie, "One Flew over the Cuckoo's Nest."

The next day when I went in, the white board that listed her meals and how much she had eaten, read that she had refused her breakfast and lunch. I went to the nurse on staff and asked her if she knew why Rita hadn't eaten. The nurse explained that when they asked Rita what she wanted to eat she didn't answer. By this time I was concerned and I asked if she had ever taken care of someone with a brain tumor. She didn't respond and stared back with a puzzled look. I explained that in Rita's condition she was unable to answer, and sometimes even simple questions were too much. She could not make multiple choice decisions. I was frustrated that I had to arrange for automatic meals for Rita because it should have been taken care of in the first place, given her condition. When I had interviewed the hospice representatives, they assured me that they had extensive experience with brain tumor patients. And yet given their track record after a few days, it was apparent that it was a blatant lie.

Another time, one of the nurses was scheduled to take Rita for a shower. She said it was fine for me to go too, so we readied Rita for the trip. When we got to the shower room I was shocked at what I saw. There were wet towels lying on the floor and hanging on the wall racks. I thought about how unsanitary it seemed and imagined all the bacteria and germs on the towels. I became concerned that Rita was there barefoot. Yet the nurse seemed oblivious to the terrible conditions. I thought that perhaps it was an isolated incident.

> My best advice to you if you're looking for a hospice service, is to be very careful. Check with your local BBB. A tour of the facility may not give you all the information you need to make an informed decision. Ask any patients you see if they like it there. If you see family members walking around, ask them how they like the services and if they feel comfortable having their loved one there. Don't just take the word of the hospice representatives. Trust your instincts. If you suspect anything unusual, don't hesitate to call someone on it. If you find that no one is answering your questions to your satisfaction, *get your loved one out of there as soon as possible.*

Never Accept Mediocre Service

From the first time he told me of Rita's prognosis, I wondered if our first neurosurgeon had some morbid desire to watch people suffer. Each time we went in for a consultation, we would be led into an examination room. The secretary would then clip Rita's most recent MRI results on the lighted board, next to her previous ones. It was hard enough to have to look at the images, but to make matters worse, we were always kept waiting fifteen to twenty minutes until he arrived.

During one visit the scans showed what might be some new tumor growth. The doctor stared at Rita with a smirk on his face.

Then he sighed and said, "Hmm… what to do, what to do," as though he were playing a game with our emotions. He went on to tell us that we should be prepared to consider another surgery. He recommended Rita stay off of chemotherapy for a while, to let her blood counts level-out. Then as we left his office, he said someone from his office would be contacting us the following week.

On Tuesday we hadn't received a call so out of frustration I called his office and left a message with his receptionist. An hour or so later, when he called back, I asked him about Rita's second surgery.

He bluntly stated, "What are you talking about? I didn't say anything about your wife having another surgery!"

I was taken aback and felt completely dumfounded. Not only did I clearly hear him talk about another surgery, but Stacey had also heard it. After thinking carefully about my exchange with the neurosurgeon, and the way he treated us, I decided to take Anne Frähm's advice. In her book, *A Cancer Battle Plan*, she states that when it comes to your life and health, the medical staff is nothing more than *hired help*. I decided right then and there that we would never go back to that rudely behaved, unprofessional doctor.

> If for *any* reason you're not one-hundred percent satisfied with the care you receive from your medical team, get as far from them as you possibly can, as fast as you can. Remember, they are at your service, not the other way around. If you're going to be charged hundreds of thousands of dollars—or even if you don't spend that much—it's your right to be treated with respect and dignity.
>
> Coincidently, that same neurosurgeon had referred us to the radiologist I mentioned earlier in the book. Because of the hopeless attitude of that radiologist, we never considered him for Rita's care. Our lives had already spiraled out of control enough and the last thing we needed was an insensitive neurosurgeon with a god-complex making us feel like pawns. Within a week of leaving the neurosurgeon's office, we were working exclusively with the staff at the Colorado University Hospital. Looking back, it was one of the best decisions we had ever made during Rita's care.

CHAPTER 22

Stranger Than Fiction

The next section covers an experience I never wanted to write about. But from the beginning, I promised myself that I would detail *all* of my experiences as a caretaker. I had already been writing this book for more than seven months when the following events occurred. So, based on my commitment to write a complete story, I have included it. More importantly however, is the fact that these events really happened. When they say truth is stranger than fiction, I can honestly say I agree. I believe it is critical for this information to be included in this book, because what I have endured was much more than just the illness and loss of someone I dearly loved. The following is a detailed account of how I was tried in a way I never could have imagined. I feel it is my responsibility to educate the reader about a system that answered to no one, especially my family and I. At their hands, I experienced emotions of confusion, anger and even hatred at times. I want to share this because I believe that there is someone, somewhere, that could be living through similar circumstances.

Halloween 2007

In 2007, Halloween fell on a Wednesday. Rita had been in hospice since the eighteenth of October. By then, she was to the point that it was necessary to secure her to her wheelchair, otherwise she would try to stand and walk. More than a few times I barely saved her from falling face first into the floor or a wall. In the last thirteen days, Rita had gone from being able to walk, to being completely dependent. She had gone from sleeping in a bed with me, to sleeping in a hospital bed with bedrails at night to keep her from injuring herself. At times even feeding herself with a fork was impossible. I was just starting to accept the fact that Rita was in hospice and was getting used to providing the new level of care she required.

It was a mild yet beautiful fall day and my spirits were up. Rita was more alert than usual and as I dressed her I was surprised to find myself having a pleasant, yet concise conversation with her; something we hadn't done in weeks. There was also a glimmer in her eyes and a smile I had almost forgotten. After I bathed and fed her, I put a sweater on her and wrapped her up in a blanket. I buckled her into her wheelchair and took her into the sunroom. From there I would be able to keep an eye on her while I raked the leaves since the sliding glass doors face the backyard. I would make faces at her and smile as I raked, and I took frequent breaks to make sure she didn't need anything. She would chuckle each time I passed by the window and peeked in to see her.

After I finished, I went into the sunroom and wheeled Rita back into the house. She giggled as I took off her blanket and sweater and joked with her. I pushed her wheelchair to the dining room table for a mid-day snack and some juice. She was very alert and seemed to be more aware of her surroundings than usual. I was surprised when she said she wanted to see what was on television. At that point she was so lucid that I thought I'd try to make some small talk, so I knelt down in front of her and we shared a smile.

I looked in her eyes and asked, 'How is it with your soul?' It had always been a question that I asked myself and it helped me stay grounded.

She didn't answer or even look at me, instead she stared at the floor for what must have been two minutes. I became more and more uneasy and I could only guess that she was pondering her response. All the while, she shook her head and stared at the floor. She slowly picked her head up and looked into my eyes.

She exhaled and said, "I have to tell you, I haven't always loved you like I should."

At first, I thought she was kidding, but I knew that after the sixteen months of grueling procedures she had been through her sense of humor was pretty much nonexistent. Besides she had trouble with simple sentences, it must have taken everything she had, to say what she just said. Then I thought of the possibility that she was making it up; she had had a large portion of her brain removed, maybe she wasn't thinking clearly. Or perhaps it was the cancer. Could it be that the tumor had grown so much that her brain was playing tricks on her? As I looked at her, I knew I'd better listen very carefully to what she was about to say. My mind was racing and I was becoming more confused with each moment of silence.

She looked down again as she took another breath and looked back at me. I could tell she desperately wanted to say something, but it was as though she was having trouble finding the words.

"I… I…I've been with someone else." Numbness swelled throughout my body, and for a minute I thought I would pass out. Anyone who knew her would never believe she would do such a thing.

I asked, "Did you have an emotional affair?" For a moment she just looked down again.

After another long pause she answered, "An affair."

When I asked her who he was she didn't say a word. Then, slowly, she told me it was a man she used to work with, and that I knew him. I became furious when I thought of how he had the audacity to send me an email wishing blessings on us just a few days prior to what I now knew.

"Are you making this up?" I asked. Her face became even more somber, and she looked at me with eyes that spoke louder than her words.

Then, solemnly she sighed, "It's true." I felt like my heart might burst in my chest and I wasn't sure what to do or say.

I left her alone in the living room and walked to the bedroom. I picked up my cell phone and speed dialed the hospice nurse assigned to us from the hospice center. I asked her if it were possible for someone with a brain tumor to make delusional statements. She said it depended on what it was they were saying.

After explaining, I expected her to say that *she probably made it all up*, or, *I'll have to put you in touch with a chaplain*. Even if she had said, 'this is out of my realm of expertise' I would have felt better. But instead she said that *in her experience*, Rita was making a confession. She said that the only reason for her having said this could be that it was the truth. Her message was loud and clear, there was no room for even the slightest possibility that Rita had made the whole thing up.

The nurse went on to say that her husband too had been unfaithful. The confidence in her voice, despite how opinionated and biased her words were, was so convincing that I never even considered that she could be wrong. Besides, the vice-president of the hospice center had personally told me that his staff was experienced with brain tumor patients. So she *must* have known what she was talking about.

I told her I needed a chaplain to contact me right away and I asked if there was a grief counselor I could speak with. She said she would see what she could do. I couldn't imagine that the staff from the hospice center would leave me alone with Rita when they knew how volatile the situation had become. I thought surely someone would call but I never heard from her or anyone else. My mind wandered, as memories of my life with Rita flashed through my mind. When could it have happened? Was I *that* blind? Had I been a bad husband? I wanted to blame myself, but I knew that Rita was responsible for her own actions. After I had literally sacrificed my entire life to take care of her full-time, for months now, how could she tell me this? How dare she!

We sat in silence as I fed her dinner. She methodically picked over her food as she always did; one tiny piece at a time. My hands trembled in her presence and honestly I wanted to just leave and never return. But thanks to God I was able to remind myself that she was completely helpless. I knew I had to take care of her till someone could take over for me.

I desperately wanted to call someone, but who could I call? I thought of calling my pastor, but I felt as though I couldn't tell him. I was the adult Sunday school teacher once a month at our church; how could this have happened in my family? I couldn't stand the thought of him or anyone else knowing, and yet part of me was also ashamed to admit that I was so blind to it. I started to call Amanda but hung up before it rang and I knew that Stacey would never be able to take the news. Calling my mom was an option but I knew the news might kill her. So, I sat alone.

I prayed for the phone to ring, I wanted to be able to just talk to someone, anyone. Finally, after waiting in futility, I put Rita to bed. As I tried to sleep, thoughts of leaving kept racing through my head and around three o'clock I heard Rita moving in her hospice bed. That meant she needed to use the bathroom and so I lowered her bed, sat her up, and walked her to the bedside commode. I had to hold her close to me as I half carried her. Her face was so close to mine that I could feel her breathing on my neck. She tried to kiss my cheek, as she had done since hospice, but all I could do was turn away. As I waited for her to finish, I looked down at the floor until I returned her to her bed. Back in my bed, I closed my eyes but I couldn't sleep. My mind was nothing more than a ball of confusion, and all I wanted to do was run away.

Suddenly, the thought that I had been used and taken advantage of crept up from the depths of my mind. I sat up and reached for my pants. I began to dress, but I had no idea where I would go. Then, I snapped back to reality. Rita was one hundred percent dependent on me. Feeling alone and forgotten, without a single call from anyone, I didn't sleep a wink that whole night.

The next morning I was even more distressed as I waited for Rita to wake up. As soon as she was awake, I asked her if she could understand what I was saying, and if she had made the story up. Again, she told me it was true. I then handed her a tablet and pen and told her I wanted her to write a confession. She wrote a sentence that confessed having the affair, and the name of the man. Though it was almost illegible, you could still read it and know what it was saying.

At eight o'clock, I called my mom and told her she needed to come over right away. Then, with phone book in hand, I searched for the home number of the man she confessed to having the affair with. I dialed it and put him on the speaker phone. I wanted Rita to hear what he said when I confronted him. Again and again he said it wasn't true, and repeatedly Rita said, "He's lying," her voice though little more than a whisper, was much more convincing than his. I can't remember every detail of the conversation, but I will admit that I used profanity and a few choice words. I couldn't believe myself, I was a person who normally would never call another person a degrading name, but I had resorted to name calling. I had let my rage take complete control of me. I knew that if I went on, I might become so angry that I'd threaten him, so I called him one last name and slammed the phone down.

By this time, my feelings had completely blinded me. I went to the head of my bed and got my .38 caliber pistol. I started to unzip the case. In spite of my fury, something inside me was telling me to think about what I was doing. As I unzipped the case I looked at Rita, lying in her bed. I hadn't noticed the pink pajamas I had dressed her in the night before and how they brought out the red in her hair. I remembered her contagious laugh which was by now a distant memory. It had been taken from her by the cancer which I called the *monster*. Suddenly, I became aware of my trembling hand which was reaching for the now exposed pistol handle. There was a three foot separation between my bed and the hospice bed. Without hesitation, I began to walk between the beds toward her.

Halfway there, I asked myself, "What are you going to do with that now? Words from the Bible suddenly filled my mind, *"Vengeance is mine sayeth the Lord,"* In an instant I came to my senses as I heard myself say out loud, "I'm not a killer!" I thought of how much had been taken from her already and how she had suffered more than any person should. Who was I to think I had the right to take her life? God had stopped me in my tracks.

By His grace, I never pulled the gun out of the case. I zipped it closed, and put it back under the bed. I fell to my knees, crying from the depths of my soul. I knew I needed to pray for God's strength to calm me down, but I couldn't manage to call out to Him. All I could do was revel in my sorrow and bitterness. Rita simply lay there in her hospice bed and looked on, void of all emotion. She never turned her head to look at me. I left her in the bedroom and went into the living room to wait for the nurse and my mom.

At around eight thirty, my doorbell rang. It was the nurse, and right behind her was my mom. The nurse obviously sensed something was wrong, and my tear filled eyes told my mom of my distress. As they stood in the living room, I told them about what had happened just prior to their arrival. They both followed me into the bedroom and they watched silently, as I walked to the head of the bed. I bent down and pulled the gun case out. I handed it to my mom and said, "Mom, you need to take this." I didn't see where she put it. All I knew was that it would be out of my house, and out of my reach.

Through my sobs, I asked the nurse what had happened the night before. Why hadn't she sent help when she knew my situation, but it was like talking to a wall. She said nothing as she helped Rita sit up in her bed and began dressing her. I told her that Rita needed to be someplace else; I didn't care where, I just knew she had to go. Honestly, I wasn't sure I could be alone with her for another day, and I knew beyond a doubt, I couldn't last another night. The nurse went outside and made several phone calls. After about forty five minutes, an ambulance came and the attendants proceeded to remove Rita from the house. I was sitting in the hallway, crying uncontrollably, almost the whole time. I couldn't even look at Rita as they rolled her out. Then, the nurse left without saying a word. I wondered if perhaps, secretly, she hoped I would kill Rita that night. Perhaps it was her twisted way of trying to get revenge on cheating spouses. I mean, why else would she do such a careless and irresponsible thing? How could she have left me all alone with Rita, knowing full well, the potential danger of the situation?

The system had failed me miserably. My mom and I sat together in the living room, an awkward silence filling the air. She insisted on staying but I told her to go, even though I knew it wasn't the best thing for me. Reluctantly, she went to her car and drove away. I was alone again, bewildered and confused. I thought to myself, "Aren't hospice facilities supposed to provide support for the patient *and* their family? Where is *my* support?" At 11:00 a.m., I received a call. The man on the phone said he was the head chaplain at the hospice center, and he apparently knew about my situation. Why in the world did he wait until 11:00 the next morning to call me?

He advised me that I should hire a lawyer as soon as possible. He explained that someone he knew had put a gun to his wife's head once, and he got in a lot of trouble for it. His friend had gone to jail for a long time. I told him I never pulled the gun out, but he again insisted that it would be smart to call a lawyer right away. Before hanging up, he gave me the number of the hospice grief counselor. I was appalled by the apathy and disregard for *my* well being, especially from a hospice chaplain. I sensed that he had absolutely no concern for my situation by the way he rushed the call and quickly gave me the grief counselor's number. *What a piece of work*, I thought. Here I was, experiencing the worst kind of anguish I had ever experienced in my life, and this excuse for a chaplain was dumping me off onto someone else's plate.

I called right away and left a message on the grief counselor's phone. That whole day I never heard a word from anyone from the hospice center. But then, at around 8:30 that night I got a call from a woman saying that the grievance counselor would definitely be calling me the next day, first thing in the morning. But he *never* called. In fact, he didn't call until Saturday, November second.

When he did finally call, he was brief and unfriendly. He told me he was "busy" and that he would get back to me on Monday. But when Monday came there was still no contact from him. *What could possibly be more pressing than a situation like this?* I thought. The hours were like a hazy blur and I could hardly think straight as I tried to regain my composure.

I realized how tremendous stress causes some people to just lose it and go off the deep end. I remembered seeing news stories about people snapping and going on rampages. Fortunately, I was depending on the Lord's strength and I believe He is the only reason I was able to withstand such an onslaught of circumstances without the dire consequences I might have otherwise faced.

I spent the rest of that day alone in prayer, asking God what I should do. I so wished that He would just sit me down and give me His guidance, as I wandered aimlessly from room to room. *Please God*, I cried out, the whole world has abandoned me, *please tell me what to do!* After a long while the words of the Bible came to my heart, almost as if being spoken in an audible voice. "Be still, and know that I am God." I finally felt the peace I sought and I knew what I had to do. More words came to mind that I had read many times before; but now they somehow were more alive, and made perfect sense. The words from Matthew 6:14-15 came to me, "For if ye forgive men their trespasses, your heavenly

Father will also forgive you. But if ye forgive not men their trespasses, neither will your Father forgive your trespasses." *I knew, I had to forgive Rita.*

That night I drove to the hospice center. I was led to the office of the vice-president I had met with before. I told him that I had prayed about my situation all day long, and that I had forgiven Rita completely. I told him that I wished to see her and I explained that her salvation was my only concern. Then after more than an hour of questioning, he left me alone in his office to make arrangements for me to see Rita.

I was escorted to a small, dimly lit conference room. The old wooden desk, the small lamp and the decor in the room made it look like it hadn't been re-done since the sixties. Rita was in the room, sitting in a wheelchair, covered in a blanket. She was alert, and she half smiled when I walked into the room. I got down on my knees and looked into her eyes. I told her I had forgiven her and that God would forgive her if she asked Him. I told her I wanted her to know that there was no unforgivable sin; God still had a place for her in Heaven. I asked her to forgive me for the things I had said and done too. Like her, I couldn't make it into Heaven without God's forgiveness. We hugged and I cried, but for some reason, Rita never shed a tear or showed any emotion or facial expression; almost certainly the result of the fast growing tumor which was consuming her brain. A woman supervised from outside the room as I sat with Rita. She was kind hearted and told me she would do her best to give us all the space we needed. I stayed with Rita for an hour or so, then, I drove home.

The next morning, I awoke with even more peace in my heart. I couldn't stop thinking of Jesus' words when He said, "The truth shall set you free." I called the vice-president and explained to him that I had a letter of confession, signed by my wife. I told him that I had planned to give it to the wife of the man Rita had been involved with. But I explained that if I had truly forgiven Rita, I needed to destroy the letter and that I wanted to do it in front of him.

Once I got there, we waited for one of the chaplains to join us, and together we all walked out an exit door. The vice-president gave me some matches and I put the note on the ground and burned it. I felt an awesome feeling of liberation as the last of the burning note turned to ashes and floated away.

When we went back into the building, the vice-president told me that I still had some things to deal with concerning the Denver police. He said that they had no choice but to call the police concerning the matter and I asked if he could give me the name of the person I needed to talk to. He gave me the name of a detective and I called him right away.

The detective seemed to be very understanding and he told me that there were no warrants for my arrest, and that no charges had been filed against me whatsoever. He told me that he had interviewed several of my family members as well as some of Rita's but he didn't say who. He said I needed to go in so he could interview me, and that he would not detain me. I went to the police station right away, though I took Stacey with me in case they did arrest me, so she could drive my car home.

Once I was in the interrogation room, the detective told me he had interviewed two of Rita's sisters. They both said that in all of the years of our marriage, neither had ever suspected I had been violent or malicious toward her. Neither one had ever even heard me say a mean word to Rita. He had also interviewed my mom who concurred with my sisters-in-law. He told me that this was a very unique case. I was the only witness to any of it, and even if I *had* pointed the gun at Rita, there was no way I could testify against myself in a court of law. The circumstances were so bizarre, that he saw no reason to even make a file on it. He was certain that even the District Attorney wouldn't hear the case. Then he said he was recommending that Rita be discharged from the hospice, and released into my care as soon as possible. I was so filled with emotion my hands began to tremble and I couldn't hold back my tears. I had to stay sitting in his office for a few minutes to regain my composure.

After that, he told me I was free to go. Stacey and I returned to the hospice center. When we walked into Rita's room, we saw that her pull-up diaper was soiled. I closed the door and took a clean diaper from the drawer and changed her. Her red skin told me she hadn't been changed in a while, and right when I was finished, a nurse appeared. She told me I was not allowed to close the door to Rita's room again. I asked if anyone had offered to help Rita use the bathroom. She said that no one had, and that unless a patient asked for help or to be changed, no one would. I sensed that there was not a thing I could do about it, so I just kept quiet the rest of the day. But it was further confirmation of the ineptitude of the facility representatives. Rita was released into my custody the next morning.

Hospice workers visited our home every day for the next week, with no complaints or problems. On Tuesday, November 6, a chaplain named Michael came over. He promised he'd send a volunteer to help me out. Yet no volunteer ever called or came. Then, that same day, I got a visit from Tony, a social worker assigned to us from the hospice center. He was a muscular man with a raspy voice. His tight-fitting polo shirt and slicked back hair made him look like he may have been a gangster, and by the way he spoke, I perceived him as a coarse man who was raised in the streets.

He asked me what had happened and I told him everything. I told him how Rita had confessed and what I had done. I told him about the letter of confession and how I had destroyed it. He listened to my words and then he told me to stop. He told me that I should just, "Forget about it." He said it was, "water under the bridge." Then he laughed as he told me he too had committed adultery and confessed it to his girlfriend. He casually told me again, that I shouldn't make such a big deal out of it. I felt like he was trying to trivialize the whole situation. He told me I was overreacting. I felt like he was telling me I had no right to be hurt or feel the way I did. His words were stinging and it was like he was peeling the scab from old wounds that were just starting to heal. Tony alienated me on our first meeting I didn't trust him anymore. After getting to know him better, I viewed him as a mean spirited and untrustworthy man whose uncaring words divided my family. He turned my life into an "us-versus-them" nightmare and I was very disturbed by what he had told me about his personal life. To him, adultery was no big deal. After hearing his comments, he was the *last* person I wanted handling my case. Before he left, he also told me he would send a volunteer to give me an hour to go buy groceries. Like all of the other representatives from the hospice center, he never kept his word. Throughout the following two weeks, their promises of support kept coming, but the only thing consistent was their lack of follow-through. Even though they sent "visitors" to check up on me every day, none would volunteer to give me even half-an-hour to recharge.

Finally, on Friday, November 9, I was so stressed out from the unfulfilled promises from the hospice center, that I called and told them I was firing them. Within minutes of the time I hung up, Tony, the social worker called.

He never said hello, or asked of Rita's or my condition, instead, he abruptly asked, "Are we in or out?"

I asked what he meant.

He said it again, "Are we in or out?" Then he said, "Because, if we're fired, I'm going to call the police right now, and they will be at your house in twenty minutes to take protective custody of Rita—and I'll have them arrest you and charge you with felony menacing."

I said, "All week, you couldn't get someone out here to bring me fresh diapers, but you can certainly get someone here right away to have Rita taken away from me... Who *are* you people?" I knew he was trying to scare me into keeping Rita in their hospice care. The police had assured me that there was no case filed, and that I was not charged with *any* crime.

Tony demanded that I meet with him. I told him I could be at a café just north of my home in one hour. I had a feeling he was up to no good, so I immediately called my cousin Pauline and asked her to sit in on the meeting as a witness. On my way to the restaurant, I took Rita to Stacey's apartment so she wouldn't have to be out in the cold. We met at the restaurant, and the first thing I told Tony was that I didn't like him and that I definitely didn't trust him. He was very abrupt and persistent and told me that I had *no choice but to keep Rita in the care of their hospice center.* I told him I was tired of them telling me one thing and doing another. I was tired of not having any support and that I hated having to answer to a man who didn't have any morals.

At the café, I had to go to the bathroom. While I was gone, Tony spoke at length with Pauline. I had no idea what he had been telling her while I was gone, but when I returned, I asked him why he was punishing me like this. He never mentioned that he was concerned for Rita's safety; instead, he again said that he was only concerned with keeping Rita at the hospice center where she was. When I reminded him there were never any charges against me, he very threateningly said he could press charges if I *didn't cooperate.* I told him I refused to let them take Rita again and he ordered me to get someone to supervise Rita and me all weekend. Pauline spent the next two days with us at our home. I was ordered to return Rita to the hospice center on Monday morning.

Later that night, Pauline told me that while I was in the bathroom, Tony had told her I was bi-polar—a slanderous statement. Even if it were true, he would have been in violation of the HIPPA laws that are meant to protect my privacy. Surely his training as a social worker had not given him the authority to diagnose medical conditions, too.

Then she told me he had slandered me again by telling her that I had been charged with felony menacing by the Denver police. I also learned, that just minutes before we met, Tony had called Stacey and told her that I was a wanted man, and that felony menacing charges had been filed against me.

The next day was Saturday, November 10, and I decided to call another hospice center called Porter Hospice. I spoke with the director. She listened intently as I told her my whole story. Then I told her that I wanted to move Rita into their care. She told me what I needed to do to get the wheels rolling, and on Monday, November 12, after I retuned Rita to the first hospice center, I called Rita's neuro-oncologist, and got approval for a transfer.

Later that morning, I went back to the hospice center. As I sat in her room, a strange man walked right in and just stared at Rita. He was about six feet two inches tall, and except for his robe, you'd never guess he was ill. He stood there for about fifteen seconds and he never said a word. Then he turned around and walked out. I was so stunned I went straight to the nurses' station to report the incident. A social worker and another woman greeted me. I told them I had some concerns. They told me they wanted to hear them, but that we needed to talk about some other issues first, and they escorted me to a private room.

Once I sat down, the social worker said, "You needn't waste any time looking at Porter Hospice. They don't offer routine care." I didn't question her about it any further. I figured if it was true, I would find out soon enough. But I wondered how they knew I had been trying to get Rita transferred to the other hospice center. We must have been quite the topic of discussion in the past few days.

As we talked, I told them I was concerned about the strange man that walked into my wife's room. The other woman who was there asked if he was a patient. I said he must have been because he was wearing a robe. Then she said, "We allow our patients to visit the other patients as they wish. We don't like to restrict them." I couldn't believe my ears! How could they insure Rita's safety if <u>anyone</u> walking down the hall had full permission to enter her room at any time? What if she were using the bathroom? What if she had removed her clothes? After all she was a brain tumor patient and even I knew that she could possibly do that in her condition.

I explained that Rita was not of sound mind and could do nothing to protect herself should a predator enter her room. I told them Rita could neither stop, nor identify a perpetrator if someone would try to molest her. If this man were dying, he had nothing to lose. He could do whatever he wanted, and no one would or could do a thing about it. He couldn't even be arrested if he were to harm Rita. It was almost as if what had happened was nothing more than a side note. To them, my issue was not important enough to even speak about, again. Their only response was, *that could never happen.* I discovered that they too were not willing to hear my concerns. My decision to remove her from their facility was again, confirmed.

After my experience with those two staff members, I decided I'd best ask the people at Porter Hospice about the extent of their care. A staff member of Porter Hospice told me they did in fact give routine care. I met with a representative from Porter Hospice that afternoon and signed the papers for transfer. Then I went in to see Rita. I was so tired from all of the events that had taken place that I decided to take a nap next to Rita in her bed. Just as I was about to fall asleep, a woman and a man came in and told me I needed to go with them to their office. Once the door was closed, the woman said that because there was an open case with the Adult Protective Services (APS), they couldn't release Rita.

Then she hinted that there was a felony menacing case against me. I said, *"Now I'm pissed off!* If there was any case at all, I would not even be able to see Rita." I also told them that if their accusations were true, I would have been incarcerated. I told them that I had gone to the police station and that the D.A. had refused to even hear the case regarding the events of November 1st.

I told them that the incompetence of their staff was the only reason there was any kind of hold on Rita, and I demanded they let her go. I told them they were all liars. I said I wanted them to give me the number of APS so I could clear this whole thing up, and they adamantly refused. Their refusal to give me the number for the person I needed to contact at APS further convinced me that they were not telling me the whole truth.

By this time I was so beside myself that I didn't know what to do. I looked at her and told her I was prepared to go to the local media and tell them the whole story. I explained that it was their fault I was even in that room in the first place. She said, "The reason you're here isn't our fault at all Paul, it's because of your own actions." I reminded her that it was their nurse, social worker, chaplain, and their staff that had left me alone, knowing the potential danger to both my wife and myself. She abruptly cut me off. She asked if there was anything else she could do. I said I just wanted to be left alone. I said I didn't want any more *support* from their chaplains, counselors, or social workers. I didn't trust anyone from the facility after that.

Early the next morning, I received word that Rita's transfer to the Porter Hospice was approved. I went to the hospice center early to ready Rita for the trip. When I got to her room, I looked in from the hallway. To my horror, the door to her room and the bathroom were wide open. I could see Rita, barely standing in the bathroom, hanging onto the bar. Her pajama bottoms were down to her knees and she was fully exposed. I couldn't believe what I was seeing! Was this really happening? How could so many things have gone so wrong? How could this facility be in business with this crude excuse for professionalism? The nurse was the same one I had had an argument with before and I already knew she had a bad attitude so I didn't say a word. I knew Rita would be out of their care soon enough, so I closed the hallway door and helped Rita get dressed. Once I finished, I carried her to her bed and asked the nurse to leave us alone. She left the door open as she exited. I closed it as soon as she disappeared. I didn't care what they said; I wanted to be alone with my wife.

All morning, people went back and forth, telling me the ambulance was on the way, and then, that it had been cancelled, then it was back on. By eleven o'clock that morning, my nerves were raw and I was angered like I had never been in my life. Finally, she told me that because of the circumstances, the APS required that Rita be taken to a hospital for seventy-two hours of observation and psychological review. Then they would decide if she could be moved to Porter Hospice.

I asked her, "Haven't I been through enough?" I felt like I was in a horror movie and I was the victim, like a pawn in some sort of warped game of chess.

Around eleven a.m., I saw the vice-president in the hall. I walked up to him and said, "You told me you were experienced with brain tumor patients. Your staff has done a lot of harm to me and my family. I want you to know I intend to write a letter to the Better Business Bureau about your lack of professionalism and service."

He asked me to go with him into his office and I refused. He turned his back and walked away. As he turned, he said, "I'm sorry you feel that way, but go and do what you have to do." I never saw him again.

Throughout the morning, the chaplain and the social worker on staff kept coming back over and over—each time telling me a different story. I literally begged them to please just leave us alone, but they both persisted. The last time the chaplain came in to Rita's room, I said, "I'm going to sue this place." I looked at him though my tears and he smiled at me as if I was joking. I closed the door on him and said, "For the last time, please just leave us alone."

Finally the ambulance arrived. I watched, as the attendants stood in the nurses' station laughing and joking as I waited. One of the attendants glanced at me as I walked to the doorway. He scowled at me as if I had done some awful thing to him. After waiting more than forty-five minutes, the attendants slowly came in and loaded Rita up. I asked one of them which route they would be taking. He said they would take Colfax to I-25 south to Broadway. I told him I was going to be following them because I wasn't too sure where the hospital was. As we walked out, perhaps fifteen staff members had gathered outside of Rita's room. Everyone was staring at us like we were their entertainment.

When they finally got Rita loaded and we were going out into the hall, I looked at the now even larger crowd and said, "Good riddance! I hope I never see any of you, again!" They loaded Rita into the ambulance and sped off. As soon as they got onto the highway they accelerated to over eighty-five miles per hour. They zoomed in and out of traffic, seemingly trying to lose me but they never turned on their lights or siren. I wasn't sure what they were doing, so I sped up in an effort to catch up with them.

Thanks to God, while I was on my way to the hospital I called Porter Hospice and spoke to a representative. I told her that I was on my way to Porter Hospital (not the same facility as the Porter Hospice) and I asked if it were possible for a chaplain and counselor to meet me there.

I had transfer papers for Rita to be received at Porter Hospital and I took them to the receptionist as soon as I arrived. I worked on my laptop as I sat in the waiting room. While I was sitting there, I noticed a man looking at me, but he never approached me. He was well-dressed and he slowly walked past me at least six times, each time, looking at me as if he were studying me.

After about thirty or forty minutes, I put my laptop away and started reading a book. Suddenly I looked up and was startled to see that no less than ten cops were surrounding me, all with their hands firmly on their weapons! I jumped to my feet and raised my hands as high as I could. At the top of my lungs, I yelled, "*I'm unarmed, I'm unarmed*!" Three policemen approached me as I stood there. I was searched from head to toe then my computer bag was searched. I was so humiliated I didn't know what to think. I asked the officer who seemed to be in charge if there was someplace private we could go.

Then I was led to a secure room which required a security code to enter or leave. I was detained for over one hour with two uniformed guards and four cops in the room, as well as a group of five to seven other police officers, administrators and other people who stood outside.

I explained the details of the events leading up to that point again and again. I told them that Rita never feared me. If I had ever stricken her surely, she would duck if

I moved toward her face. I challenged them to take me to Rita and let me raise my hand to her and see how she would respond. Finally, I said that I had told them all I was going to. The man who had been walking past me in the lobby turned out to be the chaplain I had requested from Porter Hospice. Prior to that time, he had never spoken to me or reached out to help me in any way, but now he asked me if I wanted to say anything. I couldn't take the stress any longer. My hands began to tremble and I completely broke down. I fell to my knees and prayed to God from the depth of my heart as I wept. "God," I cried, "I know You're there someplace. You promised I could call on You in times of trouble. I need You now, God! Please give me comfort and wisdom." I fell to my knees and wept uncontrollably again. I could do nothing but look at the floor.

After another twenty minutes or so, one of the cops opened the door and finally let me out of the room. Then the cops escorted me to my car and ordered me to open it up. I was surrounded the whole time. There were twenty or more onlookers standing around, as well as another eight to ten police officers nearby. One of them told me to open the trunk and they searched my car inside and out. Seeing the looks on their faces, I was literally fearful for my life. No weapon was ever found, not even a pocket knife. And to this day, there has never been a single legal charge against me.

I was then told that Rita would be held in *protective custody* for seventy-two hours. The social worker from Porter Hospice had now come, and I told him that I wanted to give Rita her things, but he ignored me. As I was being released, a Denver policeman gave me a stern warning not to return to the hospital, or even call. Rita's condition would not be given or discussed with me, my daughters, or anyone else. He said that I would be arrested if I made any attempt to make contact with Rita, or even come within one block of the hospital. I later found out that this was just another intimidation tactic. The law required legal procedures, and they had no right to keep me from my wife without written documentation. Based on heresy, I had been tried, and convicted without a trial or even one shred of evidence.

I drove away. When I was four blocks away from the hospital, four police cruisers surrounded me with their lights and sirens on. By that time, I was literally terrified. I pulled to the side of the road and turned the car off. I opened the window and took my keys from the ignition. I stuck both hands out the window, showing the keys and didn't move a muscle. By this time, I thought I was going to have a heart attack if they didn't shoot me first. The officer who approached me happened to be one of those present while I was being interrogated, so he knew the whole story. He told me to put the keys back into the ignition, but I refused. I told him I didn't trust the police and that I had been terrorized by them enough. I said I feared they would shoot me if anything went even remotely wrong in their eyes. He told me he had heard the entire thing and that he believed me. He took me by surprise when he said, "I believe better men would have done a lot worse than you did." They never told me why I was again being stopped, they just told me to "sit tight." Then, after ten or twelve minutes, they all drove off. I was left sitting there, humiliated, horrified, and most of all, confused.

I decided that it would be best if I got as far away from that place as I possibly could, so I called my brother Terry, in Craig, Colorado, and asked if he felt like some company. I drove four-and-a-half hours to Craig that afternoon and spent the next two days with him and my sister-in-law, Colesta. I returned to Denver on Thursday, November 15th.

Upon returning, I discovered I had several messages from a supervisor from Adult Protective Services. She had left the messages over the past two days but I didn't get them from northern Colorado. When I finally reached her, she told me to stay calm, and that she had set up a meeting for the following Monday morning at ten. She assured me that after hearing all of the facts and talking to the officers who had interviewed me, she was definitely on my side. She said the officers were also on my side. I called a lawyer right away.

The next day, I went in to see the lawyer. I told her the whole story from beginning to end. As I spoke, I sensed that she didn't believe me, but she listened to all I had to say. I was a little surprised that she didn't believe me since I came with a detailed description of the 24-hour care I had been giving Rita, including every ounce of food she ate to every vitamin. I listed every hour of sleep to every bowel movement and even every visitor. I also had dates, time and complete descriptions of every event. But when I finished, she looked me in the eye and came right out and said, "I'm sorry Mr. Lane, but I'm having trouble believing you. Either there's something you're not telling me, or there is something really screwy going on. I need to talk to APS." I gave her the name and number of the APS supervisor. She picked up her phone and dialed the number. Someone answered right away, and as the lawyer asked question after question, I could tell that she was starting to believe what I had said. When the lawyer started saying, "I see, an amazing caretaker huh?" I knew she was starting to see that I was telling the truth. Then the lawyer mentioned the name of the social worker, Tony. There was a long silence as she listened to the woman on the other end of the line. After a long pause, the lawyer said, "Four cases against him right now? Oh, I see, thank you for your time, that's all the information I need." The lawyer hung up and looked at me. She told me that she couldn't handle this type of case but that once Rita had passed away I definitely needed to contact a lawyer. She agreed that I had clearly been slandered by the social worker and that he was definitely guilty of defamation of character.

> The six days that Rita was taken from me were nearly unbearable. I didn't get more than two or three hours of sleep each night. Over the next three months, every time I saw a police car, my heart jumped. I kept telling myself I had done nothing wrong but still, I was terrified of law enforcement officers for a long time after that. I became so depressed I thought I might die before Rita was released back to me.
>
> I decided that rather than sue the social worker for his actions, I would rather include the details of his actions in this book. I never sent a letter to the Better Business Bureau. I thought it would just be a waste of time. I figured by including the specifics of the ordeal in my book, I could reach many more people than composing a simple letter. Most people never think to call the Better Business Bureau when faced with a situation like hospice, anyway.

Of course, I have not named the first hospice center, because of legal reasons, but I wanted to share this information as a warning to those seeking care. Before you select a hospice provider, I strongly recommend you tour their facility. Don't just interview their administrative staff in your home. If possible, try to interview families who have, or have had loved ones in their care. Take time to check them out with the Better Business Bureau. But don't be fooled, just because they have no registered complaints, doesn't mean they will provide all they promise. Once you are in their care, they have a lot more control over you and your situation than you think. Getting your loved one transferred to another hospice facility could prove to be a difficult if not impossible task.

As for the Denver police, I called their records department and asked for a police report of the events that happened at Porter Hospital that fateful day. Oddly enough, there was no file *or* record of anything having ever happened there.

I met with APS that following Monday, November 19. The supervisor told me that the police had given me a positive recommendation. They advised that no action be taken against me.

I was overcome with joy when she said that the APS was also behind me. She told me I was going to be interviewed by an APS lawyer. She assured me that as long as I was the person the police said I was, everything would be alright. The meeting was short and they assured me they were working on having Rita released as soon as possible.

Later that day, I got a call from Porter Hospice. They told me that Rita would be discharged from Porter Hospital that evening.

I was so excited I called my daughters and my mom right away. I gathered all of Rita's personal belongings and loaded them into the car. I packed two large poster boards covered with photographs of our family. I had built a stand to hold an under-the-counter compact-disk player. I loaded everything I thought Rita might need. Stacey and I got to the hospice center an hour early so we could set her room up before she got there. The single room was just about the same size as the ones at the other hospice center, only they held two patients. Rita was taken to the Porter Hospice Center in Centennial, Colorado around six forty-five p.m.

When the ambulance attendants brought her into her room, I could do nothing but weep. I was so happy to see her, I was a mess. She looked so weak and frail it was scary. I looked at her arm. The band-aid in the fold of her elbow told the story. She had been fed through a tube for the whole week while she was in Porter Hospital. The attendants also told me she had been on a catheter. Prior to her being taken from us, she had been eating solid foods and was able to make it to the bathroom with some assistance, though it was necessary to change her adult diapers.

I believe that there are situations where a family needs to be separated by the powers that be. But after the in-depth interview I had with the police; the positive recommendation of APS from the beginning; and the fact that there was never any weapon found, a seventy two hour hold should have been sufficient.

Because of the conversation I had with the director of Porter Hospice the day I followed the ambulance, there was never any restriction placed upon me. From the first day Rita arrived, to her last, the staff was better and more professional than I could have ever asked. They were certainly one of the reasons I was emotionally able to keep going back to the hospice center every day she was there.

As for my ordeal with the Denver police, I was so deeply impacted, that over the next two weeks, I slept at the hospice center almost every night because I was afraid to drive.

I was very disturbed that, as her Medical Power of Attorney, they refused to give me any details of Rita's condition, status, or any other information during her entire stay. Worst of all, our daughters were kept from seeing their mother for an agonizing period of six days.

> There is always the possibility Rita made up her whole story about having an affair. But given the circumstances, I believe she told me the truth. She never made anything else up and never wavered from her statement. Regardless, I will always love and respect Rita with all my heart. I have forgiven her for everything I felt she has done and I pray God will forgive me of my own sins.
>
> In the Bible, when Jesus was asking the adulteress where her accusers were, she said they were gone. Jesus then said, "Neither do I condemn you, go and sin no more." She is forgiven and that is that. I will always remember Rita fondly and think of her with high regard. She was the best friend I ever had and I will always love her.
>
> Lastly, all the time I was in distress and misery, I didn't know what to pray for. I should have been praying for wisdom.

CHAPTER 23

Forgiveness and Closure

I would be lying if I said that throughout my experience, I never struggled with forgiveness. In fact, I still pray daily for strength to forgive the atrocities that have been committed against me. One might think I have written certain parts of this book to avenge my wrongdoers, but the truth is I never intended to write a book that exposed dirty secrets or caused harm to the integrity of another.

My original intention was to write a book that told what a wonderful and beautiful wife I was blessed with, and how together, we won the battle with her cancer. In the beginning, I never gave thought to the possibility she would die of this illness. I desired to write a book that gave hope and one that aided future caretakers through their ordeal.

The story unfolded the way it did for a reason, and that's just the way it is. Though I'm saddened by the fact that there will be some people who, when they read this book, may never forgive me for having written it, I make no apologies. Neither do I make any excuses for my own behavior. But I know I must also pray the Lord forgives me for my many shortcomings; He sure has a way of keeping us humble. I must also admit that there are definitely things I wish I would have done differently. Death is incredibly stressful and taxing for everyone associated with it and emotional stress has an enormous impact on behaviors. When we are under the burden of an impending death, we may say and do things we otherwise may not have said nor done, thus producing loose ends or unfinished business.

I believe that one of the biggest complexities of death involves unfinished business. Many people die regretting things they've done to others or endured from them. Consequently, they die without closure. Survival without closure is like living with a ghost that haunts us all the days of our lives. When I use the word closure here, what I really mean is forgiveness. We need to forgive, and we need to be forgiven. I'm reminded of the words of the Lord's Prayer, "… forgive us our trespasses as we forgive those who trespass against us." What peace we might find if we truly grasped and believed those powerful words. I have known plenty of people who absolutely refuse to forgive others for even the smallest offense. Their unforgiving heart is laden with conflict and bitterness and even they themselves can't understand the uneasiness that plagues them. The following story illustrates the importance of complete and unconditional forgiveness.

Years ago, I was awakened in the middle of the night by a neighbor who told me my garage had caught fire. I ran to my backyard and pulled out my water hose, while Rita called 911. I drenched the roof and soffit of the garage till there were no more flames. By the time the firemen got there, the fire was completely out from what I could see. The firemen took their hoses into my garage and sprayed the ceiling from the inside. As they sprayed their high pressure hose, they soaked my cabinets, tools, and almost everything else in my garage. When I asked one of them why they were doing this, he said that they needed to make sure the fire was extinguished on the inside as well as the outside. If they didn't spray inside, the fire would likely start again. Then he turned the water pressure down and told me to listen carefully to the water hitting the ceiling. I could hear the hissing of hot spots.

Forgiving and being forgiven before death is like that, too. If you're the one dying, your fears are compounded by the lack of closure. If you're the survivor, you may look fine on the outside but on the inside, you're burning up with resentment and hate. You even dream about the offense committed. All the days of your life are filled with the event, if only in the back of your mind.

Take it from me; walking away from a gravesite, knowing that there are unanswered questions and unresolved issues can leave you in terrible emotional turmoil. We must find it in ourselves to move beyond the issue(s) we have faced, will face, or are facing now, no matter how difficult. Otherwise the consequences may come in the form of crippling emotional confusion. You may feel yourself teetering between feeling sad, angry and bitter toward a dead person, which is an unrepresented and for all intents and purposes, a nonexistent entity.

Personally, I must come to terms with the fact that I will go to my grave with many unanswered questions in terms of my marriage. Only then will I be at peace with the memory of a life that once was. In my opinion, a *peaceful* death is directly related to complete and unconditional forgiveness, no matter what side you're on.

I bet you know of at least one family who was torn apart, by the death of the mother or father, due to unresolved issues. Yours may be one of them. If a family was divided before an illness occurred, the division may be compounded by the death if there was no closure. Family members can re-live their hatred and hold bitterness toward the deceased, or other surviving family members for the rest of their lives. The resentment may be even further magnified if the illness is long and drawn out. Then they too die one day, and the cycle continues.

Common sense tells us that most division within any personal relationship could be resolved by simple forgiveness. When I die, I hope to have the peace of knowing that I have corrected the wrongs I have either caused or endured. I have learned that un-forgiveness at the time of death may create a volatile environment which makes peace of mind very elusive, if not impossible to achieve later on.

I knew a man whose sister was mad at him at the time of his death. She never was very forgiving, and when she received word of his death, her regret was almost more than she could bear. The night before he died, he went to his sister's husband and begged forgiveness. I don't know how she responded to the request for forgiveness that night, but it must not have been good. At his funeral, his sister cried uncontrollably, and no words could relieve her guilty conscience. Because he was a healthy young man and his death was unexpected, there was no time for closure. I believe she never forgave herself for harboring those bitter feelings.

The only logical solution is forgiveness of others as well as ourselves while we are still alive. Sadly, in our unforgiving society, humility is not a common trait.

So how can we forgive? God said His forgiveness is unconditional and perpetual. Once he has forgiven our sin, it is forgotten forever.

There is enough pain to go around, why add to it by carrying an extra burden? Let it go! Unfortunately, talking about forgiveness and living it are two different things. God's forgiveness is perfect, ours is of course, flawed as are we.

Letting the Other Person Save Face

In his book, *How to Win Friends and Influence People*, Dale Carnegie talks about letting the other person save face. Pride, haughtiness and conceit, are all counter-productive, attitudes that get in the way of our forgiveness. With these as our dominating attitudes, we can see no further than our own pain and anguish. Is it possible that at least some of those who have offended us would love the opportunity to be forgiven if they had a chance? They may live every day of their lives, wishing they could just knock on your door and say they're sorry for what they've done. Instead we gloat in our bitterness, thinking that our feelings somehow give us the authority to look down on those who have offended us. Our bitterness may last long after the offender has died and nothing is gained from it but a soul that is troubled more after the death than before.

As I've mentioned before, talking about forgiveness is much easier than actually forgiving. In fact, forgiving someone for things that we may consider unforgivable may be the hardest thing we'll ever have to do, but unless we can find a way to forgive, we may as well brace ourselves for a rough ride. You can know the peace that forgiveness brings by asking God for the strength and wisdom to forgive, even if the offender has not asked to be forgiven.

I challenge you to ask yourself, "Am I going to forgive this person/people or even yourself, and move on, or will I decide not to forgive and *seemingly* move on?" No one can make this decision for you; it must be your own. I will relate another story I once heard, that may help you to make a decision; not necessarily the right or wrong decision, but a decision nonetheless.

Once there were two boys who decided they would try to make a fool of the wise man in their village. They thought and thought, till they came up with an idea that, in their minds, could not fail. They captured a sparrow and gathered the entire village at the gate of the home of the wise man. They then knocked on his door and said they had a question for him. One of the boys asked the wise man what it was he was holding. At once, the wise man answered, "You hold a sparrow." The boys then asked, "But is it a live sparrow, or a dead sparrow?" If the wise man said it was alive, the boy would smash it to death. If he said it was dead, he would let it go. They knew they couldn't fail. But the answer was one they never expected. The wise man smiled as he looked into the eyes of the boy. He said, "My son… it is as you wish!"

The choice is yours, it is as you wish! Decide to be at peace; let it go. Incidentally, if these words are ministering to you, I want to share that they're also ministering to me. God bless your decision.

Grudge Holding

I believe grudge holding is one of humanity's biggest downfalls. Rather than talk about what grudge holding is all about and trying to analyze the dynamics of it, I decided to express the essence of it with a story I heard many years ago on National Public Radio.

"One, My Darling, Come To Mama"

There was once a woman who had four daughters. She loved the first three and despised the fourth. Each time she brought food home for her children, she would stand outside the door and sing:

> *One, my darling, come to Mama,*
> *Two, my darling, come to Mama,*
> *Three my darling, come to Mama,*
> *Stay Philemadré, stay,*
> *Stay where you are.*

The older daughters would run to the door and let their mother in. Philemadré remained in the corner. The three girls and their mother would sit at the table and eat. And if there was any food left, it would be given to

Philemadré. The three older girls grew fat and sleek. Philemadré was thin as a nail.

Now a devil had been watching the mother for a long time. He saw how the mother would arrive at her house and sing, and how the young girls would run to the door. He had secretly bee practicing her song:

> *One, my darling, come to Mama,*
> *Two, my darling, come to Mama,*
> *Three my darling, come to Mama,*
> *Stay Philemadré, stay,*
> *Stay where you are.*

At last the devil decided he was ready. He came to the door and sang in a deep gruff voice:

> *One, my darling, come to Mama,*
> *Two, my darling, come to Mama,*
> *Three my darling, come to Mama,*
> *Stay Philemadré, stay,*
> *Stay where you are.*

But, of course, the girls knew the gruff voice was not their mother's and did not open the door. The devil went to see the plumber.

"Tighten my voice", he said. "Tighten it as much as you can, so it will be as high as possible."

When the devil returned to the house of the young girls, his voice was three octaves higher and sounded like a bird:

> *One, my darling, come to Mama,*
> *Two, my darling, come to Mama,*
> *Three my darling, come to Mama,*
> *Stay Philemadré, stay,*
> *Stay where you are.*

"Some silly bird, "The girls said to each other and did not go to the door.

A little later their mother returned and sang:

> *One, my darling, come to Mama,*
> *Two, my darling, come to Mama,*
> *Three my darling, come to Mama,*
> *Stay Philemadré, stay,*
> *Stay where you are.*

The girls at once recognized her voice and let her in. As always the four ate together, leaving the scraps to Philemadré.

The devil went back to the plumber and complained, "You tightened it too much." So the plumber loosened it a bit and when the devil returned the next day, his voice sounded just like the mother's:

> *One, my darling, come to Mama,*
> *Two, my darling, come to Mama,*
> *Three my darling, come to Mama,*
> *Stay Philemadré, stay,*
> *Stay where you are.*

The girls ran to the door to let their mother in and the devil grabbed all three and ran off with them.

Philemadré remained in the corner.

After a while the mother returned and sang:

> *One, my darling, come to Mama,*
> *Two, my darling, come to Mama,*
> *Three my darling, come to Mama,*
> *Stay Philemadré, stay,*
> *Stay where you are.*

No one came to the door. The mother sang again:

> *One, my darling, come to Mama,*
> *Two, my darling, come to Mama,*
> *Three my darling, come to Mama,*
> *Stay Philemadré, stay,*
> *Stay where you are.*

Still no one came. Where were her dear ones? Then she heard:

> *One, cannot come to Mama,*
> *Two, cannot come to Mama,*
> *Three cannot, come to Mama,*
> *Philemadré is*
> *Where she is.*

The mother pushed open the door and when she did not see any one she ran from the house like a madwoman, singing her song to anyone who would listen.

Philemadré walked out the open door, down the road to town. She found work and after some time, she married the king's son.

Many years later a madwoman was heard singing in the street:

> *One, cannot come to Mama,*
> *Two, cannot come to Mama,*
> *Three cannot, come to Mama,*
> *Philemadré is*
> *Where she is.*

The king's servants tried to hurry her away from the palace. She was in rags, and her wild hair, filled with droppings of birds, looked like branches of a tree. But every day she would come back and sing:

Forgiveness and Closure

One, cannot come to Mama,
Two, cannot come to Mama,
Three cannot, come to Mama,
Philemadré is
Where she is.

Then one day the queen's servant said to the queen, "There is a ragged woman in the street who calls every afternoon for Philemadré. Do you know anyone of that name?"

The queen rushed to the window. The woman in the street, the beggar woman, was her own mother. She went down and brought her into the palace. She washed her and gave her new clothes and cut her hair.

"Mama," she said, "the others are no more. But I am here. Look at me, I am Philemadré. You did not care for me, but I am here, and now I will take care of you."

I'll leave the rest up to you to decide how you will address your grudges. I think you will agree forgiveness and communication are instrumental in a family's ability to move forward. Though the way your family reacts to your crisis will be unique unto your family members, certain behaviors and attitudes are not only predictable—they seem to be almost universal. In my short experience in the hospice environment, I have observed that almost any and all irrational behavior can be traced to the way people address and react to the situation at hand. Am I saying there may be irrational behavior displayed at some point during a serious illness or death? I'm saying it is almost a given and you must be prepared for anything.

Whether the irrational behavior is exhibited by the patient, the caretaker, the family, or anyone else, if it offends other parties involved, there will be need for forgiveness. The most desirable outcome for everyone is to be at peace, both with their family and themselves from the onset of the illness, till long after the funeral. Without the forgiveness I wrote about, the outcome can only be an emotionally painful one.

Intent Versus Perception

I believe that much of the conflict that arises from stressful situations is derived from misunderstandings. Well-meaning comments can be perceived as criticism and can easily be misinterpreted by a caretaker. While you may be meaning to say, "It's cold in this room," the caretaker may hear you say, "Don't you care enough to turn the heat up?" While you may comment, "Some grief counseling might really help you feel better," the grieving person may actually hear you say something like, "You need help—*you're all messed up!*"

In a class I once took, the instructor used an example that made me realize that people don't always hear what it is you're trying to say to them. He said a sentence that went something like this, "I never said you took the wallet." Then, he restated the sentence several times. Each time, he would say the exact same words, but he would place emphasis on a different word. For example, he said, "*I* never said you took the wallet." Then he said, "I *never* said you took the wallet." "I never *said* you took the wallet." "I never said *you* took the wallet." He then proceeded to state the sentence, emphasizing each word except the word, "the" until he had emphasized every word in the sentence. Each time he stated it, the sentence took on a new and different meaning. All of the statements were either accusatory or defensive, yet they all used the exact same words. There are two versions of every story and both may be right and both may be wrong. I've included the following example to illustrate my point.

The Coin

I started volunteering as a consultant to the Denver Public Schools back in 1985. At first I taught a class called "Project Business" through the Junior Achievement organization. But before I was half-way through the first semester, I realized that the kids I was working with needed more than the understanding of supply and demand. They needed more basic information, like why it's important to look someone in the eye when they shake hands, or how important it is to finish high school. For some, the idea of sitting for a job interview was something they could not comprehend. Most of the students were from families without a single college graduate and even the *thought* of a high school diploma was a stretch for others.

Over the years, I had taken many courses and read many books on motivation, sales, and goal setting, and I felt I could better serve their needs by sharing with them about what I had learned. I had also been a professional storyteller for several years by then, so by the time I started my second semester, I had completely designed an eight-hour motivational class called *Kick Start*.

One of the modules I wanted to teach had to do with seeing and respecting the opposing views of others. After much thought, I came up with what I believed would be a simple, yet powerful tool. I took a silver dollar to class with me. I held it up to the class and asked them all what it was. They all agreed it was a silver dollar. Then I asked if they all agreed it was heads. Of course, it was heads because that's what I showed them. I paused for a long while then I said in a loud voice, "You're ALL WRONG!" Then, as I turned the coin to the opposing side, I would smile and say, "*It's tails.*"

As I showed the coin, the point was instantly made; just like there are two sides to the coin, there are two perspectives in every situation or more if there are more than two people involved. Every perspective is right in our own eyes. Even though the kids were right in saying the coin was heads, they couldn't see the other side. In a disagreement, one person may see the proverbial heads and you may see tails. It doesn't mean either of you is right or wrong, just different.

The CAREGIVER'S HANDBOOK

CHAPTER 24

She Should Have Been Dead by Friday

I happened to be visiting with a friend one day whose spouse was receiving full-time care for Parkinson's disease. The spouse was presently at the end stages of life and my friend shared with me about the Parkinson's support group she attended. We both shared about how grateful we were and how we benefited from our respective support groups. She told me the perfect story for this section.

During one of her support groups, one of the participants mentioned that they wished their spouse would just hurry up and die, so the surviving spouse could get on with their life. Upon hearing the statement, there was a gasp from someone else in the group. Suddenly, the room was filled with loud conversation. After the facilitator calmed the group down, there was a survey taken. All but two of the participants felt the same about wishing their loved one would "hurry up and die."

My friend then reluctantly revealed to me that she was one of those who wished their spouse would die. I felt embarrassed as she shared with me. It was as though my deep dark secret had been exposed. I too had secretly felt the same way, though I would never dream of revealing it to anyone. It's not that I wished my wife were dead, but that she was no longer in the state she was presently in. I had been through so much already and she had, too. I wished we both could be free from the illness which gripped all of our lives.

If you have someone in hospice and you are burdened about wishing it were over, don't let anyone lay a guilt trip on you, including yourself. Wishing it was over is natural; besides, you're not wishing your loved one is dead as much as you're wishing they were no longer suffering. You've been through a lot. If you feel that you've fought the good fight, don't beat yourself up. That's never a good idea. God wouldn't want it that way, either. If you were to have taken that same survey, you'd see you're actually in the majority.

On the other hand, if you do verbalize your feelings, be prepared for an onslaught of attacks. Certainly, few if any of the relatives of the patient will understand or agree with you. In fact, they'll likely accuse you of not loving the patient at all. Just remember the coin. You're not right or wrong, just different, and your perspective is valid.

Handling Crisis

December 20, 2007 was a cold, snowy day. Rita had been in twenty-four-hour care at the Porter Hospice Center for thirty days. It had snowed that night and there was snow and ice on the sidewalks. While I was in the cafeteria having a cup of coffee that morning, I happened to see someone slip and fall on the icy walkway. The staff at the center had been so good to Rita and me that I was glad to be of help in any way I could, so I went looking for the snow shovel I had used the night before. It was nowhere to be found, so I asked the charge-nurse if she could show me where it was. She showed me to a small utility room. Next to the shovel was a five-gallon bucket of salt rock so I took the liberty of taking it out with me as well.

I had just returned from shoveling the snow and was sitting at Rita's bedside warming my hands when the social worker came into Rita's room. His stout frame and thick beard bore a striking contrast against the tie and dress shirt that he wore. Though he was built like a mountain man, he was very soft-spoken and kind.

The serious look on his face told me he meant business. He told me he needed to talk to me and I followed him robotically, down the dimly lit hall. No words were spoken as we walked to a conference room at the end of the building. As we walked, I wondered why we needed to go to a private room to talk.

Something told me it might not be good news. I wondered what he might have to say that couldn't be said in front of Rita. Once we were in the room, Chris closed the door and lowered the shades. I became more concerned as I watched him. I wondered: *Why is he closing the door and lowering the shades?* I couldn't imagine what he might have to say that warranted such precaution. By the look on his face, it was obvious that what he was about to tell me was not going to be good.

Did he think I would react violently to his words? Had I violated some hospice policy? I *had* taken a shower in the patient's shower room that morning and the nurses were not shy about letting me know I was not to use those facilities again. The day before, one of the nurses had given me permission to use that shower. But I had also shoveled the snow three times in the past twenty-four hours. I wondered if perhaps someone had slipped on the ice that formed after I'd shoveled. I wondered if maybe I was in trouble.

As soon as I sat down, Chris reached into his shirt pocket and pulled out a letter. It was addressed to Rita and dated November 20, 2007, a whole month before. His expression turned from serious, to an obvious sadness, as he looked at me. His eyes seemed to be saying he was sorry for what he was about to say. He took a deep breath, and in a quiet voice said, "Rita's insurance won't cover the cost of hospice care." He said he had been trying to resolve the issue in-house, but that he had done all he could. Then he said that the insurance company had even declined payment for care that had been received over the past month. That meant at the rate of one-hundred-ninety dollars a day, *we were six-thousand dollars behind already.* I didn't know what to say. I must have had a strange look on my face because Chris asked me if I was alright. I told him I was certain I had a letter at home, stating that Rita's care was one-hundred percent covered. He said that at the bottom of the letter, there was a disclaimer stating it was possible the insurance company may not cover any of the charges.

The magnitude of my situation hit me like a hard slap on a cold face. The fear of what might possibly happen became my central point of focus. What was to become of Rita's care? For the past month, Rita had been receiving 24-hour hospice care. There were three shifts of two CNAs and one RN taking care of her needs. If I took her home, it meant that I would be doing the work of nine people. On top of that, her condition had declined significantly in the last thirty days. How could I possibly manage her care all alone? I had no team assembled—*I wasn't prepared for this*!

Then, the concern about money hit me. Rita had been in hospice care since November 19. I told Chris there was no way I could afford to pay another six-thousand dollars. He told me that since they had been trying to resolve the issue and hadn't yet told me, that the entire cost would be picked up by Porter Hospice. I was relieved at first—then he dropped the bomb.

He told me I would be given two days to remove Rita from the facility. Four days before Christmas, and I had just two days to take her back home. It was the most horrible thing I could have imagined. After everything I had been through, now Rita was being removed from the hospice center. I walked down the hall from the conference room in a daze. My heart was heavy to the point of having chest pains and tears were streaming from my eyes as I walked.

When I was a few doors away from Rita's room, I heard a familiar voice coming from one of the rooms. I looked up and saw a woman, sitting in a wheelchair, wearing a bandana. I recognized her as one of the patients from our brain tumor support group. She, like Rita, had been diagnosed with a GBM. Like Mike and Judy Bahm, she and her husband had become our friends. I used to send encouraging words to him via email whenever I got a chance. She had worn a scarf from the first time we met. I guessed her hair hadn't grown back from the radiation, or maybe her surgical scar was too prominent. In any case, I wiped the tears from my eyes as best as I could. I stood in the doorway to her room and called out her name. She didn't recognize me at first. Then, after a short conversation she said, "Oh, Rita and Paul, yes, I remember you." Her voice was almost a whisper. I told her I was happy to see her, but that I was deeply saddened to see her in hospice in this condition. I sensed she was uncomfortable and she had a couple of guests, so I left.

Seeing her there brought me back to the reality of our dire situation. As I approached the nurse's station, one of the nurses happened to be walking out. She saw me and must have noticed the troubled look on my face and asked what was bothering me. As I explained my situation to her, I began to cry, again. I heard myself as I was speaking and it was almost as if I was listening to the words of a small boy, looking down at the ground, trying to talk between tears. I broke down and almost fell to my knees. She tried her best to comfort me, but it was clear... I was a completely broken man.

For a moment, I wondered to myself if I was being punished by God for some sin I committed in my past. I wondered if perhaps I might have another nervous breakdown. So many thoughts ran through my head. I was dizzy from the burden of it all. I realized that I needed the advice of someone who could see my situation better than I could. I knew I could never handle this alone, so once again, I called my pastor, Scott.

As I told him of my plight, he listened carefully. He knew all of the prior details of my situation; he knew about my family and Rita's not being a very big part of the whole thing; he knew I was going to be facing a very difficult challenge. After I finished, he repeated something I had heard him say before, but I never really thought too much about it. He had always told me that everything I was worried about *could* possibly come to pass, but that it likely wouldn't be as bad as I thought it would. I hated that he was so correct in his counsel, but somehow, I knew he was right. We prayed together and I made my way back to Rita's room. On my way there, I made the decision to find a way to make the best of my day, in spite of the devastating news I'd just received.

I didn't want Rita to know how concerned I was, so as I sat in the recliner next to her bed, I looked at her with a smile. I always kept an ample supply of nuts, crackers and assorted snacks in a night stand next to her bed. I pulled out two granola bars and a bag of raw almonds. I unwrapped one of the granola bars and gave it to Rita. She returned my smile as she took it. I searched through the CDs and found the Righteous Brothers' greatest hits collection. I closed the door to her room and played "Unchained Melody" as loud as I thought I could without someone coming and asking me to turn it down. As I listened to the music, I pushed the recliner to its full back position and closed my eyes. I held Rita's hand tightly as we listened to the music together.

Warm tears rolled down my cheeks and the sadness I had been feeling turned to a deep sense of peace. I thanked God for having provided all He had up to that point and I told Him I trusted Him, no matter what happened. I don't know if I drifted off to sleep or if I was just very relaxed, but in an instant, I found myself in a state of total calm. I was no longer worried about what would happen two days from then. As I relaxed, I felt like I was floating. It was as if all my perception of time and space had disappeared. Nothing else existed except Rita, the music, and me. The music seemed to go on forever as I meditated, and when the song finally ended, Rita was fast asleep. We sat there holding hands for what must have been thirty minutes. When I finally came out of it, I realized that I had truly experienced something profound. I had stumbled on the beauty of solitude.

Later that morning, I called Amanda to tell her the news. I wanted to let her know I was alright and when I told her we had been through worse, I did my best to let out a chuckle. Next I called Stacey and my mom and told them. Then I called my cousin Lou. She was an extremely competent, high-level triage nurse who worked for the Denver Children's Hospital. Lou had been the one who had shown me how to manage caring for Rita when she first went into hospice. She taught me how to transfer Rita from her bed to the chair and back.

She taught me to how to change bedding while Rita was still in her bed. She taught me how to change a diaper and even how to change Rita's clothing without hurting her thin, fragile arms. Had it not been for Lou's wisdom and insight, it would have been a much harder transition to hospice. After a few months, I was probably as competent as any of the hospice nurses, in terms of caring for Rita.

Actually, Lou's dad was Rita's dad's brother so in truth, she was Rita's cousin, but after all the help she had given to my daughters and me, I claimed her as my own. She told me to take a deep breath then she asked me when Rita would be sent home. She promised she would be there to help as often as she could and she assured me, her family would be bringing us dinner on Christmas Eve. All that happened on Thursday and by Saturday I was calmed down and mostly mentally prepared for Rita's arrival.

By the time the hospital bed, wheelchair and bedside table arrived at my house, I had already rearranged our bedroom to accommodate the bed and made room for the wheelchair. Rita's bed was made and I had spread a warm blanket out on her recliner.

When the ambulance attendants rolled the gurney into the house, I could see a look of confusion on Rita's face. But as she entered the house, her face began to brighten up. Once she recognized her surroundings, a smile came across her lips. I realized I was actually glad to have her home again, and as I watched them loosen the belts around her waist and carry her to her chair, Scott's words resonated through my head; *It might come to pass, but it would likely not be as bad as I thought it might be.* He was right... again.

    Rita was in home hospice for six weeks and although it was both physically and emotionally grueling, I think I handled it quite well. Then, in the second week of February, 2007, I got a call from the company Rita had worked for prior to her illness. The woman told me that the company had changed insurance carriers at the first of the year. She suggested I call Porter Hospice and ask if they could investigate if the new carrier would cover hospice care. I called Porter Hospice and told them of the changes in Rita's insurance carriers. Within an hour, they called me back and told me that the new carrier would in fact pay one-hundred percent for Rita to be returned to the center. Then they told me they had a room available. She returned to Porter Hospice the next day and remained there till her passing in May.

The CAREGIVER'S HANDBOOK

CHAPTER 25

The Magnitude of Solitude

Unless you've endured the loss of a loved one as a caretaker, it may be difficult to grasp this section. Seeing the caretaker go through the process, and going through it as the caretaker are definitely two completely different experiences. While I was revising and editing this book, my nephew Mitchell was assisting me. He had edited two novels while in college and had a strong literature background. He has taught English in Japan for over a year and was stateside, awaiting his return to Japan while he helped me. He was fortunate to have been one of the few in my family to have seen his aunt Rita in the last days of her life. But honestly, like the others, he saw very little of the reality of what I was going through as a caretaker.

I must have driven him crazy as we worked through the pages during revisions. He insisted over and over, that I was being too redundant. In every chapter, sometimes even multiple times within chapters, I wanted to tell *how devastated I was*, or that *I cried till there were no more tears to cry*. But I was steadfast in my response; I repeated these things over and over because *that's the way it feels*.

If you think this book is redundant in describing a caretaker's emotions, then it is likely you haven't experienced being a caretaker yourself. If you're currently a caretaker, I would bet that you're saying, "I know exactly how you feel." Of course, there are those who are blessed with the ability to manage crisis, illness, and death very calmly, at least outwardly. To those readers I say: Use your gift to reach out and help others who are facing the task of being a caretaker. They desperately need to be understood and validated. Your understanding may bring them peace and comfort beyond words. Too many times, I could have only hoped for wisdom such as this. Fellow caretakers I've spoken to have shared with me their deep, unending feelings of solitude. Even in a room packed full of loved ones, they sometimes find themselves longing to talk to someone who understands.

In this section, I have given some examples of my own experiences associated with solitude. You may not experience the intense low points like I did, yet we each experience some emotional struggles. Perhaps you share many of the same feelings I have. Nevertheless, I hope this helps you to better address and understand your own solitude and the pain it brings. You are not alone in the way you feel and you need not make apologies for your feelings. Your feelings are not wrong or bad and I assure you—you are not crazy.

I wrote the following in my journal on the day after I learned Rita had to be removed from Porter Hospice. Afterwards, I was able to look back at the entry and better understand myself. Consequently, I was better able to address and cope with much of my distress. Understand that the section may be painful to read; caretakers are under a tremendous amount of stress that is sometimes incomprehensible.

Benchmarks and Milestones

As I write these words, I am painfully aware of the fact that tomorrow, December 21, 2007 will be the eighteenth month since Rita was first diagnosed. I never dreamed she would be in her present state. I wish this day never came, yet another part of me wishes this day were far in my past.

Last night, I went to our annual Christmas party at our church. There was a festive atmosphere and joyful children could be heard laughing throughout the place. Parishioners were having fellowship, laughing and visiting before the activities were to begin. I sat in my chair, glancing around the room, barely able to hold back my tears. As I looked around, a powerful feeling of loneliness swept over me. It seemed to choke me like a snake which constricts its prey, not letting go until its victim has breathed its last breath.

When I got home, I couldn't find the peace I'd so hoped I would find there. I ended my day by reading from my devotional, *My Utmost for His Highest,* for a second time. I prayed for God's will and peace as I went to bed. Every time I started to drift off to sleep, I instinctively would reach over to where Rita used to sleep; only to meet with the empty place where she once laid her head. The feeling wouldn't let go throughout the night and into this day. There are some milestones which give no comfort at all… this day, being one of them. I can't imagine how much more difficult this would be if I didn't have God to call upon in these trying times.

Many times depression and heartache crept in, and would completely overtake my emotions. Another night I was so depressed, I wrote a blog on My Space. It was deep and perhaps perceived as gloomy by some but I have included it, because I believe it captured the essence of the moods I experienced during some extremely trying times.

After I wrote the blog, I looked back at it and was humbled. I realized that only the wisdom of God could have expressed my pain in such a profound way. I know it sounds like there was no hope whatsoever, but after reading the blog, I saw that He never left my side. I hope it ministers to the way you may feel or have felt. Moreover, I pray it opens your eyes to see that there is hope.

How Long, Lord?

Nothing pains my heart like the loneliness I feel. With no apparent end in sight, this grief is without mercy. I constantly find myself in the wings, waiting to be a part of it all, or on the outside, looking in. My turn has not yet come. Sadness and agony are the only sensations my heart knows. Solitude and despair are my partners in life right now, rarely leaving an opportunity for joy. I seek comfort for my soul, only to find another day of waiting. At times there seems to be no hope for me at all. Happiness and love are fleeting at best.

Oh, how I long for a kindred spirit to share in my pain, yet there is none. Hope... is it real? Or did I imagine it once in a dream? Love... is it something I gave away, only to find the well ran dry? Will it continue to elude me forever? How long? How many more days without happiness will I know? Is there an end to it all? I repeat to myself over and over, "This too shall pass, this too shall pass," but am I only kidding myself? Will it pass? Or is it here to stay? Oh Lord, ease my soul. Oh Lord, heal my pain. Oh Lord, open my eyes. *Oh my Lord*! *Oh my God*! I long for your peace that passes understanding. Nevertheless, as our Lord said, "Not my will, but Yours be done." Oh joy, find your way into my heart, again. Please God, put this feeling far in my past. Like death, it would be a step up for me. *Please God—please*!

Last, I wrote the following poem. I think it too captured my pain. Unlike the others however, this one provided hope in the end. What I wish to convey is that while there may not seem to be a light at the end of your tunnel, it is there just the same.

This Pain

This pain my heart feels
Can't be measured or weighed
It comes and it goes
And it won't be delayed

It closes my eyes
It accents my fears
It makes me confused
And deafens my ears

I've tried to control
It's merciless hand
And then I discover
It's unyielding demand

I'm trying to bargain
Its timely demise
It's all from the devil
All wrapped up in lies

So I must live this time
In my sadness and pain
But I'll trust in His promise
His love will sustain

Peace to you people
Who see this today

*Look to the promise
And turn to God's way*

*He'll soften your heart
And He'll open your eyes
He'll comfort your spirit
And snuff out those lies!*

~Paul Lane

The Beauty of Solitude

I've touched on the magnitude of solitude. Now, I wish to discuss the beauty of it. After a two-hour visit from one of Rita's sisters who hadn't seen her in a while, my sister-in-law turned to me and said, "It must be horrible when the phone stops ringing and everyone's gone."

I told her that in all honesty, most of the time, the only voice I ever heard was my own, and that solitude was my closest companion. Good thing I can sing. Ha!

After many months of bearing the burden of solitude, I finally learned to seek the beauty in it. Learning to see beauty in solitude can sometimes be like trying to enjoy having your finger smashed. A complete contradiction of terms, yet if you can develop this ability, you will be better able to maintain your composure in trying times.

For me, the beauty of solitude would sometimes present itself in the form of tender moments throughout our day, where all time and space disappeared. We (whoever "we" happened to be at the time) just got caught up in each other's presence. Usually it was just Rita and me, other times it was one or both of our daughters, their mom and me. Sometimes, it was all of us, plus boyfriends and a few select others. As we visited, we would be overcome with what can only be described as a *magical* feeling. It was like the lights would go dim, but we could see *with amazing clarity*.

All frustration disappeared; the pain of the solitude disappeared if only for a moment. During these magical times, we laughed more than usual; there was no stress in our hearts, and even time itself seemed to disappear. Suddenly we didn't have a care in the world. That's when I could truly appreciate God's word, where it says, "Be still, and know that I am God." At these times, I/we experienced a tremendous sense of peace and calm that cannot be put into words. Everyone present would leave with a feeling of being fed the perfect meal on the perfect night, with the perfect company. *Wow—it was real.*

The CAREGIVER'S HANDBOOK

CHAPTER 26

The Dance

Since there were not usually a lot of visitors, I had a lot of idle time to spend with Rita. From the time we were in our twenties, she always loved the songs: "Only You and You Alone," by the Platters and "Unchained Melody" by the Righteous Brothers, among others. As her illness progressed however, she was no longer able to tell me what she wanted to hear, so I would just play random music for her. I could tell she enjoyed hearing those two songs when I played them because she would sometimes close her eyes and get a peaceful look on her face while the songs played.

One time, while "Unchained Melody" was playing, I asked her if she wanted to dance with me. She smiled and gave me an affirmative nod. I closed the door to her room and raised her bed to its maximum height. I lowered her bed rail and slid her close to the edge of her bed. I held her close as I slowly rocked her upper torso from side to side with the music. She wrapped her arms around me and placed her head close to mine.

A wonderful feeling of peace completely filled the room. After that, it became our daily ritual and there was always a special connection between us whenever we danced.

Sometimes, I suddenly become keenly aware of our situation as we moved and swayed together and I would be overcome with emotion. When that happened, I would quietly fall apart as we *danced*. Usually, I would weep for the duration of the song, and most of the time she was oblivious that I was even crying. It was one of the most enjoyable times we shared while Rita was in hospice. I considered those times to be solitude at its best.

The Necessity and Benefits of Solitude
Without solitude, I discovered there can be little reflection and introspection. Although I mostly feared solitude, I now understand that it was necessary for my own grieving and healing process. Many times, it was when I was loneliest that I was best able to grasp the reality of my situation. It was then that I was able to realize and examine what meant most to me.

At times in my solitude, I felt as if I was in the loving embrace of God. His comforting hands never felt so absolute. Funny thing is I didn't really think about having been in God's presence till the moment had passed. Not until I was beyond the pain of it all, did I see the presence of Him. I now see I could easily have spent more time reflecting and praying.

One day while I was very down and out, I wrote a blog that told of my sadness and pain. A good friend sent a comment, quoting a beautiful passage of scripture, telling me I needed to be content in all situations, though I can't remember what scripture it was. While the message was loud and clear, it didn't settle well with me as I read it. I didn't know why my soul was so troubled at reading the words, but it was. Then all of a sudden it hit me, even though I knew the words were true and I knew I needed to be content—I wasn't ready to hear the news. I wrote a message back that said, "It is always easier to read scripture than it is to live it." I spent the next several days reflecting and meditating on the words she had sent me. Eventually I was able to grasp the incredible significance of God's wisdom. Living it however, took significant effort and even after much reflection and prayer, I still struggled with the words.

I believe there are wonderful opportunities to grow during trying times, particularly in times of solitude.

When I was a teenager, I loved to backpack. I would fill a backpack with enough food and supplies to last three or four days. Then I would ask my mom to drive me to a certain spot on a mountain road that bordered a wilderness area. She hated to do it but I told her that if she didn't take me, I would just hitchhike there. I would get out and begin walking till I got to the place I wanted to be. There I would spend three or four days alone in the wilderness. People asked me why I liked to go alone, but I could never answer them. I didn't know why I did it. As I look back on it now however, I guess I was getting to know myself. I remember when I returned home, it was as if I had grown into someone better than the person who left, just days before.

When we are at the bedside of a dying loved one, we tend to see only the pain and suffering which is before us. We may not realize it, but when we focus only on our own situation, we may be overlooking many blessings and lessons about ourselves. When we sit in self-pity—which, by the way I'm as guilty as anyone—we cannot see the beauty of the world around us. We even forget to appreciate the last minutes we have with our loved one because all we see is the fact that they're dying.

Sometimes I think God nudges us; other times He shakes us to wake us up. Still, at other times I believe He watches, and shakes His head and wonders if we'll ever learn the lessons He has placed before us.

I strongly suggest you take every opportunity to pray for wisdom, especially when you find yourself in the pits of despair. Difficult as it may seem, there will be comfort after all is said and done, if you seek it. I know—I speak from experience. I'm also experienced with ignoring the promptings placed before me, as well as the blessings and, more importantly—the lessons.

One day, while I was feeding Rita, a very large bird of prey flew by her window. It seemed to look into the room as it passed. I turned and watched as it circled. Suddenly, it came back and perched on a tree *just a few feet from her window*. I could see every feather on it and it looked me right in the eye as it rested. I felt like we were all alone in the world with this magnificent creature. The most beautiful feeling of solitude swept over me as I admired it. Then, as swiftly as it had appeared, it flew off. Had I been focused only on the dire situation I was facing, I may have missed such a beautiful example of the magnitude of God's blessings.

The point I'm trying to make is this, solitude was difficult and it was also crucial to my peace of mind. Without having experienced that solitude, I doubt I could have ever overcome my situation peacefully. I believe I would have found myself without closure and unfulfilled. Overall, I am thankful for learning to see the beauty in the solitude I experienced.

Isolation

As brain cancer progresses, the patient tends to become more and more withdrawn till at some point they only want to be in the presence of a select few individuals. The more withdrawn Rita became, the more depressed I became; the more depressed I became, the angrier I felt; the more angry I felt, the more isolated I became. Eventually, I got to a point where it felt like I was facing my daily problems all alone. Although I don't deny that a big part of my isolation was because of the way I responded to people (from inside myself), a large part if it was because people didn't know what to say to me. Whatever the case, isolation from other living beings, is not a good thing and can greatly contribute to your distress. My advice to you is to get around as many positive people as you can. You may surround yourself with friends and family or you may decide it's better to be around people you don't know; perhaps in a crowded mall or a park. Of course, there are others who need to be isolated during trying times. There are really no wrong answers, I only speak for myself.

Should I Go to Church?

I was fortunate to have had a very supportive church family that treated me with kindness and dignity throughout the duration of the illness. Our church is one where everyone knows everyone else very well and we all care very deeply for our fellow parishioners. But once Rita went into hospice, those same caring people would ask me over and over how she was doing. Every week I was asked to tell them how she was. Repeating her condition was overwhelming for me. I felt like everyone there was feeling sorry for me, consequently, I found myself becoming closed-off to my much-needed support from the church.

You may be convinced that you should stop going to church for the same reason. You may even be asking yourself if you should stop going to church right now. I asked myself that same question many times over the course of Rita's illness, until one day when I heard a story of the world famous minister, D. L. Moody. He touched many lives both during his lifetime and long after his death.

It is reported that one evening, one of his parishioners came to see him. As they sat next to the warm fire, the friend told Moody that he had decided that he would stay in his own home and worship God rather than going to church. Without saying a word, Moody got up from his chair and walked over to the fireplace. He grabbed a pair of tongs and picked up a large hot burning ember. He carefully placed the red, glowing coal on the side of the fireplace and went back to his chair. Without a word being spoken, the two watched the hot coal change from glowing hot, to a piece of ash. D. L. Moody simply looked at his friend and said, "Now, you were saying?"

I will close the section with this last thought: If you think you can go it alone, you're probably right—but why *would* you?

Of course, there were times when I went to church and it seemed like everyone pitied me and I hated the thought that I was pitied; even though I knew in my heart they didn't actually see me as pitied and they would never look down on me. If this is the case, it may be good for you to visit churches where no one knows you or your situation. Ultimately, my advice to you is to stay firmly grounded in the faith that God is here and He cares for you. He feels for you and He understands why you feel the way you do.

CHAPTER 27

Family Dynamics

With the exception of the six weeks Rita was in home hospice care, she was in a hospice facility for a total of seven months. I have no idea how many other families went through the center during that time, but it was more than a few. I was fortunate to have met many others whose loved ones were also receiving care. I talked daily to most of the family members in the same wing of the building as Rita and several from another wing. Most of the time, I could name just about every visitor and tell you their reason for being there.

Usually, someone would be in the cafeteria or in a hallway when I was going for a cup of coffee or a snack. Because of the fact that we shared a common fate in regards to our loved ones, we became more and more comfortable in sharing our feelings. More than not, people were willing to open themselves up like they may not have otherwise and after a couple of months I began to realize that there were several commonalities in family behaviors. For us, it didn't take long to see that some of our best friends and closest family members completely eliminated us from their lives. Many others shared the same feelings of being ostracized and outcast from their social and familial circles.

I noticed that a lot of people talked about their family conflicts. Some conflicts were subtle, while others were more pronounced; still a few were downright volatile. Some families, though rare, seemed to be so together, that the entire illness and death were seamless. I always envied those families because they stuck together through thick and thin. I also noticed that in those rare cases where the entire family chipped in and helped, there were fewer conflicts and consequently less resentment in the end. Of course, no one knows what goes on behind closed doors or what emotions take place beneath the surface.

There always seemed to be a spouse, child, or sibling who ended up being the only one who provided care for the ill person. Sometimes, the caretaker had a spouse to help and other times, the spouse would turn tail and run. The way your family communicates and reacts will be unique unto your family, so there is no way of knowing or predicting what will happen if, and when the time comes for your loved one to go into hospice care. I also noticed that some people had more friends than family involved in the care of their loved one.

While I can't tell you who will be there to help and who will not, I have observed certain irrational behaviors and attitudes that are not only predictable they seem to be universal in families facing a crisis situation. Am I saying there may be irrational behavior displayed at some point during your experience? I'm saying you need to be prepared for anything. When someone is experiencing unusually high levels of stress and uncertainty, rational thought may take a backseat. Whether the irrational behavior is exhibited by the patient, the caretaker, the family, or anyone else, it is important to understand that they are not being themselves and they may never have acted in the way they did had it not been for the impact of the situation. The most desirable outcome for everyone is to be at peace, both with their family, the deceased, and themselves from the onset of the illness, till long after the funeral. Without the forgiveness I wrote about, the outcome will not bring peace.

I have written about a few of the attitudes I observed in both myself and others as we progressed through Rita's illness. You may be facing similar circumstances in your situation right now. The aftermath of the illness can be as devastating as the event itself if the dynamics of the situation are not understood. People's reactions will be in direct relation to the state of mind they are in and the level of stress they are experiencing. Is it any wonder most hospice centers lock their doors?

Cut and Run

One common behavior I've seen in several families facing terminal illness is that one of the spouses (usually the husband) leaves, or becomes totally detached from the sick person. One day while my daughter Amanda was looking for statistics of married couples and terminal illness, she discovered that an astounding eight out of ten married couples divorce either during or after the terminal illness of a child! The burdens of the illness are more than the average person can handle. Running away is common to the fight or fight mentality. In my opinion, either is a choice, only one is a positive one.

In my case, I believe I was left alone with Rita for several reasons. First, the combination of my emotional pain alienating our family, second, our families had little experience with death, so they didn't know how to respond. Third, because they didn't see Rita very often, they had no idea she was as ill as she actually was.

The Blister

When I was a gas pipe-fitter, the work I did was not only very technical, it was incredibly physical. We used to call our lazy work-mates "blisters" because they always showed up when the work was done. They always seemed to find some other menial work to do in order to keep from helping with the more difficult chores. The same is true for family members who never want to help throughout the illness, only to show up when the patient goes into hospice care as if they were helping, all along.

I remember one family in particular. The mother had a fatal brain tumor that had started out as breast cancer. Everyone in the family had gathered because it was apparent she would be gone within a day or so. I had made friends with the husband because of our common situations and we spoke often during their stay. Then the brother showed up. The sisters who had been the caretakers, along with their father throughout the illness, were incensed when he walked in. He came to where the father and I were talking and sat down by his dad. He was a friendly man and we chatted quite freely. But as soon as he went in to see his mother, the sisters walked up to their father and began to complain. One of them said, "He hasn't been to see mom in three months, why is he coming now?" Another said, "I think we should tell him to just leave." The father was a sensitive man and told the daughters to please just let it go. He wanted the family to be together more than anything else at that moment.

From a caretaker's perspective the feeling of doing all the work only to have someone else come in and take all the credit can likely feel very disturbing. Being a caretaker is not only stressful, it is a thankless job. From the brother's perspective, perhaps he just couldn't bear to see his mom like that, or maybe he was just too wrapped-up in his own life to notice what was happening.

Whatever the reason, be aware, the blister may literally not have had the capacity to be there before, but toward the end, after the work is done, they somehow manage to offer assistance. Holding bitterness against them only serves to elevate your own stress levels and rarely motivates them to be any more caring or helpful. My advice to you is to move on. Save your energy for important things, such as taking care of both yourself and your loved one. You'll be heads above where you would be otherwise.

Armchair Quarterbacks

This type of behavior irritated me more than any other, because they were not only critical, they always seemed to be the most judgmental. It was as though certain family members looked for reasons to criticize everything I did. To me, this was the most common type of counterproductive behavior. For a while, I received regular emails and phone calls from Rita's family members, telling me the "family" didn't like the way I was doing this or that. Once, someone tried to tell me that they didn't like what I was feeding her. The person came over while I was feeding her and said that it was too hot for her. Another time the same person told me to stop feeding her because she had had enough, yet she was still eating every bite I fed her. I ignored the person because I knew Rita's eating habits better than they did. This, after I had been taking care of her for many months without their assistance. Sometimes, I just wanted to unload on that person, but I always held my tongue because I knew he wasn't the one doing the work.

If you're a caretaker and you're being inundated with unwelcome suggestions from an armchair quarterback, I would advise you to ignore them as much as you possibly can. Again, they will tax your emotions and even cause you to question your every decision. If you're doing all the work, you are the one best qualified to make those decisions.

I'm Too... You're Too

I just hated it when someone would call me to tell me why they couldn't make it to see Rita and me. Sometimes the same people would call every week with the same sentiments and it was never a comfort to know why they couldn't make it. The reasons people gave for not coming ranged from, "I wish you/we lived closer;" "I'm too sick;" "My kids are sick;" "It's snowing;" "It's raining;" "I'm too busy;" etc. I would much rather they simply not have called or if they did, that they said something like, "Paul, I just don't know what to say." Or, "I'm feeling nervous and I'm afraid I would feel uncomfortable there." These are valid and honest statements that would have been much more well received than the "I'm too" excuses for me. Of course, it is essential to understand that when you are in a situation like hospice you tend to be more sensitive to having your feelings hurt by things that otherwise may have never affected you.

The Nine Lepers

Years ago, I took the Dale Carnegie Course. It involved studying three books written by Dale Carnegie. In the course, the main book and topic of study was, *How to Win Friends and Influence People.* The main study involves practicing ten principles of human behavior that make people feel more valued, thus more willing to hear what you have to tell them. One of the principals of the book is on the topic of expecting ingratitude. It refers to a passage of scripture in Luke 17:11-19. The verse says, "And it came to pass as he went to Jerusalem, that he passed through the midst of Samaria and Galilee. "And as he entered into a certain village, there met him ten men that were lepers, which stood afar off: and they lifted up their voices, and said, 'Jesus, Master, have mercy on us.' And when he saw them, he said unto them, 'Go, show yourself unto the priests.' And one of them, when he saw that he was healed, turned back and with a loud voice, glorified God. And fell down at his feet, giving him thanks... And Jesus answering said, 'ere not ten cleansed, but where are the nine? There are not found that returned to give glory to God, save this stranger."

If nine out of ten men, healed of a horrible disease like leprosy never even looked back to Jesus to thank Him for what He had done, we cannot expect anything more today.

In her book, *Caregiving*, Beth Witrogen McLeod says, "Family caregiving is an emotional roller coaster that can leave a person exhausted, bewildered, and dislodged, wondering how she or he can feel so helpless in a period so supposedly grown up. Each stage of an illness presents a succession of hurdles, stretching hearts more than it seems possible to bear. At times it would be enough to just hear, 'You're doing a good job,' but even that reinforcement can be elusive." The feeling of being unappreciated is common, so don't feel alone.

I believe there is a dynamic here that we can never completely understand. It's as though no one can fully grasp the magnitude of your situation. Nor do they comprehend the extent of your commitment to your cause. Know that you're doing the best you can and that your reward awaits you. You would do well to let go of expecting gratitude and in doing so, you'll give yourself at least a degree of understanding and perhaps a better sense of peace.

Personal Dynamics

In addition to the preceding family dynamics, I have listed some things that I noticed in my own life and the way I felt at different times throughout my experience. If you are a caretaker, you may find you relate very well to the following, or you might not agree at all. The way you cope with stress and what kind of relationship you have with the person who is ill will greatly affect your emotional condition.

On Journaling

In July of 2006, Amanda bought journals for everyone in our family. I didn't start writing in mine at first, probably because I didn't know how to put my feelings into words. The first time I did fill in an entry however, I felt quite liberated from my fears and concerns. I soon found that writing a daily entry gave me more clarity and actually helped me with addressing those fears and concerns. I also found that I was better able to focus on solutions to problems that before, seemed to elude me. The benefit of filling in daily entries not only helped me to cope with my situation—eventually it led me to the writing of this book.

I would highly recommend that you purchase a journal and begin filling out daily or at least consistent entries. You may one day discover that there were true treasures in your words. You may even find treasures that may give you a unique insight as to the best way to handle a crisis or even open your heart to opportunities that you never saw before. My first entry was made on July 27, of 2007. The last entry was made on October 18, of the same year, when I brought hospice in to help with Rita's care. By that time, I was well on my way in the writing of my book, so my journaling was no longer done in longhand. Incidentally, the therapeutic value and benefit I've gained from writing the book has, in my opinion, given me an understanding and appreciation I could never have gotten if I hadn't started with a daily journal entry.

Months after her passing, I found my journal and re-read many of the entries I had made during some of the most trying times of my life. I also made an interesting discovery while reading the journal. I found that there were also many times of great joy. I was reminded again of just how much I loved my precious Rita. I can scarcely read the words written in my now treasured journal without crying. I thank God for giving me the insight to have written those journal entries.

CHAPTER 28

Serve Others, Serve Yourself

I have found that when we take our eyes off of ourselves, we don't focus on our problems as much. When I was in the Porter Hospice center with Rita, I often sat in the cafeteria and waited to see if anyone came in to have a cookie or a cup of coffee which were readily available there. As people wandered in, I tried to strike up conversations with them. I found it was relatively easy to find a common link, especially since we were all there for the same reason; our loved ones were dying. As I asked them about their situation(s) they would almost inevitably share about themselves and their pain. As they shared, their faces would sometimes light up, especially when they began talking about the love they shared with the patient. Their faces became animated as they sometimes laughed at how "silly things" made their lives special, or how their loved one was "such a little stinker" or whatever the case. We'd usually end up in a hug or at least introducing ourselves and sometimes crying on each other's shoulder. As we listened to the stories of one another, our own pains seemed to diminish. It proved to me, when we take our eyes off of ourselves, our own problems aren't so big any more. Lastly, I made some wonderful lifetime friendships.

Vicki and Her Husband

One afternoon, I met a woman named Vicki. We happened to strike up a conversation as we passed in a hallway. Her husband was a patient there. He had been diagnosed with a GBM, ten months before. She mentioned that she was very tired and had many trials in regards to the experience of being her husband's caretaker. I happened to be working on my book that day and just printed a hard copy of my manuscript. I told her I would be honored to share my book with her and she seemed very interested in looking at it. She happened to mention that she was a very good proofreader. I gladly agreed: if she were to find any typos, she could feel free to make the necessary corrections. We parted ways and I didn't think much about our conversation the rest of the day.

The next morning when I went into Rita's room, I was deeply saddened. The manuscript was laid on the chair in the room. There was no note or indication of her even having been there; nothing but the manuscript. My heart sank as I thought of the only logical reason for the manuscript being there. I took a deep breath and slowly walked to the area of the building where Vicki and her husband were. I almost hesitated when I looked into the room where he was. The room was cleaned out. No sign of Vicki or her husband anywhere. I knew what I had suspected from the minute I saw the book carefully laid in the chair: her husband had passed away the night before. I never had the chance to meet her husband or even get to know his name, but we who walked the hospice halls and met one another in the common areas, had a thread of commonality that can never be broken. We shared a loss that cannot be defined. Our lives not only crossed in those times, our spirits intermingled and for a moment, we became one.

When I returned to Rita's room I picked the book up and held it close to my heart. I opened it to see if she had had the opportunity to look through the manuscript. I'd know how far she made it by the way the pages were corrected. As I opened the book, my heart seemed to stop when I got to page 36. There was a pen clipped onto the page and the corrections stopped there. I could only assume Vicki's husband must have taken a turn for the worse when she was at that spot. So many beds were filled and emptied throughout our stay at the hospice center, I can't remember them all. So many faceless forms, in and then out, just as quickly. Their names were but a blur—a soon to be distant memory on the lips of the hospice nurses, their faces and stories never to be forgotten.

CHAPTER 29

Poor, Poor Pitiful Me

This is a characteristic you need to be prepared for. I found myself steeped in this mode of understanding for a long, long time. As a caretaker you have been through a lot already. You may be feeling tired, angry, or even bitter. Your self-talk may sound something like this, "I have a right to be angry after all, I'm here all alone facing this." Or, "No one knows how I'm feeling." Or any number of justifications for your rude and angry attitudes.

Believe me it will serve you best to listen carefully to these words. All the anger in the world will not make your loved one better, or yourself for that matter. Nor will it convince your friends or family to be more responsive or supportive. Stop pitying yourself! Stop being mad at the world! You'll be far ahead of where you are and your pain will be greatly diminished.

Before Rita became ill, when I met someone and they asked me what I did for a living, I used to tell them

I was a contractor. Then we would have a conversation and that would be the end of the question. However, after Rita became ill, and her condition worsened, I was forced to quit working and become her full-time caretaker. One day though, when someone asked me what I did for a living, I paused and wasn't sure what to say. After a moment, I felt my eyes begin to water. Soon thereafter, if someone asked what I did for a living, I began answering that I was *my wife's caretaker*. I discovered I had become one with the title. I had somehow lost my identity in the mix.

I actually forgot who I was. I was no longer Paul, but "my wife's caretaker." It wasn't an easy pill to swallow. Rita's illness had consumed so much of me that I actually forgot who I used to be. I often wonder how I'll answer the question in a year. All I do know is that I want to be the best I can be no matter *what* that happens to be.

In his book, *A New Earth*, Eckhart Tolle explains how we tend to become so enveloped in our life experiences that we allow the experiences to become who we are. After reading his book, I realized that though my wife was dying, I was not. I had allowed another part of my identity to become "My wife is dying." Consequently everywhere I went, I saw myself as, "my wife is dying." When I would meet new people, it wasn't long before I shared with them the fact that my wife was dying. I almost lost sight of the person I really am, Paul Lane.

After I began to understand that I am an entity and my experiences were not that entity, I was able to maintain a better state of mind as well as a better attitude. Within a week of my starting *A New Earth*, I had no less than a dozen people tell me I seemed "much more at peace" and less "angry." The book has been one of my biggest helps in understanding and addressing my self-pity.

Last, keeping yourself occupied with positive activity will be of great help in terms of self-pity. For me, the more I spoke with, and encouraged people whose loved ones were dying, the better I felt about my own fears and concerns. Taking our eyes off of ourselves is better for everyone involved. If you see someone having problems, give them a hand. If you see an opportunity to touch another life, your own life will inevitably be touched as well.

I'm the Only One in the World Feeling This Way
At times, when you're in the position of being a caretaker, you may feel like no one on earth can understand how you feel. The feelings of depression and isolation can be so overwhelming you may feel like you are the last person on earth. But honestly, if you think about it, there are thousands of people dying all over the

world every second. There are caretakers with many of those who are dying, and most if not all of them are feeling the same or similar feelings of isolation and anguish. That's why I say again and again how important it is to attend support groups. You've probably noticed one of the central themes of this book is, "You are not alone." I say this because it is absolutely true. No matter how alone you feel there is always someone who can relate to you.

When Rita first had her seizure I remember leaving the Intensive Care Unit of the hospital for the first time. I had been by her bedside nonstop for two days. I wouldn't have ever left except I needed to eat, take a shower, and change clothes. As I drove home, I saw a man standing on a street corner with a sign that said he was homeless and needed money. I was so angry I wanted to just stop and tell him, "You think you have problems? My wife is in a hospital fighting for her life right now, how would you like to trade places with her?" I was so furious I wanted to yell, "How dare you stand there pretending to be helpless. You have two eyes, two hands, two legs! Get a job!" My insides felt like they were being ripped-out. I felt like I was the only one in the world who felt such pain. It seemed like everyone should feel like I did.

Then I went home and turned on the television. The news was on and the anchorwoman was smiling and there was a lot of laughter on the set. I was angered to see their joy. It seemed *no one* knew the sadness and despair I felt.

Back at the hospital, I ran into my daughter Amanda. She told me she was furious. I asked her why she was so mad. She said she had just seen a panhandler and it infuriated her to see him there, able-bodied and begging. Suddenly I realized I was *not* the only one feeling the way I did. It may have been subconscious at the time but somehow, I believe that day, I decided I would write this book in hopes you would pick it up and receive benefits from its pages.

While doing my study on this topic, I realized there were some common feelings I believe most, if not all caretakers experience. I mention this because I believe if we, as caretakers, can understand that our feelings are not unique or exclusive, we can better address those feelings of confusion or frustration.

The CAREGIVER'S HANDBOOK

CHAPTER 30

I'm Nobody's Hero

During the writing of this book, there happened to be a mass shooting in two Colorado churches: one in Arvada, which is just north of Denver, the other in Colorado Springs, which is sixty miles south. The same gunman was responsible for both shootings. For the purposes of this book, the significance of this news story is not the fact that there were two separate crime scenes, or that several people were shot, it was that the security guard, a woman named Jeanne Assam, responsible for ending the shooting was doing nothing more than what she was hired to do... guard the premises.

Sometime after the incident, a local reporter interviewed Jeanne. She was very humble and never spoke of herself as anything other than a security guard. She never asked to be the one to stop the gunman, she just happened to be the one that did. I'm sure beyond a doubt, if she could have been anywhere but in the middle of a gunfight at that moment, she would have chosen the alternative. When it was all said and done, she was just another person, trying to do the best she could. She never asked to be a hero.

Almost from the beginning, people constantly told my daughters and me how *strong* they thought we were. They would send notes telling me I was an *inspiration*, an *example of true faith*, someone they *looked up to*. They told me our experience was *teaching* them a lot about love, loss, and so much more. I even remember someone calling and telling me I had taught him how to be a better husband. After hearing those words and words like these over and over, I began to become annoyed. I never chose to be where I was. I never asked to be anyone's example, teacher, and especially their hero. My daughters and I were thrust into the situation we found ourselves in; nothing more, nothing less.

We never wished to be any kind of example and like Jeanne Assam, would have gladly removed ourselves from the present situation if it were at all possible. I certainly would have run from it if I could have. I know I speak for everyone who has found themselves immersed in the situation of being a caretaker of a family member or someone who is in a fight for their lives. Admire those who face trials and tribulations, but understand it is never their desire to be a hero. They most likely won't feel better knowing their misfortune had been a fortune or beneficial discovery for you.

On the other hand I didn't want Rita's death to be in vain, so I made the difficult decision to share about our experiences. I knew I was going through a terrible ordeal and I wanted others to gain, grow, and learn from our experiences. I wanted our pain to be the substance from which others might glean benefits and could perhaps be better prepared for the trials they'll face as caretakers and those who support them.

Where is God in All of This?
Before I joined the Army, I knew a married couple whose love was a great inspiration to me. They shared a loving relationship and a closeness that was exactly what I had envisioned for my own eventual marriage. I used to watch the way they interacted so effortlessly and it seemed certain they were made for each other. He was twenty-one years old and she was twenty-three or twenty-four and they had a two-year-old son. After much saving and hard work, they purchased their first home.

He had an unbearable headache all day as they began the move to their new home. After the last boxes had been carried in, he told his wife that he needed to go the hospital. That night, he died of a brain aneurysm, never having spent a single night in his new home. To make matters worse, his young widow discovered she was pregnant shortly thereafter.

She was so distraught and hopeless that she lost all faith in God. Shortly after the funeral, she told me she would never believe or trust in a God who could let this happen to her and her family. She told me she hated the idea of God and to this day, I believe she still harbors bitterness. I pray she'll one day be able to overcome her anger and find peace. I did my best to explain to her that, in spite of her feelings, God was there and still loves her.

Then, after everything happened to me, I thought back to her words. I thought it ironic that I was now being tried. I wondered if I too might turn my back on God and my faith as a result of my experience. Through it all, however, I have been fortunate to have had a great spiritual support system and I have kept my trust in the Lord to sustain me. Oh, I can't deny that there were times when I was tempted to reject God, but the words of Job 13:15 kept coming back to my mind, "Though he slay me, yet will I trust him..."

Undoubtedly, seeing someone die of a serious illness or injury can challenge your relationship with God and certainly, it can diminish anyone's faith. The day Rita first became ill, I prayed and asked God for peace, comfort, and wisdom as we walked to the hospital. I have continued to do so from that day till this. Sometimes, when things got very complicated, honestly, it was difficult to think about God at all. I have no doubt that my faith was challenged over and over. But I promised myself from the beginning I would always do my very best to seek God's face in the midst of whatever storm I found myself. I continually announced that I would overcome my obstacles because God would take me through them. And by His grace I believe that He was there through the worst and the best of it all.

If you're feeling angered and are looking for someone to blame for your situation, whatever it is, I urge you to stop right where you are—it's no one's fault. You're not being punished, neither is your loved one. The Bible says in Hebrews 9:27, "And it is appointed unto men once to die…" each of us will someday pass through the portal of life. It also says in Matthew 5:45 "…he makes the sun to rise on the evil and on the good, and sends rain on the just and on the unjust."

As I watched the World Trade Center towers collapse, and thought of all the lives being extinguished at that moment, I wondered what the millions of other Americans and people around the world were thinking. I'm sure some were cursing God, others were just dazed. Still others were paralyzed by fear. No matter what you were thinking, I believe God saw every event and heard every prayer, even though it may seem He heard none. Every person that was supposed to die, died. I believe everything happens for a reason.

Whether we die of an illness or in an accident, we will *all die*, eventually. We must trust that God has ordained the time and place. I don't care if the world's best doctor is at our bedside, we will die when it is our appointed time. Trust that God has a plan for you. Know that He loves you. No matter how hard it gets, God is there. In Hebrews 13:5, the Word reminds us that He said "…I will never leave you nor forsake you." He will always be there.

O Ye of Little Faith

One time, Amanda told me that a friend had told her that the reason for Rita's illness was because we hadn't had enough faith. He said that if we had prayed more fervently or if we were more faithful she would have been healed. His words made me so angry, I wanted to go to him and tell him how ignorant he was. All I could think was that it was good to be young and ignorant. He obviously hadn't heard about the prayer chains that had scanned the entire globe. I wanted to go to him and say that perhaps his prayers would heal Rita, but I knew that doing so would have been just as bad as what he was saying, as it would have been in anger.

My faith was shaken by the words of that young man even though I knew he was wrong. I wondered secretly if perhaps he was right, till I heard on the news one night about a tornado that struck someplace in the Midwest.

It had devastated a town in the Bible belt and several people had been killed. I wondered if that young man would have said that the town could have been spared if they had more faith. I knew God had never left me and I believed that what happened was God's will.

The CAREGIVER'S HANDBOOK

CHAPTER 31

Is There Life After Death?

Something commonly overlooked by many caretakers, is the fact that they will, (or at least should) live on after the death of their loved one.

There may be support groups you can join, but I must warn you; be careful not to become too dependent on support groups. Let me explain. One night while I was at the hospice center I went to the cafeteria to get a cup of ice water. There was a wonderful woman there who happened to be a volunteer. She was perhaps in her mid-sixties and had a contagious smile and an enthusiastic laugh that instantly drew me to her. We struck up a conversation. She explained that she had been married to a sweet man for twenty-seven years before he passed away. A short time after his passing, she met another woman who invited her to go to a grievance support group. The woman had also lost her husband, so it seemed only right that my friend should go. The woman picked up the new widow on the appointed night and they proceeded to the meeting.

As they began the meeting, they went around the room and everyone introduced themselves. Each participant told a little bit about how they became a part of the support group. The time came for the woman who invited the new widow to the meeting to speak. She stood to her feet and confidently introduced herself. When she got to the part where she explained how she became involved, the new widow was shocked at her friend's revelation. The woman had lost her husband seventeen years earlier!

At first I thought it was very odd that someone would hang on to a group of fellow mourners for so long, but after thinking about it I realized that nothing was wrong with it. We all deal with grief in our own way and that was hers. For me however, I would rather move on and start a new life without the painful memories and thoughts of her passing.

Let me tell you about another situation that intrigued me. There is a man I used to know, whose wife had been the victim of a long, drawn out terminal illness. Then, one day he came home and found her dead. Like her illness, his grief, had been gnawing away at him for a long time. Her death was no surprise to anyone. What did raise an eyebrow or two was the fact that he remarried within three weeks of her death. To some, this may sound morbid or even unacceptable. I can only tell you that unless you're the one caring for a dying spouse, you can never understand the loneliness and depression one feels. The resulting emotions can be so overpowering you would do anything to put an end to your sadness, even if it seems irrational or abrupt to others. After the passing, you may want to find someone, anyone to fill the emptiness you felt throughout the illness.

Last, I will tell you of another friend whose husband passed away very unexpectedly. They were happily married and one day he had a massive heart attack and in an instant, was gone. She never had a chance to say goodbye. His death was sudden, and then it was over. I don't know if it would have been easier than having it be strung out over a long period of time, but in the end the result was still the same. My friend made it through the next eight years, but found herself in the role of a caretaker during the week, and takes care of her mother on weekends. When she told me of this, I was stunned. I wondered if she had really ever gotten over the loss of her husband. Was she occupying herself so she wouldn't have to move on? Was this her way of coping? Or was it just her nature to be this kind of person? Only she knows. I pray for her continued peace and comfort.

The CAREGIVER'S HANDBOOK

CHAPTER: 32

A Most Beautiful Death

Between the months of February and April of 2008, Rita's appetite had diminished to almost nothing and she had become frighteningly thin. Her thighs had shriveled to the point where they were almost as thin as her ankles and her face and arms were so lean she literally looked like a Holocaust prisoner of war.

Almost every day I would apply lotion from the tops of her legs down to the soles of her feet, then I would cover her arms and hands with lotion. I was proud of myself because of the fact that in all the time she was in hospice she never developed a single bed sore. Sometimes, I would dress her in pajamas and put her in a wheelchair. I would wheel her all around the hospice center, although she couldn't tell me whether she liked it or not. She seemed to perk up when I took her to the main gathering area. From there, she could look out the large, almost floor-to-ceiling windows and see the trees and birds. It was heartbreaking to know that her life had dwindled down to this.

Some days, when I went into her room I could see a look of confusion on her face and I wasn't sure she knew who I was, so every morning I would greet her and then point to the large poster board with all of our family photos on it. I would show her pictures of herself with our daughters and me and tell her I was the guy in the pictures. Sometimes, she smiled when I showed her the picture of us kissing.

In late March, one of the hospice nurses told me that Rita would no longer eat when the nurses tried to feed her, and that she only ate when I fed her. By that time I was sleeping at home almost every night, so each morning before I went to the hospice center, I would make a salad that was big enough to feed us both. Each day, I was amazed at how much Rita would eat. She would consume the entire container of salad every time, and I figured that as long as she kept eating it, I would keep feeding it to her. Then, in the second week of April, she began to aspirate, or choke, on her saliva when she swallowed.

Once, when one of her sisters was visiting, Rita began to choke. Though she was extremely weak, she coughed and gasped so violently, her sister was visibly shaken. I sat next to Rita and held her close to me and rocked her back and forth. I patted her on her back gently till she regained her breath. I had seen it so many times that it was hardly unusual to me. Then, on April 20, the charge nurse told me that because Rita had been aspirating, I could no longer take her the salads, nor was I to feed her anymore.

In the last week of April, Rita's countenance clearly changed. She became more and more absent and her weight dropped so much, I couldn't understand how she could sustain life. By April 29, it had been three days since Rita had eaten anything. She looked so frail it was as if she would literally break if she were to bump herself. In my heart, I knew she was in her last week. I called her family to let them know of her condition. That week, she received visits from two sisters and their husbands, a sister-in-law, two nieces and of course my daughters and mom. I was very blessed to see her family coming to see her and my heart was set at ease.

By May 1, Rita had become so weak, I was positive she was in her last twenty-four hours. Her sister Delfinia and her husband had spent the prior day and night with us at the hospice center, but they had to return to Pueblo. Her brother Albert and his wife Mary Ann arrived less than three hours after Delfinia left. Even though Rita was totally unresponsive I was comforted to have someone else there with me through those days, especially Rita's family. I called Amanda and Stacey at work around three and told them I believed their mom was getting close. I told them that they should get to the hospice center as soon as they could. Stacey got there right after she got off work. Amanda and Josh got there a short time later. The mood in the room was peaceful considering what was happening. Everyone took turns sitting close to Rita and holding her hands. We listened to quiet music through the day and into the evening. Our cousins Ben and Joanne Madrid, who had held the fundraiser for us, sent several boxes of food from their restaurant so there was plenty of food and sodas for everyone.

At around ten o'clock, Rita began to hyperventilate. It was extremely difficult to watch as she gasped over and over for air. I called the nurse in and she gave Rita something to help calm her down. Within an hour, her breathing became more relaxed. The nurse told us that we needed to remove Rita's fingernail polish so that they could see her nail beds. From the time Rita had first gone into hospice, Stacey had always done her mother's nails so there was never a second thought as to who should do it. She meticulously wiped her mom's nails clean on one hand.

Since Rita's cousin Lou had been such a great supporter through it all, I called her around eleven. She was at work but said she would get there as soon as she could. Then, I called Rita's sister Bertha. She was always Rita's favorite sibling and I had promised her I would call if and when Rita was ready to pass. At two that morning, I called our pastor, Scott, to tell him Rita would be gone by morning. I told him he needn't come but he was there within an hour. By then, there were ten of us in the private room gathered around Rita's bed.

The feeling in the room was one of complete unity and love. Everyone was there for the same reason, to be there for Rita. I played her favorite music and we all spoke softly as we comforted one another. The nurse would come in every once in a while to make sure we were alright. We were ten souls, lending prayer and love to one as she left this world. I had never thought about what it would be like when the time came, but the spirit in the room was so sweet it was as if I was in a dream. Rita's breathing had slowed down to an almost normal pace and she looked at peace.

Sometime around four-thirty that morning, Lou suggested I tell Rita who was there in the room. I scooted closer to her and quietly told her that there were a lot of people there with her. I named everyone and told her it was alright to let go whenever she was ready. Then, Lou asked me if I would like for everyone to leave us alone with Rita for a while. Her words were not only welcome, they were very timely. I agreed. Everyone but Amanda, Stacey and I filtered out of the room, leaving us alone with Rita.

It was around four-thirty-five a.m. when the last person left. Rita was so tiny she only took up a small area in her bed. Amanda and Stacey had taken turns lying beside her throughout the night. Now I took my place next to her while Stacey cuddled at her feet and Amanda sat in the recliner I had spent so many nights in. It was scooted close enough to her bed that Amanda could reach out and lay a hand on her mother, whose breathing had now become even less labored. It was as if she were completely aware of what I was saying. There was an amazing clarity in the room. It was almost as if the seconds had been stretched out for us to grasp what was happening.

I asked Stacey to play the song, "Poetry Man," by Phoebe Snow. I looked at the clock and saw that it was four-forty-four a.m. I quietly explained to Rita that everyone had left, and that only Amanda, Stacey, and I were in the room with her. I crawled up close to her and told her that everything was going to be alright. Then, I told Stacey to tell her mom she was going to be alright.

She moved to the top of the bed and hugged Rita. "Mom," she said, "it's Stacey. I want you to know, I love you and I'm going to be alright." Then she kissed her mother on her cheek.

Next, Amanda hugged her mom and said, "Mom, it's Amanda. I want you to know that I love you and I'm gonna be alright, too." Then she kissed Rita's cheek.

Finally, it was my turn. I held Rita for what seemed like a long time and said, "Rita, I want you to know, you've been a wonderful mother and you are the best friend I ever had. I couldn't have asked for a better wife. I love you honey and I promise, I'm going to be alright, too." Then I kissed her and hugged her, once again. Up to that point, no one had cried a tear, but as I spoke, I could feel the emotions building in all of us.

The second I finished kissing her, Rita inhaled deeply and let it out. As she exhaled, her head slowly leaned forward. She opened her eyes and looked up and into Stacey's eyes. She didn't inhale again. It was all so surreal, yet so peaceful, we all sat there in disbelief. There was an incredible feeling of peace and calm in the room as we all laid our heads on Rita's chest. No one moved. Somehow we knew the time was upon us. As if on cue we all looked at each other. Not a word was said at first, yet it was as if we were each asking, "Is that it?" For a moment, at least for me, every sad feeling was replaced with a mixture of relief and joy.

I sent one of the girls to get the nurse. The other went to gather all of those who had left the room just minutes before. The nurse came in and asked when Rita had taken her last breath. I told her it was four-forty-four a.m. She had a notebook in which she wrote Rita's time of passing *officially* as four-forty-nine a.m.

Just then, everyone started to come back into the room. I asked Stacey if she wanted to repaint her mom's nails. She wiped the tears from her eyes and said she would be honored. She took Rita's hand and carefully began to paint her nails. As she painted, she giggled, saying "Now I can finally get them painted without mom messing them up." We all laughed through our tears and I was relieved to see that Stacey really was alright. Seeing my baby girl holding her mother's hand while she carefully painted her nails was a beautiful sight.

The nurse told me that she had called the funeral home and that they would be there within an hour. Then she asked me if it was alright if one of the CNAs came in and combed Rita's hair and made her look a little nicer. I said it was fine as long as I was there. I stayed with her till the hearse came and I helped them put her body on the gurney and load her into the car.

As I said the last goodbye, my heart was overcome with emotion once again and I cried tears of deep sadness, coupled with tears of complete relief. But as I drove away from the hospice center, the thought of what would become of me filled my mind.

All the way home, all I could think of, was everything my girls, Rita, and I had gone through since June 21, 2006. Twenty-two months and eleven days. Images flashed through my mind like an unending reel of movie trailers. I saw her face in my mind over and over: from the first day I met her so many years before, to the last moment of her life.

I just wanted to call her on the phone and tell her how I felt. I was in awe of God's goodness, humbled in knowing that with His strength, I had never left her side. I asked myself, had done all that I could? So many thoughts filled my mind that when I got home, I could think of nothing but the night before. Through all of my struggles, I admit, I failed many times, but I also did a lot right.

The next few days were grueling. I wavered between feelings of relief, to anger and everything in between. I had to go to the funeral home to make arrangements. It was intimidating how much there was to do, from picking the coffin and flowers, to telling the mortician the way she combed her hair. I had to select an outfit to bury her in and what jewelry she would wear. Since I am a veteran of the U.S. Army, I didn't have to pay for the burial plot, but still, before they would even do a thing with her body, full payment was required for the coffin and all other expenses.

I had told the funeral director I wanted a closed casket because Rita would never have wanted anyone to see her like she was, but when I got to the church, I found the coffin open. I was so angry I chewed the host out. I demanded they close it right away.

The church had a seating capacity of over three-hundred-forty, and there was standing room only. I had selected Rita's niece Lisa to present the eulogy long before she passed because since she was a child, Lisa was just like our adopted daughter. She really loved Rita and her words were warm and well organized. When she was finished, I knew I had chosen the right person for the job.

After the service, the funeral director had the pall bearers push the casket along the perimeter of the church. It was embarrassing to have the entire church watching me and my daughters as we followed the casket, crying the whole way. Then, to make matters worse, the casket somehow came to a spot in the floor, where it wouldn't go straight. Instead, it banged into the wall and no matter how many times they tried to straighten it out, it hit the wall again and again. Everyone in the church could see what was happening and I was becoming frustrated. Finally, the church became silent as the casket banged into the wall. You could hear a pin drop, when I exclaimed, "She always was a stubborn woman!" There was laughter throughout the place as they finally straightened it out. I know it may sound a bit inappropriate, but I was so stressed out, I needed some relief and I didn't know any other way.

The next day, when I went to settle all of the details with the funeral home, they told me that Rita's was the largest funeral procession they had even seen. When Rita's body was placed in the ground that day, I held my head up high as I walked away.

In Gratitude: Loving Hands of Grace

The one group of people who never got the recognition they deserved were the hospice nurses we dealt with on a day-to-day basis. For the most part, they were as dedicated and compassionate as I ever expected anyone to be. Though their names might not be remembered by the families of the patients over the course of time, their gentle care and kind hands will forever be etched into my heart and mind. After my experience with the mediocrity of some of the nurses and staff at the Hospice of Saint John, I was very cautious and guarded upon Rita's arrival. I soon learned my fears were unfounded. The Porter Hospice nurses had a spirit of cooperation and respect, for themselves as well as for the patients and their families. I felt respected and valued every time I entered the facility and was never disappointed.

I would sometimes come around the corner and hear a nurse talking sweetly to Rita, laughing and smiling at the way she responded. One area of peace for me was the knowledge that Rita was in the capable hands of the staff at Porter Hospice.

The names, Shannon, Elizabeth, Joyce, and Heather, Dianna, Lisa, and Melissa, may have no meaning to you the reader, but these are the names of just some of the real heroes in my eyes. There were many others, too many to tell of them all; these are the ones who most clearly stood out for me: thank you. They say some angels don't have wings, they call them hospice nurses.

References and Further Reading:

Baum, L. Frank, *Wizard of Oz*, George M. Hill Company, 1900, Chicago

Black, Peter, M.D., *Living With a Brain Tumor*, Owl Books, New York, 2006

Callanan, Maggie and Kelly, Patricia, *Final Gifts*, Bantam Books, New York, 1992

Carnegie Dale, *How to Win Friends and Influence People*, Simon and Schuster, New York, 1936

Chambers, Oswald, *My Utmost For His Highest*, Discovery House Publishers, Grand Rapids Michigan, 1992

Chapman, Gary, *The Five Love Languages*, Moody Publisher, Chicago, 1992

Diamond, Harvey and Marilyn, *Fit For Life*, Kensington Publishing Corp, New York, 2001

Frahm, Anne E. with Frahm, David J., *A Cancer Battle Plan*, Tarcher Penguin, New York, 1992

Keyes, Daniel, *Flowers for Algernon*, Bantam Books, New York, 1959

McLeod, Witrogen, Beth, *Caregiving*, John Wiley and Sons Inc., New York, 1999

Schuller, Robert, *Tough Times Never Last but Tough People Do*, Bantam, Books, New York, 1984

Tolle Eckhard, *A New Earth*, PenguinGroup, London, 2005

Wolkstein, Diane, *The Magic Orange Tree and other Haitian Folktales Schocken Books*, New York, 1978

Ziglar, Zig, *See You at the Top*, Pelican Publishing Co, New Orleans, 1982

I'd Have Gotten More Kisses

If I could do again I'd have gotten more kisses
More holding hands, I'd do more of the dishes
More intimate dinners and heart to heart talks
More mushy love letters, I'd have taken more walks

I would do much more laughing,
I'd do less complaining
More quiet times. I'd go out when it's raining
I'd have pampered her more and looked in her eyes
I'd have cooked her more dinners and
baked her more pies

More intimate talks, more walks in the park
More romps in the hay and love after dark
Now the past is behind me, I can't change it at all
I'll do better next time if love ever calls

So don't waste a minute
In this life that you live
The day that it ends
You'll have no more to give.

~Paul Lane

Young Paul Lane

Paul & wife; RIta

A Most Beautiful Death

Rita

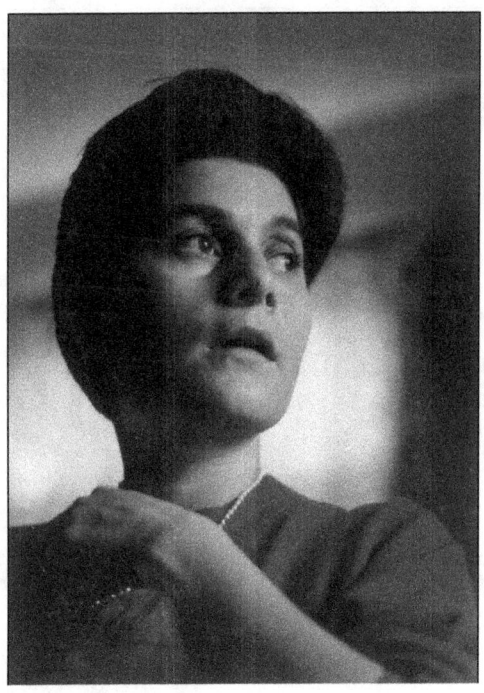

The CAREGIVER'S HANDBOOK

Paul and Rita

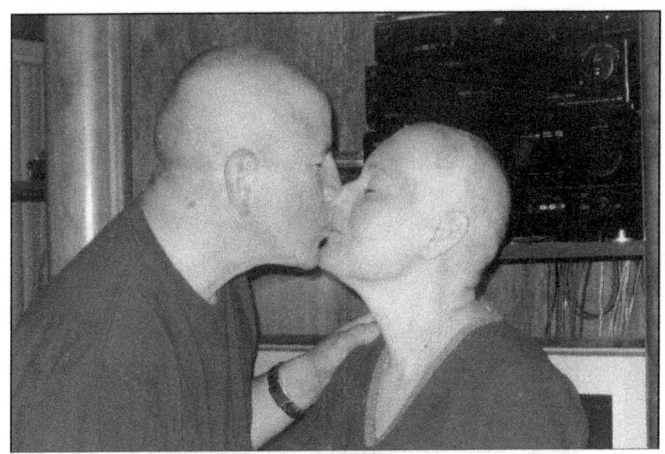

Paul and Rita

Paul and daughters

Paul & brother; Joey

Paul Lane & Robin Williams

Contact Paul Lane

Certified Life Coach & Public Speaker

* * *

AVAILABLE FOR RADIO, TV, DIGITAL AND SPEAKING ENGAGEMENT

* * *

please email or visit:

www.PaulLane.net | info@paullane.net

—

This book is also available in large print, eBook & audio.

Don't forget to order your Caregiver's Journal.

www.ingramcontent.com/pod-product-compliance
Lightning Source LLC
Chambersburg PA
CBHW071647160426
43195CB00012B/1381